Subfloor Pits and the Archaeology
of Slavery in Colonial Virginia

Subfloor Pits and the Archaeology of Slavery in Colonial Virginia

Patricia M. Samford

THE UNIVERSITY OF ALABAMA PRESS
Tuscaloosa

Copyright © 2007
The University of Alabama Press
Tuscaloosa, Alabama 35487-0380
Manufactured in the United States of America

Typeface: ACaslon

∞

The paper on which this book is printed meets the minimum requirements of American National Standard for Information Sciences-Permanence of Paper for Printed Library Materials, ANSI Z39.48-1984.

Library of Congress Cataloging-in-Publication Data

Samford, Patricia.
    Subfloor pits and the archaeology of slavery in colonial Virginia / Patricia M. Samford.
        p.   cm.
    Includes bibliographical references and index.
    ISBN-13: 978-0-8173-1586-3 (cloth : alk. paper)
    ISBN-10: 0-8173-1586-1 (cloth : alk. paper)
    ISBN-13: 978-0-8173-5454-1 (pbk. : alk. paper)
    ISBN-10: 0-8173-5454-9 (pbk. : alk. paper) 1. Slaves—Virginia—Social life and customs. 2. Slaves—Homes and haunts—Virginia—History. 3. Root cellars—Virginia—History. 4. Hiding places—Virginia—History. 5. Sacred space—Virginia—History. 6. Material culture—Virginia—History. 7. African Americans—Virginia—Antiquities. 8. Excavations (Archaeology)—Virginia. 9. Virginia—History—Colonial period, ca. 1600–1775. 10. Virginia—History—1775–1865. I. Title.
    E445.V8S26 2007
    975.5′00496073—dc22

                                                                            2007016291

Cover illustrations Courtesy of the James River Institute for Archaeology, Inc.: Subfloor pit in Utopia IV's Structure 140 with in-situ copper frying pan. Utopia IV's Structure 140, circa 1750–80, prior to excavation. Carved bone container from 1700 to 1730 occupation at Utopia II, 2 7/8″ in length.

Contents

Illustrations

Figures

Tables

Acknowledgments

Completion of this book would not have been possible without the assistance of many individuals. I feel incredibly fortunate to have the advice and guidance of Vin Steponaitis, Carole Crumley, Robert Ann Dunbar, Glenn Hinson, and James Peacock.

Since much of my analysis focused on previously excavated archaeological sites, various institutions in Virginia made their collections available to me. I would particularly like to thank Garrett Fesler and the staff at the James River Institute for Archaeology in Jamestown, Virginia, where the Utopia Quarter collections are curated. The Kingsmill Quarter collections are stored at the Virginia Division of Historic Landmarks in Richmond, where Elisabeth Acuff, Keith Egloff, Dee DeRoche, and Catherine Slusser assisted me in working with these collections. Thanks are also in order to Gregory Brown, Marley R. Brown III, William Pittman, and Kelly Ladd at the Department of Archaeological Research at the Colonial Williamsburg Foundation, where the Carter's Grove Quarter assemblage is curated. This book has also benefited from comments and insights from Amy Young at the University of Southern Mississippi and Laurie Wilkie at the University of California, Berkeley. A Sigma Xi grant and a Mooney Award from the Research Laboratories of Anthropology at the University of North Carolina helped fund this research.

Many other individuals also deserve recognition and thanks here. The maps and graphs were done by Tamera Myer-Mams, and Kim Kelley-Wagner drew the Eden House shrine. Various scholars served as sounding boards during this project. My thanks go to Eli Bentor of Appalachian State University, Bolaji Campbell at the Rhode Island School of Design, Herbert Cole, Henry Drewal at the University of Wisconsin at Madison, Reverend Eze Ndubisi, Dr. Richard Henderson, Dr. Chika Okeke of University of South Florida at Tampa, and Robert Farris Thompson at Yale University. Jane Ellen Baker, Carol Richardson, and Johnie Carol Williams—my Bath neighbors and friends—helped me during the final manuscript preparation. I would also like to thank Ann, Carl, and Kate Martin, John and Kara Metz, Reverend Morgan and Nancy Smart, and Nancy, Alana, and Matthew Durham, and the staff of the University of Alabama Press. Colleagues at the University of North Carolina at Chapel Hill who deserve thanks are Sara Bon-Harper, Steve Davis, Jane Eastman, Tom Hargrove, Joe Herbert, Annie Holm, Diane Levy, Trish McGuire, Tom Maher, Tim Mooney, Chris Rodning, Martha Temkin, Amber Vanderwarker, Greg Wilson, and Alicia Wise. I am honored to have worked with each and every one of my Chapel Hill colleagues. Last, but not least, my extended family has been understanding and supportive during this long process.

Subfloor Pits and the Archaeology of Slavery in Colonial Virginia

1
Introduction

> The slave's history—like all human history—was made not only by what
> was done to them but also by what they did for themselves.
>
> —Berlin 1998:2

Prior to 1863, enslaved African Americans performed much of the manual
labor that powered the American South. Millions of Africans and subsequent generations of their descendants toiled in the tobacco, cotton, and rice
fields of the South, while others were employed in skilled trades and industries. Despite their crucial roles in the economy, the lives of slaves, in many
respects, are shadowy and inaccessible. Because most of the enslaved were
kept from learning to write, their thoughts and emotions come to us only indirectly. A few slaves were allowed opportunities to tell their stories; some of
them were relayed in the context of nineteenth-century abolitionist-backed
autobiographies. Other former slaves had to wait over half a century before
Works Progress Administration workers in the era of the Great Depression
undertook an extensive program of interviews with elderly African Americans (Perdue et al. 1976; Rawick 1979). Because only a handful of the millions
of enslaved African Americans were able to put their stories on paper, the
narratives of the rest have to be gleaned from other sources.

These other sources of information are varied and, surprisingly, quite
abundant. Analyses of slave trade records reveal regional concentrations of
individuals from specific African cultural groups (Chambers 2000; Lovejoy
2003). The enslaved make frequent appearances in court records throughout
the seventeenth and eighteenth centuries. Plantation accounts penned by
slaveholders record seemingly mundane entries: slave names and ages, work
assignments, punishments meted, and rations apportioned. Hidden behind
the often spidery and faded ink strokes are the rich textures of individual
and community life. In the hands of a skilled historian, these plantation records can be used to weave compelling stories of the tenacity of the human

spirit in an unjust system and the often creative means by which the enslaved worked to improve their lives.

Historical research over the last several decades has focused on the development of families and communities (Gutman 1976), the formation of individual and group identities (Rucker 2006), African influences on attitudes toward time, work, identity, and spirituality (Gomez 1998; Sobel 1979, 1987), acts of resistance (Mullin 1972; Sidbury 1997), the roles of women (Brown 1996), community and social relationships (Penningroth 2003), and the development of distinct African American cultural practices (Berlin 2003; Mintz and Price 1992; Morgan 1998). In these studies, the enslaved are shown forming their own families and communities, resisting ill treatment and overwork, and reacting in individual and creative ways to enhance their own well-being. Far from being passive recipients of their marginalized positions, the enslaved are portrayed as individuals who were active players in the scope of their own lives.

Each of these studies reveals human actions occurring within specific historical contexts with each individual's choices constrained to varying degrees by circumstances (Trigger 1991). These circumstances occur on a number of scales and include environment, economic, political, and social conditions at local, regional, and national levels, and personal factors such as gender, ethnicity, age, and religion. In the case of most African Americans, the aforementioned constraints also included the power differentials and racism that accompanied being marginalized in a slave society. Despite these restrictions, however, even enslaved individuals possessed some degrees of choice about how they structured their lives. Critical in these individual and plantation community choices were African traditions, as Africans and their descendants drew upon memories and shared knowledge of their homelands.

Recent historical scholarship has focused on how groups of enslaved peoples, both Africans and their descendants, formed distinct cultures on the plantations of the South. These studies owe their increasing sophistication, in large part, to the adoption of a regional approach to slave life. Over time, these studies have become more refined, particularly in their handling of the presence and transformations of African traditions (Brown 2001; Chambers 1996), and how regional agricultural economics, labor management, and plantation demography affected daily and seasonal work patterns (Berlin 1998; Morgan 1998).

Since the 1970s, archaeology has also come to the forefront as a means for studying the past of enslaved African Americans. At the grouped dwellings known as quarters, the bonds of family and community were strengthened and reinforced as children were born and grew, men and women fell in and out of love, and the sick and elderly were nursed. Most slave quarters, not built to withstand the test of time, have long since fallen to the ground or otherwise been destroyed. These quarters are visible now only to archaeologists, who carefully record and excavate the soil stains and brick foundations and preserve the thousands of artifacts revealed by their digging.

Just as historians make it possible for the words written by long-dead individuals to come to life, so too a skillful archaeologist can coax silent artifacts to speak. Patterned soil stains and rows of masonry delineate houses, gardens, yards, and the larger landscapes within which the enslaved lived and worked. Firepits and scatters of artifacts found in an enclosed yard between two houses indicate a gathering place for work and socializing. There, a woman could tend her garden while talking with other men and women engaged in the daily activities that made up the substance of community life—cooking, child care, crafting items for personal use or sale, and simply relaxing. Fragmented dishes, bones, and other debris aid archaeologists in recounting stories about life in the quarters during the hours following the completion of planter-assigned tasks. These short spaces of time, free of planter obligations, were surely the most important hours of the day for the quarter's occupants. The fragmented animal bone and the hunting and fishing implements found in household refuse reveal the strategies used by the enslaved in their struggles to provide adequate sustenance for themselves and their families. Other items, such as beads and cowrie shells, speak both of the desire for adornment and individualization of dress and of African-based spiritual traditions of protection and healing. These archaeological discoveries reach out from the past and help scholars paint a vivid picture of slave life. Used in combination with ethnohistoric, ethnographic, and documentary sources, archaeological findings are a vital component in shedding light on the African American past.

This study uses the archaeological findings from five quarters on three eighteenth-century Virginia plantations to examine the material circumstances of slaves' lives, a process that in turn opens the door to illuminating other aspects of life: family and community, individual and group agency, spirituality, acts of resistance and accommodation, and symbolic meanings assigned to material goods. Analysis, grounded in a contextual approach that uses material culture to reconstruct meaning in the past, allows the development of hypotheses about how West African cultural traditions were maintained and transformed in the Virginia Chesapeake. To place this analysis with the broader context of African American archaeological research, the story must begin in the 1970s with the earliest archaeological interest in enslavement.

African American Archaeology

Over the last four decades, increased interest in understanding the diverse cultures that formed our nation has sparked extensive research in African American history, material culture, folklore, religion, and archaeology. Archaeological sites of the African diaspora—the places in the New World where peoples from Africa or their descendants lived and worked—have been the focus of extensive research since the 1970s, ranging from tenant farmers in Louisiana (Wilkie 2000) to enslaved communities in the Caribbean (Armstrong 1990; Delle 2000; Haviser 1999; Wilkie and Farnsworth 2005). Recent archaeological research has been informed by theories concerning the formation of distinct African American cultures through processes of creolization, adaptation, and syncretism (Dawdy 2000; Edwards-Ingram and Brown 1998; Franklin and McKee 2004; Mouer 1993), ethnicity (Baumann 2001; Brown and Cooper 1990; Ferguson 1992), race (Blakey 1988; Epperson 2004; Orser 2004), resistance (Davidson 2004; Orser 1988), and individual and group identities (Fennell 2000; Franklin 2001; Larsen 2005).

The earliest slave archaeology in Virginia dated to the early 1970s, with the discovery of the Carter's Grove Quarters (44JC110). Since the late 1970s, a large number of the slave quartering sites have been explored in Virginia (Appendix A). These sites have been concentrated in the Tidewater region, and many have been eighteenth-century quarters on large elite plantations.

Early archaeological studies in Virginia examined housing, foodways, and material culture, comparing enslaved households with sites whose occupants were of non-African descent (Crader 1990; Heath 1991). The development of regionally based research has demonstrated local and regional variations, affected by the different staple crops, work patterns, economic and political circumstances, labor management practices, the demographics of the enslaved population, climate, technology, the internal economies of slave households and consumerism, and myriad other factors (Heath 2004; Martin 1997; Orser 1994). Interest has focused on gender roles within plantation communities (Samford 2004) and the development of families and households at the quarters (Fesler 2004; Franklin 2004). By shifting attention away from slavery as a monolithic institution to focusing on regional approaches, archaeologists have been able to draw substantial conclusions

1.1. Subfloor pits in Structure 1 at Kingsmill Quarter (Virginia's Division of Historic Resources)

about how regional environmental, economic, social, and political factors, as well as the African backgrounds of the enslaved, shaped the institution of slavery in various parts of the South.

The Present Study

This study focuses on one particular type of feature—subfloor pits—that commonly occurs on African American quarter sites in Virginia. These features were flat-bottomed pits, cut into the soil under the floors of the houses. Generally rectangular, but sometimes square or circular, these pits were scattered across the floors of eighteenth- and early nineteenth-century slave houses, occurring singly or in groups. The 1,150-square-foot floor space of the Kingsmill Quarter, for example, contained 20 pits cutting through the clay within the building's footprint (Figure 1.1). Other slave quarters with multiple subfloor pits have been found at Carter's Grove, Utopia, and Rich Neck Plantations and throughout Tidewater Virginia. Over 250 subfloor pits have been excavated on eighteenth- and nineteenth-century African American slave sites in Virginia.

Subfloor Pits in Tidewater Virginia

The strategy of using subterranean storage has risen independently in many cultures across the world and through time. There is historical precedence for the use of underground storage facilities by each of the three main cultural groups that populated colonial Virginia. Storage pits are frequently present on pre–European contact Native American sites throughout the eastern United States (DeBoer 1988; Stewart 1977), although they do not appear to have been used by Tidewater Native Americans during the contact period (Mouer 1993:147). The Igbo, one of the West African cultures whose members were brought to Virginia in large numbers, are documented as using underground pits in the nineteenth century to store personal belongings (Yentsch 1991). Subterranean storage pits have also been found in Iron Age Britain (Fowler 1983; Reynolds 1974).

Subfloor pits have been found on sites in Virginia dating as early as the second quarter of the seventeenth century. While there has been a tendency among archaeologists to equate the appearance of these features with African American occupants, caution should be used before assigning such blanket ethnic affiliations (Kimmel 1993). Archaeological and documentary evidence indicates that such features were also used by white colonists in the seventeenth and eighteenth centuries (Mouer 1991). Despite these caveats, Virginia archaeological investigations have demonstrated significant differences between pits in slave and nonslave structures. The vast majority of the recorded subterranean pits appear within the footprints of eighteenth-century structures that quartered African Americans. Table 1.1 depicts data on 79 excavated structures that contained subfloor pits, listing the known or probable ethnic background of occupants. Subfloor pits appear sporadically in seventeenth-century structures and only become a regular feature at the end of the century, a date coinciding with the increased importation of Africans into the Virginia colony.

An analysis of 33 Virginia sites compared numbers of subfloor pits in 54 structures (Fesler 1997). The structures were divided into three categories: buildings from documented quarters, structures that were highly likely to have housed enslaved African Americans, and dwellings either known to have been occupied by white tenants or whose occupants were unknown. Analysis showed that subfloor pits were more commonly associated with slave than nonslave households and that the presence of multiple subfloor pits in a structure was "strongly associated with slave households" (Fesler

Table 1.1. Total numbers of subfloor pits on Virginia sites[a]

Period	Known slave structures		Probable slave structures		Nonslave or unknown structures	
	# Pits	# Structures	# Pits	# Structures	# Pits	# Structures
1 (1620–1635)	[b]	[b]	0	0	2	2
2 (1680–1700)	[b]	[b]	19	2	1	1
3 (1700–1720)	19	3	11	6	2	2
4 (1720–1760)	15	2	38	11	4	2
5 (1760–1780)	49	6	56	10	1	1
6 (1780–1800)	28	13	17	5	1	1
7 (1800–1830)	[b]	[b]	6	5	1	1
8 (1830–1860)	0	3	1	3	0	0
TOTAL	111	27	148	42	12	10

[a]Sites and data used in this table available in Appendix A. One site from the North Carolina coastal plain, the Eden House site, was included. Sites were assigned to the date ranges having the closest fit. Sites were assigned as "probable slave" based on what was known about the property owner, size of landholdings and labor force, and known location of main plantation house.
[b]No known excavated quarters from these periods.

1997:39). Table 1.2 illustrates numbers of subfloor pits per building for 70 known and probable slave structures, using the dataset from Table 1.1.

Subterranean pits found archaeologically in the homes of Anglo-European colonists were larger and more substantially constructed than African American pits. In addition to greater dimensions (6 feet or more in length and width), they were generally deeper and had been constructed with some type of floor. These features, called "butteries" in the seventeenth century, were used to store dairy products, beer, and wine (Mouer 1993:149).

Interestingly, the increased appearance of pits on sites coincides with the rapid expansion of the Virginia slave trade at the beginning of the eighteenth century. In the first half of the seventeenth century, small numbers of Africans labored as indentured servants alongside similarly employed European peoples in the Chesapeake. Some of these Africans were able to work out their periods of indenture and set up small plantations of their own (Breen and Innes 1980). After 1660, a combination of factors, including the increased demand for tobacco and decreasing numbers of English indentured servants arriving in the colony, led to restrictions and laws that eroded

Table 1.2. Number of subfloor pits in African American structures

Period	Structures with no subfloor pits	Structures with 1 subfloor pit	Structures with 2–3 subfloor pits	Structures with >3 subfloor pits
1 (1620–1635)	0	0	0	0
2 (1680–1700)	0	0	1	1
3 (1700–1720)	1	2	3	4
4 (1720–1760)	0	2	4	5
5 (1760–1780)[a]	0	5	1	10
6 (1780–1800)	3	7	5	3
7 (1800–1830)	1	3	1	0
8 (1830–1860)	5	1	0	0
TOTAL	10	20	15	23

[a]Four structures with dates spanning the period 1740–1780 were included in this category. This table includes kitchens on urban and rural sites, such as the Brush-Everard kitchen in Williamsburg, Virginia.

the freedom of Africans, as colonists came to realize that enslaving Africans answered their need for a stable labor force. The importation of labor directly from Africa, rather than through the West Indies, began in the 1680s (Kulikoff 1986:320), the same period in which subfloor pits begin to appear regularly on Virginia sites.

The black population in Virginia increased from 2 percent of the total population in 1660 to slightly over 13 percent by 1700 (Blackburn 1997:269). Most of this increase came about through the direct importation of Africans. Of the 54,000 blacks brought to Maryland and Virginia between 1700 and 1740, 49,000 were African, resulting in Africans comprising more than 90 percent of the Chesapeake enslaved population between 1727 and 1740 (Kulikoff 1986:320). The cultural impact of such a massive influx of individuals on the already-established black population can only be imagined.

The regular appearance of subfloor pits on post-1680 Virginia sites, combined with the tremendous numbers of Africans arriving in the Virginia colony, suggests that the use of these features was tied to the presence of Africans there and arose largely in response to the conditions of slavery. The geographic distribution of subfloor pits, viewed in conjunction with the history of expansion by the United States during the early national period, holds clues for answering these questions. At the end of the eighteenth century and extending into the opening decades of the nineteenth, some Virginia planters began moving west and south into Kentucky, Tennessee, Missouri, and Mississippi in search of new agricultural lands along the frontier. Archaeological excavations of slave quarters in these states have revealed subfloor pits, suggesting that enslaved Virginians carried this cultural practice with them to these new areas (Wilkie 1995; Young 1997). Excavations in areas of North Carolina settled by planters and slaves from Virginia have revealed quarters with multiple subfloor pits (Lautzenheiser et al. 1998). Interestingly, subfloor pits have not been found on slave quarters in South Carolina, Georgia, or Florida, areas whose slave trade drew upon different parts of Africa than Virginia's trade. Chambers (1996) has suggested that the initial creation and use of subfloor pits was related to the ethnic heritage and food preferences of the enslaved in Virginia, linking Igbos in Virginia and their preference for yams with subfloor pits. Thus, it becomes possible to formulate an explanation for the geographic range of these pits based not on external ecological factors but on a combination of culture, demographics, and environmental factors. This connection will be discussed later in more detail.

The use of interior subfloor pits appears to have virtually vanished by the end of the first quarter of the nineteenth century. Similar pits, located in the yards outside of houses, have been found on late nineteenth- and early twentieth-century sites in Maryland, Virginia, and North Carolina (Ryder 1991; Westamacott 1992). Larger than subfloor examples, these exterior pits were used as root cellars and for overwintering live plants. The reasons interior subterranean pits presumably fell out of use on Virginia plantations in the nineteenth century are outlined in Chapter 9.

When found as archaeological features, the subfloor pits are filled holes that appear as darker soil stains against the undisturbed subsoil clay. After falling out of service, they were filled, presumably by the occupants of the house, with garbage. Archaeologists have offered several plausible functions for these subfloor pits, including their serving as root cellars for the preservation of fruits and vegetables, as "hidey holes" for stolen or valuable goods, and as personal storage units (Franklin 1997; Neiman 1997). Some of the pits, however, displayed characteristics suggesting they may have been used in yet another way—as spiritual spaces. In this study, each of these proposed functions is examined and tested in more detail.

A cursory perusal of artifacts from a number of the pits suggests that most of the debris could be characterized as secondary refuse, those small bits and fragments of household garbage swept up from yards or fireplace cleanings. But some of the pits contained a number of serviceable items, such as bottles, tools, and pottery. If the material life of the enslaved was as impoverished as eighteenth-century accounts suggest, then why were enslaved people discarding useful items along with broken debris in subfloor pits? A possible answer may be found in the West African cultural traditions of Virginia's enslaved. Since the construction and maintenance of shrines is critical in these cultures, some of these subfloor pits may have been serving spiritual functions. If this hypothesis is correct, items placed on the floors of the pits were shrine objects left intentionally by the individual or family who created the shrine.

The physical characteristics and spatial patterning of subfloor pits raised other questions as well. Why were there so many of these features found on sites associated with African Americans? While underground pits are present on some Native American or Anglo-American sites from the same period (DeBoer 1988; Fowler 1983; Reynolds 1974), they are much more numerous on sites associated with the enslaved in Virginia. While the need for storage in slave quarters is a feasible explanation for these pits, the homes of colonial-period yeoman farmers of European descent were often just as small and cramped as quarters, but subfloor pits were less typical in these structures. When interior pits do appear on these sites, they are generally larger, more substantially constructed, and located close to hearths (Fesler 1997; Mouer 1991). In some of the slave quarters, however, pits literally covered most of the floor space. Were the numbers of pits reflective of slave demographics at these individual quarters? Did each enslaved individual or family maintain its own pit? Could changes be seen over time in numbers of pits per structure and in the objects they contained, and, if so, could they be related to changes in the enslaved population? These features seemed to be a response to enslavement—whether their creation stemmed from a need for food preservation, a desire for private space, a perceived spiritual need, or some other yet unknown factor.

In this study, subfloor pits from thirteen Virginia sites are examined in detail. Because the slave population of Virginia's eighteenth-century plantations consisted of Africans as well as first- and second-generation African Americans, it is critical to consider the African heritages of the enslaved when studying their lives. Thus, this study uses an interdisciplinary approach that combines archaeological, historical, ethnographic, and ethnohistoric evidence from both Virginia and West Africa, the area from which many of Virginia's slaves were taken. In their encounters with white colonists, the enslaved brought with them cultural traditions and practices very different from those of their oppressors. What were these encounters like?

How did these different beliefs intersect in the Virginia colony, particularly given the power differentials that characterized these encounters?

Slaves in Virginia

Earlier historical research posited that the random patterns of slave trade placed Africans from many different cultural groups together on plantations, a demographic factor that would have led to the rapid abandonment of African cultural practices (Kulikoff 1986; Mintz and Price 1992). Presumably, the new creolized African American cultures that formed on plantations of the South were more American than African, as individuals from diverse African cultures would have found little to unite them other than their common plight. These works overlooked two important factors: the presence of broad-based cultural similarities within some of the regions of Africa tapped during the transatlantic slave trade (Thornton 1992), and evidence that patterns of slave trade and purchasing tended to concentrate individuals from the same cultural groups in specific areas of the North American colonies (Chambers 1996; Curtin 1969; Walsh 1997). It is critical to combat what Chambers (1996:9) has called "historical amnesia"—the idea that Africans abandoned all that was known by them after stepping onto foreign shores.

This study focuses in particular on the culture, history, and traditions of one group of West Africans, the Igbo of southeastern Nigeria. The Igbo, a people from the Niger River area, were concentrated in the eighteenth century in Virginia's lower tidewater (Chambers 1996; Curtin 1969). Igbo cultural traditions will be viewed within a larger West African context to isolate practices that could have been reproduced and transformed in Virginia. Africans in other parts of the Diaspora did not abandon African beliefs (Drewal 1988; Thompson 1983, 1993), so the suggestion that this erasure happened in Virginia is implausible and offensive.

Chambers has posited that the enslaved in colonial and early national Virginia formed an "Igboized" culture, particularly in the interior tidewater and piedmont counties along the James, York, and Rappahannock Rivers (Chambers 1996:401). He also argues that their numbers and concentrations were so great that they even "Igboized" individuals from other African cultural groups who had been enslaved. Igbos were by no means the only African cultural groups present in the Virginia tidewater; at different periods Senegambians, Ibibios, and other West African peoples were also brought to Virginia. The cultural traditions of these groups will also be addressed, although in somewhat less detail. The Igbo in Virginia interacted with fellow Igbos and with members of other cultural groups to refashion familiar actions to help them in the new, often intolerable situations in which they found themselves. What social, ideological, and material resources did Igbos and others enslaved in Virginia draw upon in creating new lives for themselves?

Because many West African cultures, particularly those in the southern forest regions, did not develop written languages until recent times, one of the primary sources used by scholars in writing West African histories is oral tradition (Isichei 1976; Osae et al. 1973). The rich oral traditions of West African cultures recount the creations of the universe, the origins of particular peoples, the founding of kingdoms, and the stories of gods and goddesses. Taking the form of stories, songs, proverbs, and ceremonies and often transmitted by elders, these traditions are used to explain and perpetuate elements of West African culture (Davidson 1977). Although some may appear to be fantastic recountings of imaginary events, careful analysis suggests that many of these traditions do represent actual occurrences. For example, the legend of Oduduwa and his seven sons seems to be a simplified rendition of a chain of events that led to the formation of the Yoruba kingdom (Osae et al. 1973). Other traditions within Igbo culture seem to explain and validate social relationships (Isichei 1976).

For past West African cultures, the written records that do exist were largely the product of outsiders traveling in the area. West Africa's long history of contact with other cultures has left a number of such sources. The first known written descriptions of West Africa date from the eighth century A.D.; prior to the establishment of direct trade with Europe in the fifteenth century, most of these sources were Arabic (Davidson 1977; Osae et al. 1973). Descriptions from the period of the fifteenth to nineteenth centuries, on the other hand, were primarily European (Connah 1990).

One of the difficulties encountered by Western historians studying West Africa is placing certain events recounted in oral traditions within a time frame. Traditional Western concepts, such as linear time or the use of certain standards of behavior as a categorizing tool may have no meaning in West African worldviews and therefore are not valid for the study of West African history. Since this study is deeply embedded in both the West African and the European-based worlds, scholars need to have an understanding of both.

Slavery should not be viewed as a system of personal domination that stripped the enslaved of the coping mechanisms so crucial for survival. Far from erasing such survival strategies, enslavement called forth creative, but

traditionally based, solutions to the problems slaves encountered. Being African, their frame of reference was African, and they interpreted their new
worlds based on what they knew from their traditional cultures. In the Caribbean, for example, the enslaved typically associated with others of their
own ethnicity, "re-grouping" to cope with the stress of enslavement (Schuler
1979). In order for this strategy to succeed, it often meant that subethnic
differences had to be collapsed and panethnic cultures created (Chambers
1996). The Igbo of West Africa, for example, were a stateless society during
the period of the Atlantic slave trade, with village-level political and social
organization. Because of this local-level organization, a great deal of cultural
diversity existed among the different villages and regions inhabited by the
Igbo. Despite these differences, however, overarching similarities provided a
sense of cohesiveness and common identity among the different areas. Ex-
plorer W. B. Baikie wrote in the 1850s, "In I'gbo each person hails . . . from
the particular district where he was born, but when away from home all are
I'gbos" (Baikie 1966 [1856]:307).

   How did enslaved individuals adjust to bondage, and how did change occur in slave communities? Which aspects of life were most likely to bring
about reworking and transformation of traditional West African elements,
and which were more likely to bring about disappearance altogether? How
did a West African heritage function for the enslaved in response to individual needs for personal freedom and identity in the face of restrictions
that imposed limits in these areas? Given the importance of kinship in West
Africa and among enslaved African American communities, did the West
African–based spiritual tradition of ancestor veneration survive, albeit transformed, in the Virginia Chesapeake? If so, what purposes did it serve? What
can archaeology reveal about how African Americans struggled to resolve
cultural differences and form community bonds and a collective identity on
plantations in the South?

   These questions are best addressed working within the theoretical frameworks of creolization (Chambers 2000; Edwards-Ingram and Brown 1998),
ethnicity (Baumann 2001; Lovejoy and Trotman 2003; McGuire 1982), individual and group identity formation (Fennell 2000; Franklin 2001; Larsen
2005), race (Epperson 2004), and power (Givens 2004). These frameworks
are used in combination with material culture studies that address how the
meanings and uses of material culture are transformed and recontextualized by individuals and social groups, particularly under new circumstances
(Beaudry et al. 1991; Miller 1987).

   A creolization model is a good vehicle for studying change, because it recognizes "the contribution of pre-existing cultural traditions to entirely new cultural formations" (Edwards-Ingram and Brown 1998:2). Creolization studies arose out of linguistic analysis, with models of culture change paralleling the development of pidgin languages occurring when groups speaking two or more languages came into sustained contact. Out of necessity, a shared cultural language based on some sort of shared grammar developed (Mintz and Price 1992). Creolization models in African American archaeology focus on how Africans remade themselves through creative adaptation with culture as a social construction. In this study, the enslaved understood "their new world using the cultural vocabularies they brought from their old world" (Sidbury 1997:48). Historical creolization is nonrandom and developmental, with an initial stage of simplification—selective borrowing between groups and leveling within groups—followed by later elaboration, reinterpretation, or even extinction of some cultural practices (Chambers 1996:411).

Individuals from different West and Central African cultures interacted on Virginia's plantations, seeking cultural similarities, working through differences, and over time forming a creolized culture that allowed individuals from these different cultures to form common allegiances. In Virginia, African ethnic affiliations were subsumed into a more general Afro-Virginian identity, in the interest of coming together under common circumstances (Franklin 2001). Concentrations of individuals of Igbo descent in Tidewater Virginia, however, may have informed the composition of this Afro-Virginian identity to a greater degree than other West African cultures (Chambers 1996). Chambers argues for a process of historical creolization (1996:397) where a *bricolage* (Lévi-Strauss 1966) of mixing and matching old and new ways formed an Igboized regional tradition. Thus, in this part of Virginia, the enslaved were able to find some common cultural ground upon which to build new lives.

The processes of creolization are far from simple. Viewing creolization and processes of culture change in a unilineal fashion—one of seeing successive generations of Africans and African Americans as moving farther and farther away from their descendant culture—is unproductive. More fruitful is an approach that examines contextual information, viewing creolization as a more erratic process. Various levels of creolized beliefs and practices, as well as incorporation of both European and African-based components, were all part of the plantation experience. Movement could "reverse" itself, as illustrated by burial practices at a nineteenth-century African American cemetery in Philadelphia. There some burials showed a revitalization of African-based spiritual practices attributed to growing racism, economic stress, and the in-migration of African Americans from the South (McCarthy 1997).

As newly enslaved Africans sought to understand and create meaning in their lives, they crafted new identities. While identities are complex, multi-faceted, and in a constant state of negotiation, background and place of origin play a large role in defining how an individual characterizes his or her self and uses these elements to negotiate daily life (McGuire 1982; Sid-bury 1997). Collective identities emerge when individuals recognize com-mon traits and come together in opposition to others (Nishida 2003). On the plantations of Virginia, enslaved African Americans created and re-created distinctive collective and individual identities based on concepts of ethnicity, race, and gender. Fluid and situational, these identities were crafted within the broader political, socioeconomic, and cultural conditions in Virginia. Race, a social construction that developed in Virginia over the course of the seventeenth century as the legal conditions of African Americans deterio-rated, was an identity imposed on the enslaved by Virginia planters (Epper-son 1999). Enslaved African Americans turned this imposed racial catego-rization to their advantage, using it to come together to further their own interests (Epperson 1999; Franklin 2001).

Identity formation on Virginia quarters invariably took place within the context of power relations. Anthony Giddens (1979:88) has defined power in terms of an individual's capability to intervene in a set of events in order to affect their outcome in some intended fashion. Whites exercised power over enslaved people of African descent. Power, however, is rarely absolute, and, at some basic level, all individuals possess some degree of control over their lives. In this study, a heterogenous concept that views power as "multifaceted and not reducible to a single source or structure" is assumed for slaves in the American South (Bowles and Gintis 1986:23). This discussion of power ex-tends into the present, with the social and political consequences of privi-leging of the voice of the archaeologist in constructions of the past (Epper-son 2004).

It is also important to approach analysis on a number of scales, since indi-vidual experiences are situational. An individual's decisions would have been affected by his or her cultural background, age, gender, and position within the plantation infrastructure and slave community. At the same time, how-ever, individuals' situations as enslaved persons are more alike than differ-ent, providing a larger, overarching scale of analysis of life under the bonds of slavery. Regional differences—in staple agriculture, slave demographics, and interaction with people from different cultural backgrounds—also have to be taken into account.

In speaking of the history and culture of his fellow Latin Americans, author Gabriel García Márquez (1982:3) noted, "The interpretation of our reality through patterns not our own serves only to make us ever more unknown, ever less free, ever more solitary." He was referring, of course, to studies endeavoring to understand Latin American history from a Western perspective. Likewise, scholars examining the lives of North America's enslaved peoples without reference to the African cultures from which they were (quite literally) taken, pursue a similarly flawed approach. Unlike the articles of clothing they were often forced to shed aboard the America-bound slaving vessels, Africans did not abandon their cultural heritages during the Middle Passage. Ideas about spirituality, gender roles, and identity, among others, came with them aboard these ships, taking root in the New World just as surely as did the cultural traditions arriving with the English settlers. Although a number of factors, most notably the imbalances of power between enslaved Africans and white settlers, prevented the enslaved from replicating African cultures on this side of the Atlantic, they did re-create and transform distinctly African cultural practices on the plantations of the American South. Spirituality would have figured prominently in these transformed practices. According to John Mbiti (1969:15), for an African "and for the larger community of which he is part, to live is to be caught up in a religious drama."

The models of material culture study that have proven most successful in addressing how the meanings and uses of material culture are transformed and recontextualized have focused on integrating behavior with material culture. Rather than attempting to trace direct unaltered transference of objects and behaviors from Africa, this approach seeks to discover how African cultural traditions were modified by slaves' experience of the new environments, different social groups, and altered power structures. Emphasis is placed on interplay and exchange between the cultural backgrounds of enslaved people and plantation owners. Exchange was not unidirectional, as had been believed by early twentieth-century historians; enslaved blacks, Native Americans, free blacks, and white colonists participated instead in a symbiotic relationship that produced new and distinct cultures forged from elements of each. Archaeologists have begun to ask how slaves used and thought about material objects, how uses and meanings changed with time and circumstances, and what roles physical items played in the formation of African American culture.

This framework of inquiry originated in anthropological concern to recover cultural meanings, as decipherable particularly from components of the material world (Hodder 1986). Humans are viewed as individuals with differing expectations and experiences, each negotiating social rules and influencing social structure. Social structure is produced and reproduced through the arrangement of the material world, which people use to define themselves and others. Material culture, actively and meaningfully produced, is viewed as a text whose meanings can be read within the context of the human societies in which these objects functioned (Leis 2002).

Archaeologists interested in identity are faced with the task of teasing out how the material remains found on sites are expressions of such identities (Beaudry et al. 1991; Fennell 2000; Hodder 1986, 1987). An interpretive analysis, by which the symbolic meanings of artifacts are recovered through careful analysis of historical and cultural contexts, is used here. To show how objects found in subfloor pits were symbols of ethnic and spiritual identity requires an approach that views material culture within the context of Igbo cultural and spiritual practices. Understanding the meanings of certain objects in Igbo and other West African cultures whose members were present in colonial Virginia is crucial for determining how objects were used in ways that maintained and transformed ethnic identities there. Particularly important is information on which objects typically are found in association with one another and whether particular colors, materials, shapes, or designs are significant. In this research the symbolic meanings of artifact assemblages are inferred by examining them contextually, both within a system of colonialism and power and within the historical context of precolonial to postcolonial Igboland. While recognizing that Igbo culture has undergone enormous changes over the centuries, the existence of long-term continuities in core beliefs is visible archaeologically in ritual iconography (Ray 1987). Although there are certain risks in drawing analogies between the present and the past, careful reading and comparison of multiple sources can surmount some of these problems.

Enslaved Communities in Tidewater Virginia

This study focuses on five slave quarters from three eighteenth-century plantations in the Williamsburg area: Utopia Quarter Periods II–IV, Kingsmill

Quarter, and Carter's Grove Quarter. These three plantations were chosen for several reasons. Perhaps the most compelling is that they were connected through descent and marriage of their white owners. Because of these connections, the enslaved communities on these three properties also shared kinship ties. Lorena Walsh's study (1997) uses historical records from these plantations to re-create a multigeneration history of the enslaved communities there. Since most of the excavated structures were only occupied for twenty to thirty years, household-level analysis was possible. In addition, taken together as a group, the three quartering sites were occupied throughout the span of the eighteenth century, a period when slavery became institutionalized and expanded throughout Virginia. Looking across the span of a century provides an opportunity to examine change across time on interconnected plantations and create a regional context for slavery in eighteenth-century tidewater Virginia.

Methodology

Statistical analyses of size, shape, placement within structures, and other physical characteristics were conducted on a sample of 103 subfloor pits from quarters at the three Virginia plantations. Detailed analysis of pit soil strata and artifacts from these features allowed a smaller number of pits to be selected for functional analysis. As a comparison to these three related sites, physical characteristics of 49 subfloor pits from 8 additional sites were analyzed (Table 1.3). These sites expanded the temporal and regional scale of the study and brought the total number of subfloor pits analyzed from all sites to 152.

A detailed analysis was conducted on the subfloor pits. Careful study of notes, maps, and photographs of the pits created a sequence for the construction, maintenance, repair, redigging, and abandonment of the features within specific structures, as well as information on pit location, size, depth, shape, and construction techniques. In addition to gathering information on the specific physical characteristics of each pit, detailed analysis of the artifacts from the features at the three plantations was conducted. Attributes included artifact type, material, and technological and decorative data, as well as a number of variables believed important in determining the function of the subfloor pits. These variables included artifact size and relative completeness, vessel form and body component of ceramic and glass objects, color, modifications, and, in the case of ceramics in particular, any information on design or decorative elements.

Table 1.3. Archaeological sites analyzed

Site number	Name	Dates	Location	# Structures	# Subfloor pits
44JC32	Utopia Period II	1700–1725	Tidewater Virginia	3	18
44JC32	Utopia Period III	1725–1750	Tidewater Virginia	2	20
31BR52	Eden House	1720–1750	Tidewater N.Carolina	1	5
44HE677	Curles Neck	1740–1775	Tidewater Virginia	1	2
44JC787	Utopia Period IV	1750–1780	Tidewater Virginia	3	24
44JC39	Kingsmill Quarter	1760–1781	Tidewater Virginia	2	26
44AB89	Monticello	1770–1820	Piedmont Virginia	4	4
44JC110	Carter's Grove	1780–c. 1800	Tidewater Virginia	3	16
44PW80	Monroe	1790–1869	Piedmont Virginia	3	1
44JC298	Governor's Land	1680–1720	Tidewater Virginia	3	19
44WB52	Richneck	1740–1780	Tidewater Virginia	1	15
CWF29F	Brush–Everard	early 19th c.	Tidewater Virginia	1	1
44CF344	Magnolia Grange	1800–1830	Piedmont Virginia	1	3

In order to assist in determining the nature of the fill within the features, information was recorded on the relative size of each object. This task was accomplished by measuring the artifacts largest linear dimension. By recording size information, it was anticipated that the fill layers within the features could be identified as primary or secondary deposition, and thus allow separation of objects associated with the primary function of the pits from items discarded after its abandonment. In conjunction with the physical size of each artifact, data on its relative completeness was also recorded, expressed as a percentage of the complete object. These percentages were based on a visual assessment of the object itself and previous experience with the size and appearance of complete objects. These assessments were not scientifically accurate to the percentage and were never intended to be; they were merely an estimate for analysis purposes. No number smaller than 10 percent was assigned, even if the artifact was felt to represent less than 10 percent of the complete item.

Also recorded were any modifications to artifacts that suggested they had been used in ways other than originally intended. Examples would include bottle glass flaked to make cutting implements, worked animal bone, or piercing or notching on coins or buttons. Also noted was any evidence of incising or etching on artifacts that might suggest their use as objects of personal adornment or spiritual significance.

Organization of Book

The following chapters detail the results of subfloor pits analysis, with several goals in mind. The first is to determine how African Americans used subfloor pits and whether these pits can be viewed as a specific response to enslavement. Larger goals include using archaeological remains to illuminate other aspects of slave life, such as the formation of slave identities, changes within the enslaved community, and the material and symbolic aspects of creolization processes.

Chapter 2 reviews the physical setting and history of the Virginia Chesapeake, the region chosen for study. The breadth of historical and archaeological research done over the last several decades makes this one of the best-studied regions in the American South. Using these works, it is possible to construct a detailed context within which to frame this study. Analysis of plantation records and other eighteenth-century documents shows how the increasingly equitable ratios of female to male slaves allowed the formation of family groups around the mid-eighteenth century (Kulikoff 1986), while other studies contrasted English and African work patterns and concepts of time and space (Sobel 1987). Other important works have been prepared on the effects of the Great Awakenings on the religious experiences of the enslaved and their acceptance of Christianity (Raboteau 1978; Sobel 1979). A study of the enslaved communities at the interconnected plantations chosen for detailed analysis (Walsh 1997) added a dimension to this study that would have been difficult to replicate in other regions. Archaeological excavations specified the physical and material conditions under which enslaved Virginians lived (Fesler 1997; Franklin 1997; Kelso 1984). Having access to a detailed regional context crafted from multiple sources provided a firm base upon which to ground this work.

Because some of this work focuses on how West African cultural traditions were maintained and transformed in the Virginia Chesapeake, Chapter 2 also includes a section on the demographics of slavery in Virginia. This discussion provides information on the parts of Africa from which the enslaved originated, the periods of heaviest immigration, slave purchasing patterns, and how slaves were dispersed on Virginia's plantations. Without knowledge of the cultural practices of the specific groups enslaved in Virginia, it would be impossible to trace if and how the enslaved were transforming African-based practices in this colony.

Chapter 3 provides a historical and archaeological overview of the five study sites. The sites—Utopia Periods II–IV, Kingsmill, and Carter's Grove Quarters—are examined chronologically. Using documentary evidence, a context for each plantation is created, including what is known about their enslaved populations, their work, and their social environments. Archaeological and historical data provide this contextual background and set the stage for the discussions of subfloor pit functions in the following chapters.

Chapter 4 briefly examines the physical evidence from the five sites, looking at change across time in architecture, material goods, and diet. Data from other slave sites are contrasted with the results of analysis at the Utopia, Kingsmill, and Carter's Grove Quarters.

Chapter 5 examines the physical characteristics of Virginia subfloor pits and the conditions under which they occur. The results of quantitative analysis on physical characteristics are examined first. Using the results of this analysis, several hypotheses are offered for pit function, based on location within structures and other physical characteristics. This chapter details the results of testing these hypotheses on data from the study sites.

In Chapters 6, 7, and 8, the three hypothesized functions of Virginia subfloor pits—as root cellars, as storage units, and as West African–based

shrines—are examined in detail. Each chapter begins with an in-depth discussion of historical, archaeological, and ethnographic evidence to support
the hypothesized functions. After building a model against which to test
each presumed function, features from the five sites that fit each model are
examined in detail.

These chapters open with three brief narratives, included as a means to
engage the reader with the past. These narratives are imagined stories—
albeit based on real people and situated within specific historical and archaeological contexts. The creation of these narratives arose from a desire
to imagine more fully the lives and emotions of the people who once lived
at these plantations and created these subfloor pits. Recent archaeological
scholarship on dialogue and multivocality in archaeological interpretation
and writing (Hodder 1989; Joyce 2002; Stahl et al. 2004) informed the creation of these narratives. Appendix B contains an explanation of the historical basis for each narrative, as well as a discussion of current interpretive
issues on the use of archaeological narrative.

Chapter 9 draws conclusions about how subfloor pits functioned within
the larger context of Virginia plantation slavery. Critical to these conclusions are acts of resistance, concepts of personal and ethnic identity, how the
enslaved envisioned their relationship to their African pasts, and the development of African American Christianity. This chapter addresses why these
pit features began disappearing from slave houses, beginning in the early
nineteenth century.

In the words of historian Ira Berlin (1998:3), "understanding that a person
was a slave is not the end of the story but the beginning, for the slaves' history was derived from experiences that differed from place to place and time
to time and not from some unchanging transhistorical verity." This story
about to unfold looks at a particular region within Virginia, providing a time
depth of five generations. Its intent is not to tell the story of all enslaved
people of African descent in the Americas but to provide some degree of
understanding about how a particular group of people negotiated the circumstances of their lives. Archaeology reveals the material circumstances of
slaves' lives, which in turn opens the door to illuminating other aspects of
life: spirituality, symbolic meanings assigned to material goods, social life,
individual and group agency, and acts of resistance and accommodation. The
time for telling these stories is long overdue.

2
Regional Context

The Virginia plantations that are the focus of this study were located on a small peninsula stretching between the James and York Rivers, two tributaries emptying into Chesapeake Bay (Figure 2.1). By the late eighteenth century, this Tidewater peninsula was characterized by dispersed plantations and farmsteads set among agricultural fields, pasture, and forests of pine and hardwood spread over a flat to gently rolling terrain. Towns and clustered settlements were scarce. Jamestown, the colony's first capital, had largely disappeared. Williamsburg, located eight miles upriver, had replaced Jamestown as the capital in 1699. The only other settlement of any size on the peninsula was the small river port at Yorktown.

By the end of the eighteenth century, the landscape, still largely rural, had been fashioned by the forces of almost two centuries of colonization. But at the beginning of the seventeenth century, when the first English settlers arrived looking for gold and other wealth, they found a forested wilderness bisected by numerous broad creeks flowing into wetlands and large rivers. While the English failed to find the mineral wealth they had come seeking, they did discover gold of another sort, in the color of cured tobacco. This crop, the regional environment, and the political, social, and economic ambitions of the English colonists and the Royal Crown were all to intersect in shaping the development of the Chesapeake throughout the colonial period.

Agriculture was the primary factor shaping the early Virginia Chesapeake, and within that agricultural framework, tobacco was king. The English demand for tobacco was considerable, and Virginia's climate, with its hot summers and temperate winters, was particularly suited for the cultivation of this crop (Morgan 1998:33). Colonists rushed to establish tobacco

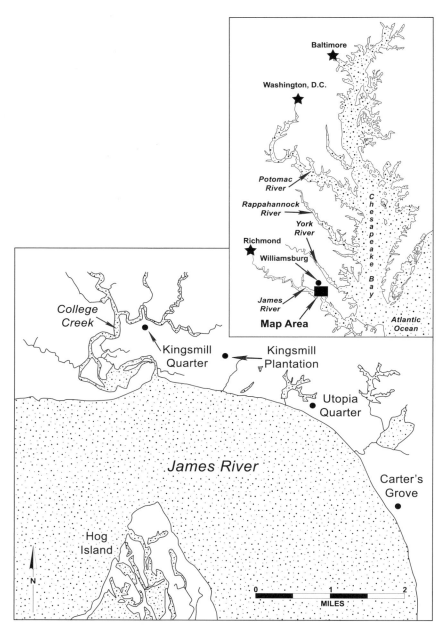

2.1. Map of Tidewater Virginia and James/York peninsula showing Utopia, Kingsmill, and Carter's Grove (drawn by Tamera Myer-Mams)

plantations, even delaying the construction of durable homes in order to acquire as much land and labor as possible (Carson et al. 1981). Since tobacco rapidly depleted soil fertility, the acreage demands of this crop, combined with the field rotation methods employed by Virginia farmers, required large tracts of land be held in reserve for future tobacco fields (Morgan 1998:33). English and European demand for tobacco was high, and even during periods of depressed prices in the middle half of the seventeenth century, planters were able to clear profits (Kulikoff 1986:5). By the late 1670s, Chesapeake planters exported an annual average of more than 20 million pounds of tobacco (Menard 1980).

The need for agricultural land led to a dispersed rural settlement pattern in the Virginia Chesapeake. Plantations were distributed along the fertile lands adjacent to rivers and creeks, and since planters could sell their tobacco to English ships directly from their own plantation wharves, there was no real need for large commercial centers. Thus, few towns developed, even when a series of town acts meant to stimulate centralization of the tobacco trade and manufacturing were enacted during the early eighteenth century (Reps 1972). Many other business and legal transactions were conducted at courthouses, taverns, and churches located at rural crossroads. While Williamsburg and Yorktown prospered as service centers where goods could be exchanged, information obtained, and services rendered, they never even remotely approached the size of cities and towns in neighboring colonies, such as Charleston and New York.

In addition to shaping the physical form of settlement, tobacco also molded the labor needs of the colony. Throughout most of the seventeenth century, indentured labor from England supplied the need for agricultural workers. Through the headrights system, a prospective colonist or an established settler could underwrite the cost of transporting individuals to the Virginia colony. For every person brought over, the underwriter would be granted 50 acres of land. If these individuals had also been bonded as indentured servants, the underwriter would gain from four to seven years of labor from each.

In the early years of settlement, a man arriving as an indentured servant stood a good chance, once his servitude was completed, of purchasing land and becoming self-sufficient, perhaps even wealthy. But as economic conditions improved in England and opportunities were reduced as available open land diminished, the numbers incoming decreased sharply. Colonists were left with labor shortages they were desperate to fill. Native Americans had proven to be unsatisfactory workers and had never comprised a large part of the labor force in Virginia (Morgan 1975). Increasingly, therefore, the colonists turned to African labor to supply their needs, with the colony evolving from what Berlin (1998) calls a "society with slaves" to a "slave society."

The first Africans arrived in Virginia in 1619 aboard a Dutch trading vessel. Numbers of Africans, who were at first considered indentured labor, remained small throughout much of the seventeenth century, supplementing the white indentured labor force. As numbers of English indentured labor diminished, the importation of Africans increased, with slave imports tending to coincide with tobacco market booms (Walsh 1993:170).

Coupled with the increasing importation of Africans came ever-tightening restrictions on their freedom. By the early eighteenth century, laws had been passed guaranteeing that planters had the right to hold Africans and their descendants in slavery (Walsh 1997:25). By 1700, the black population of Virginia and Maryland had increased to just over 13 percent, up from 2 percent in 1660 (Blackburn 1997:269). The largest numbers of slaves arrived between the 1720s and 1740s, and by midcentury at least half the householders in the Tidewater owned slaves (Kulikoff 1986:6). Slave families began to form, and by the middle of the century the larger Chesapeake planters no longer needed to purchase extra hands owing to natural increase. Enslaved Africans and African Americans comprised between 50 to 59 percent of the total population in James City and York Counties in 1750 and rose to over 60 percent in James City County by 1775, where it stayed for the remainder of the century (Morgan 1998:98–99).

In the eighteenth century, Virginia agriculture underwent a series of changes that reflected a combination of environmental, demographic, and economic factors. Since long settlement in the region meant there was little new land available for acquisition, expansion had begun in the Piedmont to the west (Kulikoff 1986). Tobacco farming had so reduced the soil fertility that planters were forced to work larger amounts of land to produce the tobacco yields of the previous century. This factor, combined with fluctuating tobacco prices around the turn of the eighteenth century, led most planters to diversify their agricultural base, never again relying solely upon tobacco.

In the 1720s and 1730s, many Virginia planters began alternating between monocropping tobacco and the planting of corn, wheat, and other grains, crops whose prices declined more slowly than tobacco during periods of economic depression. Tobacco continued to be raised, and an increase in tobacco prices between the 1740s and the American Revolution brought about prosperous conditions for many Chesapeake planters, especially those individuals with larger estates (Kulikoff 1986:118). With this wealth, planters constructed fine homes, added to their labor forces, and improved their landholdings.

The Revolutionary War brought about hardships for many planters, as their external markets were cut off by the hostilities. By the 1790s, Chesapeake planters had abandoned tobacco production and made the switch to grains, cotton, and livestock (Walsh 1997). A combination of factors, including wars in Europe and depleted soils, contributed to the long-term economic decline the Chesapeake entered by the 1820s.

In the eighteenth century, the Virginia Tidewater was characterized primarily by landowners farming modest tracts with the assistance of limited numbers of enslaved individuals (Walsh 1997:14). Such small farms were able to survive because tobacco could be successfully grown in small units, requiring little initial outlay of equipment or labor (Kulikoff 1986:23; Morgan 1998:36). Despite the numbers of small landholders, Virginia's economy, politics, and society were under the control of a minority—the gentry landholders. Virginia society had gone from a relatively egalitarian society in the early seventeenth century to an increasingly hierarchical one beginning late in the same century (Kulikoff 1986). The dominance of the egalitarian system had been supported by the steady supply of indentured labor, and with its disappearance and the reliance on African labor, the stage was set for a new gentry class to develop (Kulikoff 1986:37). These wealthy planters, descendants of some of the region's early settlers who prospered and gained political power, inherited land and labor wealth. At the turn of the eighteenth century, two-thirds of the land was owned by the wealthiest 5 percent of the population (Blackburn 1997:359). The elevated positions of the gentry allowed them to purchase additional labor and make improvements to their properties, as well as garner political power of their own. It is on several of these elite planters that this study will focus, examining quarters on three large James River peninsula plantations whose free and enslaved communities were connected across time and space.

The Plantations

The histories of the land and people of Carter's Grove, Kingsmill, and Utopia plantations are complex and intertwined, including consolidations of both real estate and human properties. Initial settlement of the lands along the north shore of the James River south of Williamsburg, where these plantations were later seated, was by early seventeenth-century English colonists. Carter's Grove Plantation had originally been the site of Martin's Hundred, one of the settlements destroyed during the Native American uprising of 1622 (Noel Hume 1991). The quarters at Utopia and Kingsmill were located on lands that later came to be known more generally as Kingsmill Plantation, as earlier, smaller plantations were consolidated by the Bray and Burwell families. Initially, however, settlement of the lands located in a slight bend in the James River southeast of Williamsburg's future location, had been in small landholdings by tenants and yeoman farmers. By the 1640s, several of these small farms had been joined into one of two plantations (Figure 2.1).

At the turn of the eighteenth century, the Bray family purchased the Utopia lands, thus setting in motion the sequence of events that was to connect so intricately the properties studied here. Utopia remained in the Bray family until almost midcentury, when it passed by marriage into Burwell family ownership. Burwell already owned the Kingsmill tract, located west of Utopia. The marriage consolidated the two tracts into what became known as Kingsmill Plantation. Twenty-nine of Bray's enslaved laborers were also part of the wedding dowry (Walsh 1997:43), thus merging two groups of African Americans that are the focus of this study. The Virginia colony's inheritance laws allowed planters to entail or tie slaves to particular tracts of land, usually passed on to the eldest male heir (Walsh 1997:44). The Burwell family continued to own the Kingsmill tract for the duration of the period encompassed by this study. Thus, the enslaved communities at the Burwell plantations remained constant over multiple generations of Burwell heirs, allowing the tracking of change within a fairly stable group of related enslaved individuals. A few years after Burwell consolidated Utopia and Kingsmill, his nephew Carter Burwell constructed a large mansion at Carter's Grove Plantation, located several miles downriver. The late eighteenth-century quarter on this plantation is also analyzed.

The quarter communities studied here span the breadth of the eighteenth century, a period that encompasses both the large influxes of Africans in the first part of the century and the later decline of the external slave trade into Virginia. At Utopia, three distinct communities, separated both temporally and spatially, provide a glimpse at one plantation through almost a full century. A group of three houses dated to the first three decades of the century, while two additional structures were occupied between 1730 and 1750. The most recent quarter, with three buildings, dated between 1750 and 1775. This latest group, known as Utopia Period IV, can be contrasted with two contemporaneous quarter buildings at Kingsmill Quarter (ca. 1750–1780) and three houses at Carter's Grove Plantation (1770–1800). On each of these

plantations, the enslaved lived in communities separated from the main plantation house, in circumstances where they were allowed some flexibility in
creating lives for themselves beyond the gaze of the planter.

Demography of Virginia Slavery

To understand the development of African American culture in the Virginia Chesapeake, it is critical to determine the African origins of its enslaved population, as well as the regional contexts of slavery. In Virginia, the
first Africans arrived in 1619, and their numbers expanded slowly throughout most of the century. Importation increased at the end of the century,
rose steadily until the mid-eighteenth century, then fell as native-born Afro-
Virginians began to predominate (Westbury 1981:82). Most Africans were
purchased either singly or in small groups, even by gentry planters (Walsh
1997). During the eighteenth century, more than half of the enslaved on Virginia's middle and lower peninsulas lived on quarters of fewer than 20 slaves
(Morgan 1998:41). On large plantations the enslaved predominantly lived in
settlements or compounds adjacent to agricultural fields called "quarters."
Isaac Weld, traveling through the Northern Neck of Virginia in the 1790s,
wrote that quarters were "usually situated one or two hundred yards from the
dwelling house, which gives the appearance of a village to the residence of
every planter in Virginia" (Weld 1799:84). Here, the enslaved formed families and communities, composed initially of individuals from various West
and Central African cultures. Before the Virginia colony's legal importation
of Africans ended in 1778, American-born blacks began to comprise the bulk
of the enslaved population (Kulikoff 1986; Westbury 1985).

Various West and Central African cultures came together on Virginia's
plantations; a number of excellent studies on the slave trade (Curtin 1969;
Manning 1990; Westbury 1985) and the compilation of data from over 27,000
trans-Atlantic slave ship voyages (Eltis et al. 2000) have enabled researchers
to draw broad conclusions about the cultural backgrounds of Africans enslaved there. Large-scale export patterns out of West Africa corresponded
with analysis of known importation into Virginia, allowing generalities to be
made about the cultural identities of the enslaved in Virginia.

Westbury's research (1985) divided the Virginia slave trade into several
periods spanning the last quarter of the seventeenth century through the
third quarter of the eighteenth century. Similarly, the demographic profile
of the Africans enslaved in Virginia can be divided into major groups, linked
largely to time of importation. Place of export was tied with slave prices and

population decline in various parts of Africa (Manning 1990:94), as well as economic conditions in Virginia (Chambers 1996). Between 1670 and 1698, approximately 1,300 Africans arrived in Virginia, largely through trade with the English Royal African Company (Westbury 1985:229–230). During the second half of the seventeenth century, the Africans brought to Virginia were gathered through trading along the entire length of the West African coast (Walsh 1997), with a second, smaller trade between the Virginia colony and the West Indies.

As importation rose in the first two decades of the eighteenth century, an almost exclusive direct trade between Africa and Virginia developed. Between 1727 and 1769, 91 percent of the enslaved entering Virginia arrived directly from Africa (Westbury 1985). During the late seventeenth century and first two decades of the next, many slave ships arrived in Virginia from Senegambian ports and included members of the Mandingo culture (Manning 1990:49; Walsh 1997:55). The decreasing population in Senegambia, the Gold Coast, and the Bight of Benin led to increased trade in the Bight of Biafra (Manning 1990:94; Walsh 1997), with trading focused around the Niger Delta in the first half of the eighteenth century (Figure 2.2). The greatest influx of Africans into Virginia occurred in the second to fourth decades of the eighteenth century, with approximately 17,000 individuals arriving in the 1730s alone (Westbury 1985:234). The largest numbers of Africans disembarked at ports on the York and Lower James Rivers (Westbury 1981:71). Nearly half of the African slaves arriving at Port York during the early eighteenth century were from the Nigerian tribes of the Igbo, Ibibio, Efkins, and Mokos (Curtin 1969). Despite the dominance of trade from the Bight of Biafra, slaves from other areas also made their way into Virginia: Mande and Western Bantu in the 1730s and 1740s, Angola and Akan in the 1760s (Chambers 1996:284). Slavers also tapped Benin and Sierra Leone for slaves destined for Virginia ports (Curtin 1969:128–130; Manning 1990:69; Walsh 1997).

A combination of factors interacted to affect the demographic composition of Virginia plantation quarters during the eighteenth century. The slave trade in Virginia, like that in other places, was intricately tied to the political, social, and economic conditions of the larger Atlantic world (Thornton 1992). Slaving ships plying the North American coast during the eighteenth century included vessels of the Royal African Company and of independent traders based in London, Liverpool, and Bristol (Walsh 1998). In Virginia, slaving vessels traveled up the Chesapeake Bay and rivers, docking at towns and even individual plantations, auctioning their human cargo as they went.

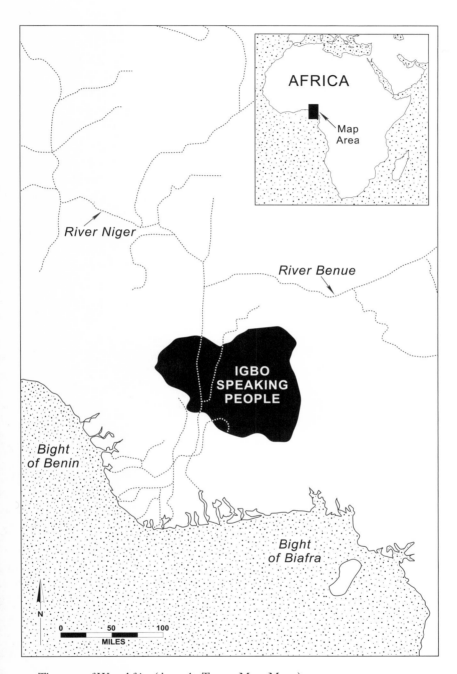

2.2. The coast of West Africa (drawn by Tamera Myer-Mams)

Because even the largest Virginia planters were often cash poor, they were forced to pay for slaves using a system of deferred remittance. The Royal African Company, with its well-established system of trading along the west coast of Africa, offered only short-term credit on slave purchases, terms most Virginia planters could not meet. Bristol merchants, on the other hand, consigned slaves to wealthy Virginia planters, who sold them locally on terms of six to twelve months' credit, payable in tobacco (Chambers 1996:215–216).

Bristol merchants came to replace London merchants as the primary players in the Virginia slave trade, shipping approximately 33,000 slaves, gathered primarily in the Bight of Biafra, to Virginia between 1698 and 1769 (Chambers 1996:12). Bristol merchants trading along the York River brought Igbo and later Angolans into the upper reaches of the Tidewater and central Virginia (Chambers 1996:286–287). Approximately 40 percent of the enslaved brought to Virginia between 1710 and 1760 were from the area around the mouth of the Niger River (Gomez 1998:115), with members of the area's Igbo culture numerically dominant in the Virginia trade in the period between 1710 and the 1740s (Chambers 1996:11). Chambers (1996:247–248) notes, "In the crucial first three decades (1704–1730), shipping records show that the proportion of Igbo in Virginia's import-trade approached 60 percent. Between 1704 and 1745, moreover, Virginia planters imported three times as many Igbo as they did any other African ethnic group." Conservative estimates place the entry of at least 25,000 Igbo into the Virginia colony between 1698 and 1778 (Chambers 1996:282). Although some American colonies, such as South Carolina, avoided purchasing Igbos, Virginians accepted Igbos and fellow Biafrans in large numbers (Rawley 1981:334–335).

Since many of the enslaved were purchased singly or in small groups, it is likely that members of at least several African cultures were represented at any one time on individual plantations. Lorena Walsh's study of the enslaved population at Carter's Grove plantation revealed that individuals from at least three West African cultural and linguistic regions (Senegambia, Igbo, and Sierra Leone) were present there during the second quarter of the eighteenth century (Walsh 1997). At Utopia Quarter, some of the enslaved during the first half of the eighteenth century were Igbo, while others were Angolans, Koromanti from the Gold Coast, and Mandinga from Senegambia (Fesler 2004:182). In some instances, names of the enslaved recorded in wills, probate inventories, and plantation accounts allow cultural backgrounds to be assigned to individual slaves. For example, Virginia planter Robert Carter (1663–1732) listed two men described as "Ebo" (Igbo) as foremen, and Lewis Burwell III purchased a Mandingo man named Jumper in 1736 (Walsh 1997:86, 116).

Concentrations of peoples of Igbo descent led to the formation of an "Ig-boized" culture among the enslaved in colonial and early national Virginia, particularly in the interior tidewater and piedmont counties along the James, York, and Rappahannock Rivers (Chambers 1996:401). To understand the social, ideological, and material resources that Igbos enslaved in Virginia drew upon in creating new lives for themselves, it is essential to have an understanding of Igbo culture. What follows draws upon historical, archaeological, oral, and ethnographic sources to portray Igbo society in the eighteenth century.

The Igbo

Social and Political Structure

In precolonial West Africa, the Igbo formed a stateless society characterized by small-scale social units with limited and localized concentrations of authority (Horton 1972). At first contact with Europeans, they inhabited the savanna woodlands and rain forest of the Guinea coast around the Niger River. Linguistic analysis and oral tradition suggest that the Igbo arose as a separate ethnic group 4,000 to 6,000 years ago in the region of the Niger-Benue confluence and, over time, spread southward from there (Afigbo 1980: 311; Oguagha 1984:197). This migration has been attributed to population pressures and the effects of centuries of agriculture, as soil exhaustion forced people to move in search of fertile land. Exploration led some of the Igbo southward across the savanna and into the rain forest east of the Niger River. Igbo economy was based in yam agriculture, supplemented by fishing, hunting, and limited tending of livestock (Cookey 1980:339). Specialized craft industries, including iron working, wood carving, and textile production, were important (Afigbo 1980).

Each village was generally composed of familial descent lines, with village leadership falling to the head of the senior lineage, with all lineage heads participating in making village decisions (Cookey 1980). Since precolonial Igboland operated under a dual-sex political system, authority was dispersed among a variety of men's and women's organizations, with women forming powerful organized groups that settled marriage disputes, imposed fines on defaulting lineage members, and took charge of death rituals (Amadiume 1987; Isichei 1978; Oramasionwu 1994).

The highest form of political organization among the Igbo was the clan, comprised of a group of villages deriving their identity from shared ancestors (Forde and Jones 1950). In times of joint need or common trouble, clans came to one another's assistance (Osae et al. 1973:139). With a social structure composed of a number of villages and clans, it is unlikely that the Igbo conceived of themselves as a single group in precolonial times. Nevertheless, common origins as evident in language, spiritual beliefs, subsistence, and sociopolitical organization validate the legitimacy of discussing the Igbo as a group (Isichei 1976:20). Despite the high population densities of some areas, most groups of the Igbo never developed cities or nation-states until recent times, preferring to live instead in small villages (Afigbo 1980; Connah 1990:138). The development of their small-scale social and political organization was owed, in large part, to a combination of their agricultural subsistence and the forest environment in which they lived. Since the scale at which land could be administered in the rain forest was limited, village settlements with descent-based political structures became the most effective unit of Igbo sociopolitical organization. With little reliance on centralized government, the Igbo political organization required no kings or emperors. Instead, a segmentary political system based on family and extended family units linked by the spirits of deceased ancestors was in place (Davidson 1977:115–116). Both men and women constructed ancestor shrines, consulting ancestors for guidance and support (Henderson 1972:169; McCall 1995:260). A family was comprised of a man, his wife or wives, unmarried sons and daughters, and married sons and their families. In Igboland, the household was a matricentric unit consisting of a woman and her children (Amadiume 1987), living with one or more other household units in a male-headed compound surrounded by an earthen wall (Oramasionwu 1994:28).

In addition to the lineage- and kinship-based governmental system, the Igbo also used age sets, a system of dividing village residents into groups based on age. Each age set had its own set of rights and duties within the community (Davidson 1977:115). The political institution of title-taking (*ndinze* or *ndi ozo*) allowed prosperous men and women to purchase titles, thereby gaining prestige and redistributing wealth around the village (Isichei 1976).

The primary economic activity was farming, and both men and women played critical roles in agriculture. While a clear sexual division of labor existed, men's and women's roles were seen as complementary. Yam and cocoyam were the two most important crops produced by the Igbo. Yams were viewed as male, and men controlled all aspects of producing and distributing this ritually important crop (Amadiume 1987:29, 35). Women, on the other hand, were in charge of producing the "female" crops that formed the primary dietary staples, such as cocoyam, cassava, and plantain, as well as all other vegetables grown (Anyanwu 1976). Women's work was critical for the maintenance of the family, and they derived power and distinction from successfully controlling and managing these crops (Amadiume 1987:30), as well as from raising and selling livestock, dogs, and domestic fowl (Achebe 1994:14). According to Olaudah Equiano, an Igbo enslaved in eighteenth-century Virginia, women also produced cloth, pottery, and tobacco pipes. Since pottery was used both for household and ritual purposes, it formed an important female-controlled industry (Anyanwu 1976:51).

Although women were in charge of the subsistence economy, men traditionally owned and allocated the property upon which these crops were grown. Men's work included clearing bush and constructing house compounds, making baskets, trapping animals, and tapping palm trees for wine production (Anyanwu 1976:139). Men held a monopoly over ritual knowledge, craft specialization (such as blacksmithing), and external relations (Amadiume 1987:30).

Spiritual Beliefs

As in most of West Africa, spirituality permeates every aspect of Igbo life, making it impossible to separate spiritual beliefs, social organization, and political authority. Religion not only provides explanations for the origins of the world and the humans inhabiting it but also supplies social power for making and enforcing laws (Oramaisonwu 1994). The beliefs of today reflect those of the past, passed down through stories, proverbs, ceremonies, prayers, and other mnemonic devices (Davidson 1977:163).

The Igbo believe in one supreme god (*Chukwu*) with dominion over the living, as well as a pantheon of less powerful deities (*Mmuo*), spirit forces (*Alusi*), and ancestors. *Chukwu*, the creator of all things, is also the designer of human destinies. Upon conception, each individual is granted a decreed-upon destiny entrusted to the personal spiritual guardian (*chi*) that oversees his or her life (Metuh 1985). Although one's destiny is largely predetermined from birth, appropriate actions taken by individuals in their lifetime, including constant petitioning and veneration of ancestors and moral behavior, can change one's destiny in a favorable fashion. Conversely, ignoring the spiritual forces and taking inappropriate actions can negatively alter one's destiny. Thus, the living are locked in a continuous cycle of birth, life, death, and rebirth, with their actions on earth determining their fate there and in the afterworld. In Igbo religion, the ultimate goal of every individual is to join his or her ancestors after death and enjoy the veneration of descendants before eventually being reincarnated back to the land of the living (Metuh 1985:106).

Igbo spiritual beliefs, like its political system, were noncentralized, with power shared among different descent lines held together by religious rituals (Davidson 1977). Oracles or diviners communicate the wishes of the deities, as well as control the supernatural through sacrifices and explain mystical events (Isichei 1976:24–25; Metuh 1985). Archaeological findings indicate the presence of individuals who were authorized as mediators between the deities and humans as early as the ninth century A.D. (Shaw 1970).

In the central areas of Igboland, a religious-political organization known as *Nri* held sway from the thirteenth to the eighteenth centuries. Representatives of *eze Nri* traveled around Igboland to perform rituals connected with material and agricultural concerns. They began to be replaced in the late seventeenth and early eighteenth centuries by a new religion based on *Chukwu*, the supreme god, and on oracles. This new subgroup called the *Aro* became important players in the Atlantic slave trade (Chambers 1996:147–148).

West African Trade and Igbo Culture

Centuries before their unfortunate contact with European slave trading, the Igbo had been involved in the exchange of commercial goods within the larger context of West African trading. Trade occurred mostly through bartering, with agricultural surplus and manufactured goods exchanged for necessities such as salt and iron ore and for luxury items (Davidson 1977:158; Oguagha 1984:195). The continued expansion of trade in West Africa through time, with its market for luxury items, helped to sustain and expand social stratification in West African cultures.

Prior to contact with the world across the Sahara Desert, an extensive trading network existed within West Africa, particularly between the forest and the savanna (Connah 1990:119). Relationships developed through the trade of agricultural products between these two regions fostered specialization and economic interdependence for each area, thus laying the groundwork for emergent social and political stratification (Shaw 1984). Regional trade developed within Igbo-occupied lands by the ninth century A.D., with the trans-Saharan trade established by the end of the first millennium (Connah 1990:146). West African gold, ivory, kola nuts, and slaves were exchanged for cowries, beads, silks, knives, alcohol, tobacco, horses, books, copper, and mirrors (Connah 1990:147; Davidson 1977:153). A string of commercial centers developed along North Africa's caravan routes in Ghana, and other market towns sprang up along the Niger (Davidson 1977). By 1600, there was an extensive local and long-distance trade throughout West Africa, with firmly established direct trade relations with Europe. Advancements in maritime technology allowed the development of trade with the Portuguese at the end of the fifteenth century, setting in motion an important and tragic period in West African history (Osae et al. 1973:156). The French, Dutch, and English shortly followed the Portuguese, all hoping to profit from the rich resources of West Africa.

The Europeans, at first interested in trading guns for gold, soon refocused their attention on the market for slaves to provide agricultural labor for New World plantations. By the second quarter of the seventeenth century, a regular system of slave trading had been established, and as this coastal trade expanded, the trans-Saharan trade declined (Davidson 1977:210, 212). Coastal West African cultures, in cooperation with European traders, would acquire slaves from the hinterlands to the north through combinations of peaceful trade and raiding (Alagoa 1972). Although devastating to the social and political structures of the cultures heavily raided for slaves, the Atlantic slave trade was a factor in the emergence of some West African states and city-states, including Bonny, Nembe, Benin, Oyo, and Dahomey (Osae et al. 1973:169). The slave trade transformed the delta city-states from fishing communities into centers of redistribution for European goods, slaves, and agricultural products (Alagoa 1972:291). The slave trade also dramatically changed relationships between West African cultures, moving in many cases from a mutually beneficial commercial exchange of natural commodities to one of political imbalance, as groups raided one another for slaves (Oguagha 1984:190–191). The trans-Atlantic slave trade had an enormous impact on Igbo culture in the seventeenth, eighteenth, and nineteenth centuries.

The Igbo in the Seventeenth and Eighteenth Centuries

By the beginning of the seventeenth century, the five primary Igbo groups— who shared common cultural elements but had regional differences— inhabited the geographical areas that they now occupy (Cookey 1980:336). During the sixteenth and seventeenth centuries some Igbo groups were invaded by Benin, which sought to control trade routes within Igboland to exact tributes (Oguagha 1984:187). Contact with neighboring peoples, particularly Benin and Igala after the fourteenth century, caused some minor changes in Igbo language, material culture, and title-taking systems, with a few Igbo states developing political systems ruled by kings (Henderson 1972; Isichei 1976). Although the Igbo were involved in trading with outside regions from an early period, agriculture continued to form their primary economic base. After centuries of farming the shallow soils of the tropical forests, however, land exhaustion forced the Igbo to take a more active role in trading (Dumett 1980:293). This commerce was primarily in the Atlantic slave trade.

Also during this time, the growth of Igbo states developed as a result of the trans-Saharan and (slightly later) trans-Atlantic trades (Isichei 1976:51). A number of new states were established on the Niger, particularly in the lower reaches of the river where there was greater access to European traders. Some of these states rose to positions of great power and wealth during the seventeenth and eighteenth centuries as the slave trade accelerated (Isichei 1976:55–56). Groups of slaves from the interior were brought to the trading settlements, such as Bonny, Elim, and Kalabari established at the Niger delta, where the West African backers traded directly with the Europeans. The slave trade allowed a greater accumulation of wealth to these kings, enhancing their power and furthering the growth of these delta states.

The number of Igbo peoples leaving West Africa as slaves was fairly small in the sixteenth century but increased throughout the seventeenth century, rising to a peak in the eighteenth and early nineteenth centuries (Isichei 1976). The _Aro,_ a group of Igbo middlemen, facilitated the slave trade, beginning around the mid-seventeenth century (Alagoa 1972:299). Because of their association with the _Aro-Chukwu_ oracle, they were afforded protection and allowed by the Igbo to procure slaves freely for the Atlantic trade.

The experiences of most Igbo individuals arriving on Virginia shores at the beginning of the eighteenth century followed a pattern that was repeated innumerable times over the next several decades as large numbers of Africans were brought to the Chesapeake. If an individual survived the excruciating physical and mental conditions of a three-month passage over the Atlantic, the next indignity that waited was the sale to a planter. During this period in the Virginia Chesapeake, most of the sales took place on board the slavers' ships, which were moored in the rivers or docked at a plantation wharf. Robert "King" Carter's description of one such sale that occurred in 1727 provides an idea of how these sales proceeded (see Mullin 1972:14–15). For a three-week period in May, Carter spent his afternoons on board the slaving vessel that was anchored in the river at his plantation. Area planters in the market for new laborers would board the ship and conduct negotiations with Carter and the captain of the ship. Carter received a 10 percent commission on each sale, with his contractual obligation being to cover the debts not paid on the sales he supervised.

The typical individual sold would have likely been an adult male, since Chesapeake planters were importing twice as many men as women during the last years of the seventeenth century and opening decades of the following. He would have been purchased either singly or with one other individual and, because newly arrived slaves were generally placed at the most menial tasks, transported to an outlying field quarter (Berlin 1998:113; Morgan 1998:78). Since most of the slave trade into Virginia occurred in the late spring and summer, the individual would have immediately been set to work tending and harvesting crops (Mullin 1972:15).

Wealthy planters, like those men who owned the plantations studied here, kept enslaved individuals with special skills in cooking, blacksmithing, gardening, weaving, spinning, or carpentry quartered near or adjacent to the main plantation house. These skilled laborers were almost never newly arrived Africans but individuals who had been in Virginia for some years and could speak English. The enslaved communities on outlying quarters, like the ones analyzed in the following chapters, were comprised primarily of agricultural workers. The daily and monthly schedules of these individuals revolved around the needs of the crops, in this instance, tobacco and various grains. An individual arriving on an early eighteenth-century outlying quarter would have seen a motley collection of timber-framed or log buildings adjacent to agricultural fields, usually located on some small piece of land unsuitable for crops. Most outlying quarters on large Virginia plantations housed twenty to thirty individuals, so the number of buildings would have been small, generally no more than two or three dwellings, some provision gardens and poultry enclosures, and perhaps a corn crib. Because the keeping of hogs and cattle by the enslaved for their own use or profit had been outlawed in 1692 (Berlin 1998:119), any larger livestock present at the quarter were tended by the enslaved for the planter.

The other residents at the quarter would have been predominantly men and, like Olaudah Equiano some thirty years later, the early eighteenth-century individual may not have been able to communicate with any of his fellow residents. He would have shared a barracks-style dwelling, perhaps claiming a small floor space of his own for a bedroll and blanket. Like his fellow residents, he was apportioned small amounts of salt meat and corn-meal weekly. He was expected to work at planter-assigned tasks between five and a half to six days weekly, as well as some evenings. If he was one of the 75 percent who managed to live through his first year in Virginia, he might be able to choose a partner and have children, as Chesapeake planters increased their purchases of African women as the century progressed. By the 1730s and 1740s, many of the enslaved were able to create stable family relationships, and native-born individuals began to predominate. This situation fostered the formation of kin networks and the establishment of communities on quarters. It was on the large plantations, such as those properties forming the focus of this study, where local slave communities and community-based identities formed in the first half of the eighteenth century (Kulikoff 1986; Sidbury 1997).

Summary

The preceding scenario sets the stage for the analysis to follow. Political, social, and economic circumstances in Virginia and the larger Atlantic world combined to affect the contexts of slavery on Virginia's Tidewater plantations. At the larger scale, the marginality of Bristol merchants in the overall African slave trade, coupled with the finances of Virginia planters, concentrated people of Igbo origin in the Tidewater. Some physical similarities between Virginia and Igboland may have eased somewhat the adjustment of these individuals to their new, but unwelcome, homes. Similarities in the rural setting, in the types and cycles of agricultural work, in foods and animals encountered, and in some climatic factors probably facilitated the formation of Igbo-style or "Igboized" communities on Virginia quarters (Chambers 1996). In addition, fairly early in the eighteenth century, Virginia planters began to include almost equal numbers of women in their slave purchases, enabling men and women to form meaningful relationships and families on the quarters (Kulikoff 1986). Kinship would have been an important organizing principle for these communities, given the importance of family and kinship in the African societies whose members were enslaved in Virginia. Multigenerational groups of extended families residing in quarter compounds bore basic similarities to Igbo kin-based societies and villages in West Africa. The freedom to practice and adapt African traditions was less controlled on some plantations than others; Edward Kimber, visiting the Maryland colony in 1745, noted African polygynous marital practices there (Kimber 1998:327).

While in no way denying the horrors of a colonial system whose success depended upon the enslavement of others as laborers, evidence suggests that the enslaved in Virginia were able to establish family and kinship ties and forge meaningful lives. The continuity across multiple generations and interconnectedness of the labor forces on these three Virginia plantations make them an ideal setting for examining responses to enslavement and how they may have changed over time. In this study, the vehicle for examining responses and strategies will be subfloor pits: why they were created, how they were used, and how use may have changed during the course of the eighteenth century. Chapter 3 examines the study sites in detail, focusing on the historical evidence and archaeological remains found there.

3
Historical and Archaeological Overview of Study Sites

In this study, plantation slavery is examined within a regional context, focusing on quarters from three eighteenth-century plantations in the Williamsburg area: Utopia Quarter, Kingsmill Quarter, and Carter's Grove Quarter. These properties were chosen for analysis because of the intergenerational continuity among the three plantations. At these plantations were over 300 African Americans, "some of whom shared family connections as close as those of the Burwell clan on whose lands they lived and labored" (Walsh 1997:49).

Using documentary evidence, a context is created for each plantation, peopling the quarters as accurately as possible with known data on the individuals enslaved there. Discussion of the sites is arranged chronologically. Interwoven with the historical information are archaeological findings from each quarter, setting the stage for discussion of subfloor pit functions at these sites in the following chapters. This study encompasses a critical period in Virginia history, beginning at a time when the enslaved labor force consisted primarily of newly enslaved Africans in the Chesapeake and ending with a largely native-born population facing a system of slavery drastically altered by the effects of the Revolutionary War and westward expansion.

While the Kingsmill Quarter and Carter's Grove Quarter were single component sites occupied for spans of twenty to thirty years, the Utopia Quarter contained three temporal components, stretching from the turn of the eighteenth century to about 1775. Each component spanned two to three decades, and the construction of each quarter appeared to correspond with changes in plantation ownership. In addition, each component was built a slight distance away from the old housing. Residents of the earlier quarters simply moved into the new buildings, providing community continuity between the different temporal components. This continuity, coupled with the spatial separation of the three groups of buildings, made it possible to draw conclusions about change within a single enslaved community across three generations. The three components, comprising sites 44JC32 and 44JC787, were excavated in the mid-1990s by the James River Institute for Archaeology, Inc., under the direction of Dr. Garrett Fesler. Each period will be considered separately.

Utopia Quarter Period II (44JC32), ca. 1700–1730

The Utopia Quarter site, located eight miles southeast of Williamsburg, had been constructed along the edge of a high bluff overlooking the James River to the south. Ravines bisected the bluff to the east and the west of the quarters, and the forested margins of these ravines were home for deer, rabbit, opossum, and other small game that were hunted and trapped by the enslaved. The proximity of the river and marshy areas along its periphery also provided the quarter residents access to a variety of plants and animals. During the later periods of occupation at Utopia (Periods III and IV), the newer quarters were constructed to the north, likely on the former location of agricultural fields whose soil fertility had been depleted by tobacco.

During each of the three periods, the buildings were part of the plantation's outlying quarters located near distant agricultural fields or other work areas. Distance from the plantation house granted the enslaved greater degrees of autonomy than individuals living and working within sight of the planter and his family.

Probate records, wills, and account books allowed a partial reconstruction of the enslaved community at Utopia. During Periods II and III, the property was owned by the Bray family, and most of the enslaved had been acquired from West Africa (Fesler 2004), forming a multicultural mix on the quarter. During the final period (ca. 1750–1775), the property was in the hands of the Burwell family, and by that time most of the enslaved residing there had been born in Virginia.

The Pettus family owned the 1,200-acre Utopia property in the third quarter of the seventeenth century, and it passed into the hands of James Bray II when he married Pettus's widow at the end of the century (Stephenson 1963; Walsh 1997). Upon acquiring the land, Bray built a new plantation house and quarters (Fesler 2004:107). At his death in 1725, Bray's enslaved labor force numbered around 75 individuals, with 28 of those enslaved individuals—11 men, 13 women, and 4 children—in three James City field quarters in 1725. These individuals were probably African-born, purchased by the Bray family beginning in the 1690s (Walsh 1997:94).

Dividing the laborers evenly places between 8 and 10 people at each quarter, although there may have been as many as 18 individuals at Utopia prior to the acquisition of the quarter at Tutter's Neck. Enslaved individuals headed two of the James City County quarters, and the quarter at Utopia was almost certainly either the female-headed Debb's Quarter or Jacko's Quarter (Walsh 1997:94). Although planters purchased more men than women in the first quarter of the eighteenth century, the labor force at the Utopia and Littletown Quarters contained 43 women and 27 men by the end of Period II (Fesler 2004:188).

By the time the site was abandoned around the end of the third decade of the century, some of the Bray slaves may have been in Virginia for close to thirty years, more than enough time to form families. Given the male-female ratios at Utopia, it is likely that long-term relationships had formed between enslaved individuals during Period II, and the presence of children certainly hints at this possibility.

Archaeological Evidence at the Site

Three timber-framed post-in-ground dwellings and a small service building were constructed on the site around the turn of the eighteenth century (Figure 3.1). Occupied for the next three decades, the three dwellings were arranged in a U-shape around a central courtyard, a plan reminiscent of West African house compounds (Fesler 2004). Many of the daily activities that occurred at the site—cooking, socializing, and creating handcrafted items—occurred in this outdoor space. A small fenced enclosure ran between Structures 10 and 20 and may have encircled a garden or poultry pen. None of the three Utopia dwellings had wooden floors or glazed windows, and each structure had been heated with a single stick-and-mud chimney. Nineteen subfloor pits had been cut through the soil floors of two of the quarters. Excavation at Utopia Period II yielded 29,764 artifacts, with analysis of pipestems and ceramics indicating the site was occupied in the first three decades of the eighteenth century (Fesler 2004:162).

Structure 1. Structure 1, on the western side of the U-shaped complex, was a 12-x-28-foot timber-framed building constructed around eight earth-set posts (Figure 3.2). A hearth stood at the southern end of the two-room structure, heating a 10-x-12-foot room. The larger, unheated room to the north measured 18 x 12 feet. Two subfloor pits (Features 5 and 6) were located in the structure, as well as a hearth-front complex (Features 2, 3, 4, and

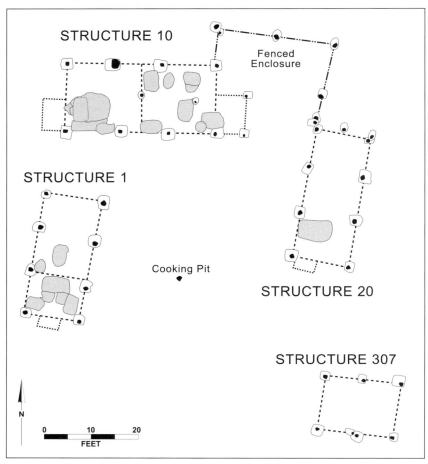

3.1. Utopia Period II (44JC32) archaeological remains

30) consisting of four separate pits built in two distinct phases. Features 5, 6, and 30, the earliest pits, had been filled rapidly while the building was still standing.

During Phase II, when Features 2, 3, and 4 were in use, a pit lay in the front of the hearth, flanked by two other pits, forming a U-shaped configuration along the front and sides of the hearth and the 3-x-2-foot pad of brick extending out from the hearth. The single layers of soil filling the Phase II subfloor pits contained substantial quantities of complete and fragmented brick, suggesting the pits had been filled rapidly sometime after the structure was no longer occupied.

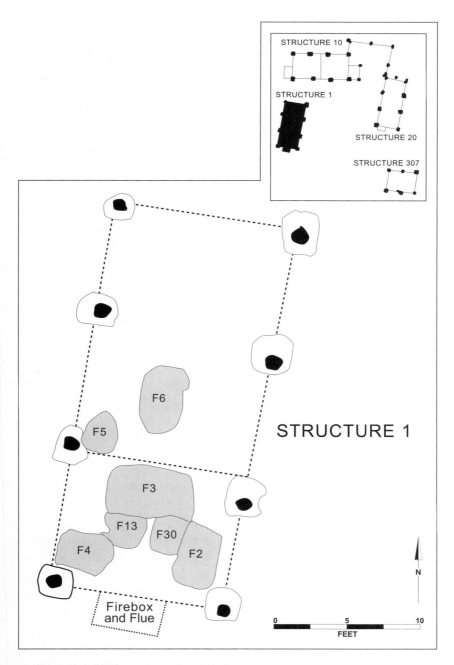

STRUCTURE 10

STRUCTURE 1

STRUCTURE 20

STRUCTURE 307

F6

F5

STRUCTURE 1

F3

F13

F30

F4

F2

N

Firebox
and Flue

0   5   10
FEET

3.2. Utopia Period II Structure 1 archaeological remains

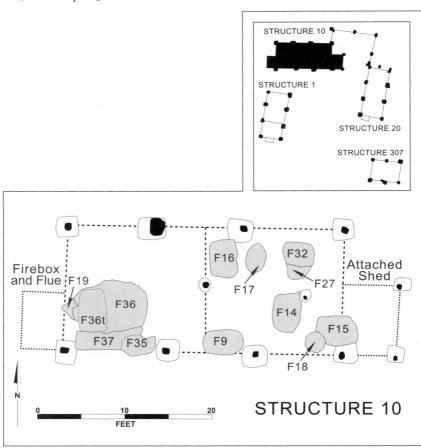

3.3. Utopia Period II Structure 10 archaeological remains

Structure 10. Structure 10, measuring 16 x 32 feet, was a timber-framed building constructed around eight major earth-set posts (Figure 3.3). Only one of two 16-x-16-foot rooms was heated. Two postholes delineated a small attached shed (6 x 8 feet) off the southeastern corner of the building.

Ten subfloor pits cut the earthen floor of Structure 10. Feature 36, the hearth front pit in Structure 10, contained at least two periods of construction and repair, with this initial 3.5-x-2.2-foot pit oriented with its long axis facing the hearth. A layer of crushed fossil shell known as marl had been laid in the bottom of this pit, possibly to provide a flooring substrate that would remain relatively dry and nonmuddy when groundwater caused moisture problems. During the last phase of construction, a 4.5-foot-square wooden box with a hinged top had been placed inside a hole cut through the backfill of the first phase pit. The other pits were scattered across the building, with eight located in the unheated eastern room and one in the western room along the south wall near the hearth.

A partially crushed padlock, a diamond-shaped iron keyhole, and an iron key, all recovered from soil that later filled the box, provided evidence that the box had been locked to prevent the theft of food supplies or personal possessions while the quarter inhabitants were working away from the quarter. Artifacts from the soil that accumulated in the box while it was in use included 1,168 (81 percent of the finds) highly fragmented animal bone, clam and oyster shell, fish scale, and eggshell. These artifacts suggest that debris from food preparation activities around the hearth had fallen into the box. Other artifacts from these two layers included small pieces of clay tobacco pipes, and a clay bead.

Structure 20. Like the other two structures, Structure 20 (28 x 12 feet) was constructed with eight earth-set posts and contained two rooms. The structure contained one subfloor pit, located at the south end of the building, where wood ash, charcoal, and burned daub from the fill of Feature 21 suggest the presence of a hearth (Figure 3.4).

Service Building. A fourth earthfast building was located south and slightly east of Structure 20. This small structure, 16 x 12 feet, containing six structural posts, probably served as a corncrib or meat house.

Archaeological Analysis of Subfloor Pits

There were two predominant forms taken by the Period II subfloor pits: hearth-front complexes with multiple episodes of cutting and filling, and single-use pits, generally located in building corners, along partition walls, or the middle of floors (Table 3.1). While most of the nonhearth pits from Period II ranged around 1 foot in depth, the hearth-front pits were larger and slightly deeper on average, ranging between .9 feet and 2.2 feet. While most of the nonhearth Phase II pits were single-cut features, there were several instances where new pits cut through earlier features.

Features 5, 6, and 30, the earliest pits in Structure 1, and Features 15, 27, and 36T in Structure 10 were abandoned and filled within a short time of the buildings' initial occupation. In general, these earlier features not only contained fewer artifacts per cubic foot of fill than did the later features (Table 3.1), but, with the exception of iron nails, they also contained very few artifacts of European manufacture. Some of the artifacts from these early pits were types that were more typically found on seventeenth-century sites, such as case bottle glass fragments and locally made tobacco pipes. The early dating, highly fragmented nature, and small sizes (under .75 in.) of these

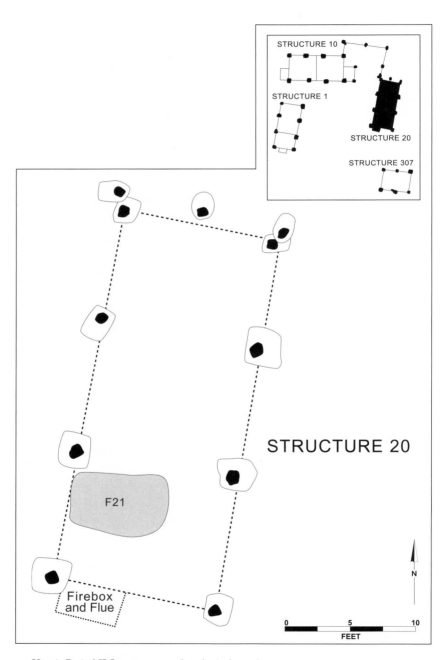

STRUCTURE 10

STRUCTURE 1

STRUCTURE 20

STRUCTURE 307

STRUCTURE 20

F21

Firebox
and Flue

N

0   5   10
FEET

3.4. Utopia Period II Structure 20 archaeological remains

Table 3.1 Utopia Quarter Period II subfloor pits descriptive details

Structure	Feature	Position	Phase	Shape	Cuts or repairs	Dimensions & depth (in feet)	Total artifacts	Artifacts per cubic foot
1	F 30	Hearth	I	Rect.	Multiple	2.75 x 2.5 x 1.0	138	20.1
	F 5	Corner	I	Oval	Single	1.1 x 2.9 x 0.7	51	22.8
	F 6	Other	I	Rect.	Single	2.75 x 4.2 x 0.8	24	2.6
	F 2	Hearth	II	Rect.	Multiple	4.3 x 4.7 x 1.1	968	43.5
	F 3	Hearth	II	Rect.	Multiple	6.25 x 4.0 x 0.9	1011	44.9
	F 4	Hearth	II	Rect.	Multiple	4.0 x 4.0 x 1.3	366	17.6
10	F 15	Corner	I	Rect.	Single	4.5 x 3.5 x 1.0	137	8.7
	F 17	Other	I	Rect.	Single	2.25 x 3.5 x 0.9	117	16.5
	F 27	Corner	I	Rect.	Multiple	2.25 x 2.0 x 0.25	95	84.4
	F 35	Other	I	Rect.	Multiple	2.1 x 4.8 x 0.3	40	13.2
	F 36T/Y	Hearth	I	Rect.	Multiple	3.5 x 2.2 x 2.25	41	2.4
	F 9	Other	II	Oval	Single	4.5 x 2.9 x 0.9	539	46.1
	F 14	Other	II	Rect.	Single	3.75 x 5.25 x 1.0	922	46.8
	F 16	Corner	II	Rect.	Single	3.0 x 4.75 x 0.9	148	11.5
	F 18	Corner	II	Round	Single	2.25 x 2.25 x 0.25	269	212.5
	F 32	Corner	II	Rect.	Multiple	4.0 x 2.5 x 0.25	48	19.2
	F 36	Hearth	II	Rect.	Multiple	4.5 x 4.5 x 1.75	4650	135.03
20	F 21	Hearth	I, II	Rect.	Multiple	7 x 4.5 x 1.25	4930	125.2

items indicates that many of the artifacts from the Phase I pits were originally present in sheet midden from the earlier occupation (1670–1700) at the
site. These objects, along with earlier Native American artifacts, were in the
soil gathered from around the site to fill these first-phase pits.

Summary

The first two decades of the eighteenth century were a period of economic
stability for Virginia, with tobacco prices holding steady. Because the lives
of the enslaved were integrally tied to that of their owners, this constancy
meant that the enslaved community owned by Bray enjoyed relative stability
as well. Conditions at Utopia in this period were favorable for the development of families and households, even with the continuing arrival of Africans (Fesler 2004:119). Detailed analysis of artifacts from the site's structures
suggested that Structures 10 and 20 functioned as family-based households,
while Structure 1 served as a coresidential structure for unrelated individuals,
perhaps largely female (Fesler 2004:377, 391).

Two postholes at the northern end of Structure 20 had been replaced and
some repair made to the service building, but otherwise the quarter's buildings seem to have stood without repair throughout their period of occupation. Archaeological and documentary evidence from the Virginia tidewater
indicates that earthfast structures generally needed major repair or replace-
ment within twenty or so years (Carson et al. 1981). The virtual absence of
such repairs on the structures suggests that they were not occupied much
more than two or three decades, a span in accordance with documentary and
artifact evidence. One of the subfloor pits contained white salt-glazed stoneware, the presence of which placed the abandonment of this feature after
1720. By the end of Period II, however, the quarter buildings were doubtless
in poor condition, as evidenced by damage to the Structure 10 hearth and the
subsequent use of an open firepit as a heat source in the building. The poor
condition of the buildings, coupled with the change in property ownership
at the death of James Bray II, occasioned the construction of a new set of
quarters in the second quarter of the eighteenth century. The four buildings
comprising this quarter have been designated as Utopia Quarter Period III.

Utopia Quarter Period III (44JC32), ca. 1730–1750

After the death of James Bray II in 1725, grandson James Bray III acquired
the Utopia property and all the people enslaved there (Kelso 1984:39). Since
Bray III was still a minor in 1725, the property remained under the control

of his father, Thomas Bray II, and his aunt until the young man came of age around 1736. He controlled operations at the Utopia property until his own early death in the fall of 1744.

During Period III, two earthfast houses and several other outbuildings were constructed 200 feet north of the earlier quarter (Figure 3.5). This quarter was home to a mixture of individuals recently arrived from Africa, other African-born individuals who had been enslaved in Virginia for several decades, and children born in Virginia to African parents. Thomas Bray II continued to purchase slaves directly from Africa through the 1730s (Walsh 1997:94). These individuals raised tobacco, corn, and possibly wheat, produced butter, cut wood, made brick, and tended livestock (McClure 1977:44). Bray's slaves raised sheep, pigs, and cattle that were sold as meat. Much of the slaves' work went into raising products that Bray sold on the market, but some of the crops, particularly the corn, came back to them as provisions.

Archaeological Evidence at the Site

Three earthfast structures, two dwellings for enslaved laborers and a small square service building, stood on a small rise north of the Period II quarter. A 36-x-40-foot ditched enclosure extended from the south end of Structure 40, perhaps serving as a livestock pen, and large trash middens were associated with each of the dwellings. The ceramics from the trash pits were primarily coarse earthenwares and stonewares made in England, Germany, and Virginia in the first half of the eighteenth century. The majority of the 21,500 artifacts were recovered from the dwellings' subfloor pits and trash pits. With the absence of a well on the site, it is likely that the enslaved used a nearby freshwater spring as their source of water for drinking, cooking, and washing clothing and bodies. Mean ceramic dating provided a date of 1734, and pipestem analysis yielded a date of 1746 (Fesler 2004:165–166).

Structure 40. Along the southern edge of the site were the remains of a 12-x-16-foot earthfast structure with three subfloor pits cutting the interior floor (Figure 3.6). While no physical evidence of a hearth was present, the placement of the subfloor pits suggests it probably stood along the western end of the building. Earlier looting of this structure had severely compromised the integrity of the subfloor pit assemblages, and no analysis was undertaken.

Structure 50. A second dwelling had stood at the northern limits of the site. Originally 12 x 16 feet, expansion at the eastern and western ends enlarged this earthfast structure to 24 x 16 feet. Its eleven postholes were arranged in a manner that suggested a three-room building (Figure 3.7). A

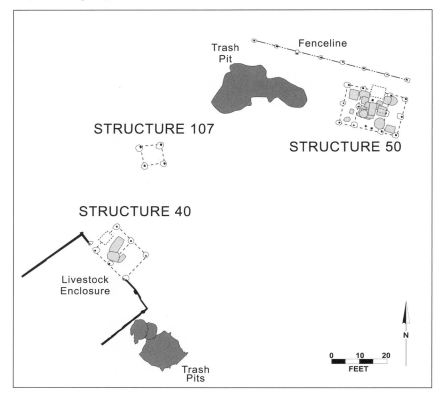

3.5. Utopia Period III archaeological remains

central room measuring 12 x 16 feet and entered through a door along the southern wall was flanked by two narrow (6-x-16-foot) unheated rooms. Eighteen subterranean pits cut through the soil floor of the building, with twelve of these pits forming a large hearth-front complex at the north end of the building. The eastern room contained two subfloor pits, and three pits cut through the floor of the western room. The hearth-front complex in Structure 50 was complicated, encompassing twelve separate pits in four phases of pit construction (Figure 3.8 and Table 3.2). During the fourth phase of pit construction, three pits with their short axes aligned with the hearth were in use. These pits cut through an earlier pit.

Residents encountered problems with maintaining hearth-front pits in good repair throughout their tenure, in part because they had placed pits too close together. A collapsed wall between Features 39 and 51 prompted residents to abandon both features. A new pit (Feature 52), cutting through the

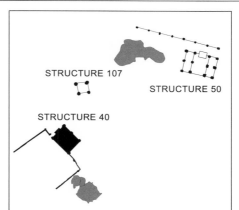

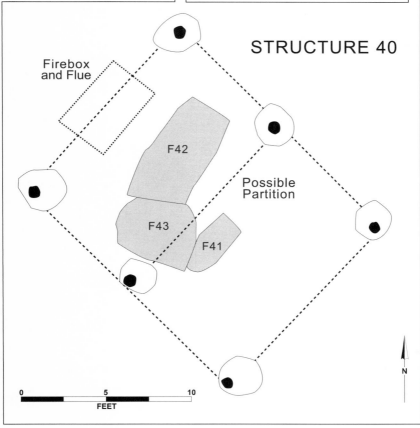

STRUCTURE 107

STRUCTURE 50

STRUCTURE 40

STRUCTURE 40

Firebox and Flue

F42

Possible Partition

F43

F41

0   5   10
FEET

N

3.6. Utopia Period III Structure 40 archaeological remains

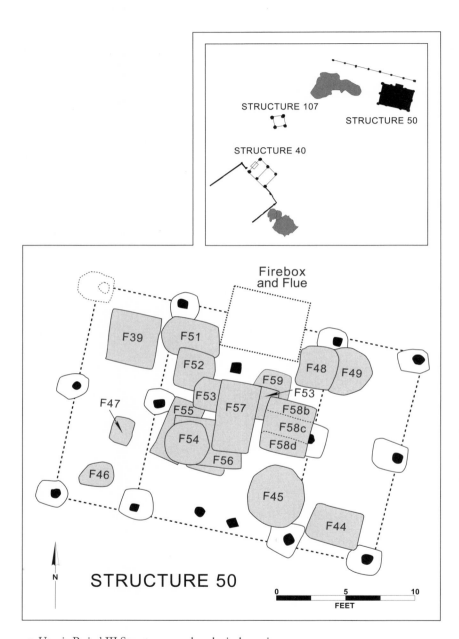

STRUCTURE 107

STRUCTURE 50

STRUCTURE 40

Firebox
and Flue

F39   F51

F52

F48 F49

F59

F47   F53   F53

F55   F57   F58b

F54   F58c

F58d

F46   F56

F45

N   STRUCTURE 50   F44

0   5   10

FEET

3.7. Utopia Period III Structure 50 archaeological remains

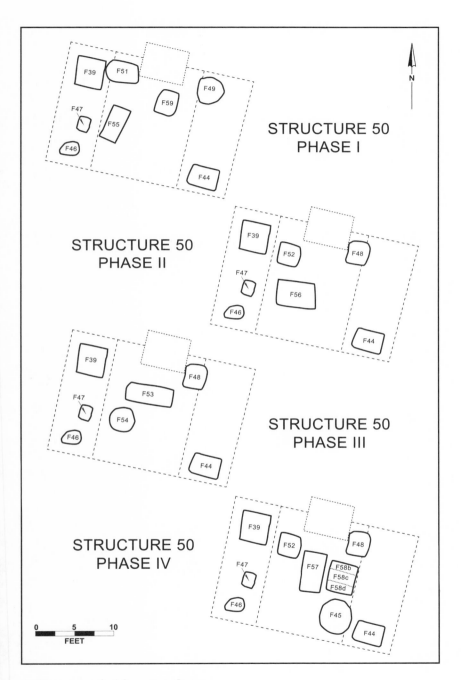

STRUCTURE 50
PHASE I

STRUCTURE 50
PHASE II

STRUCTURE 50
PHASE III

STRUCTURE 50
PHASE IV

N

0   5   10
FEET

3.8. Phase maps of subfloor pits in Structure 50

Table 3.2 Utopia Quarter Period III subfloor pits descriptive details

Structure	Feature	Phase	Position	Shape	Cuts or repairs	Dimensions & depth (in feet)	Total # artifacts	Artifacts per cubic Ft.
40	F41	?	?	Rect.	?	?	?	?
	F42	?	?	Rect.	?	?	?	?
	F43	?	?	Rect.	?	?	?	?
50	F51	I	Hearth	Square	Multiple	3.25 x 3 x 2	392	20.1
	F56	II	Hearth	Rect.	Multiple	4 x 1.8 x .5	8	2.2
	F48	II, III, IV	Hearth	Square	Multiple	2.8 x 3.2 x 1	214	23.9
	F52	II, III, IV	Hearth	Square	Multiple	3 x 3 x ?	79	Indet.
	F53	III	Hearth	Rect.	Multiple	5.5 x 3 x 2.75	1140	25.1
	F55	I	Hearth	Rect.	Multiple	3.3 x 3.3 x ?	Indet.	Indet.
	F54	III	Hearth	Rect.	Multiple	4.8 x 2.7 x ?	56	Indet.
	F57	IV	Hearth	Rect.	Multiple	6 x 2.5 x 1.75	854	32.5
	F58A/E[a]	IV	Hearth	Square?	Multiple	3.75 x 3.5 x 1.3	274	16.1
	F58A/D[a]	IV	Hearth	Rect.	Multiple	1.5 x 3.75 x .5	70	25.0
	F58A/B[a]	IV	Hearth	Rect.	Multiple	1 x 3.75 x .5	46	24.5
	F39B		Corner	Rect.	Multiple	4.3 x 4.0 x 1.4	345	14.3
	F39A		Corner	Rect.	Multiple	4.3 x 3.75 x 1.0	205	12.7
	F44		Corner	Rect.	Single	3.8 x 2.7 x 1.1	99	8.8
	F45		Corner	Round	Single	3.5 x 4.3 x 2.75	401	9.7
	F46		Corner	Oval	Single	2.5 x 1.8 x .4	13	7.2
	F47		Other	Rect.	Single	1.6 x 2 x .3	0	0
	F49		Corner	Round	Multiple	3.5 x 3.5 x .5	10	1.6

[a] Artifacts from Layer A left out of artifact totals from these three pits.

southern edges of Feature 51, was created. Feature 39 was also abandoned and filled, with a new, smaller pit (Feature 39A) created using the original western, northern, and southern walls.

There were six nonhearth subterranean pits in Structure 50, and they varied in size and shape (Table 3.2). Several of the nonhearth features were very shallow (under .5 feet below the base of the plowzone) and filled with a single deposit of brown sandy loam containing few artifacts. The small size and fragmentary nature of the artifacts from these features indicated that they had been filled with secondary refuse, probably early in the occupation of the building.

Structure 107. A small service building (10 x 10 feet) stood to the north of Structure 40. Its function was not apparent from archaeological data, but based on its small size it likely served as a corncrib or meathouse.

Archaeological Analysis of Subfloor Pits

As in Utopia Period II, the hearth-front pit complexes continued to predominate. Inhabitants were still experimenting and making modifications in pit construction and placement, particularly in the complicated hearth-front complexes. Perhaps in an effort to gain stable work space adjacent to the hearth, Structure 50 residents chose to place their first hearth-front pit some six feet away from the hearth, well back from the busiest foot traffic area. Later, a pit of similar size and alignment was placed much closer to the hearth. During later phases, the orientation of the hearth-front pits changed, as the residents dug three pits with their short axes facing the hearth. By the time these three pits were constructed, large areas around the hearth had been disturbed by earlier pit construction. Most of the nonhearth subfloor pits appeared to be shallow and, upon abandonment, filled rapidly with one deposit of soil containing secondary refuse. Pits whose use span had been cut short by the collapse of a wall were filled with a combination of household refuse and secondary debris probably swept up from the yard of the quarter.

In several cases, the residents attempted to strengthen pit walls with sheathings and walls of clay when they cut though earlier back-filled pits. The residents of the quarters were also experimenting with pit depth, particularly for hearth-front pits. The earliest hearth-front pit in Structure 50 extended only .5 feet below the base of the plowzone but was replaced by a pit that extended to a depth of 2.75 feet. Damage from groundwater rising into this deeper pit was evident as erosional undercutting around the perimeter of the feature's base. In the final period, the hearth-front pits were dug to depths ranging between 1.5 and 1.75 feet, presumably out of ground-water range but still considerably deeper than the earliest pit.

While undisturbed subsoil clay provided the sturdiest walls for subfloor pits, it was obvious that placing pits in an undisturbed area was not the only consideration in deciding pit location. After the wall collapse between Features 39 and 51, for example, a new pit could have been located in an undisturbed area along the west wall in the same room, or Features 46 and 47 could have been enlarged. Instead, the inhabitants chose to reconstruct the pits in their original locations. It would have been easier to relocate a new pit along the west wall in the same room, or simply to enlarge the old pit. Reconstruction in the original location suggests that placement was viewed as important—whether for sacred reasons or because these areas were viewed as "belonging" to a certain individual.

Summary

Combining archaeological and documentary evidence suggests that this site was active between 1730 and 1750, spanning the tenures of three property owners. The arrangement of space at the quarter during this period was more organic than in the earlier generation, and spaces between structures were used for daily activities as well as for dumping garbage. Artifacts from Utopia III suggests that Structure 50 served as a coresidence for men and women, while Structure 40 was occupied by two family-based households, perhaps headed by females (Fesler 2004:390, 403). In addition to the smaller daily humiliations of bondage, Utopia residents also faced the ever-present possibility of being separated from their immediate community. This period was one of instability for the Utopia Quarter residents, with the chance of sale away from Utopia threatening with each change in ownership. New slaves, probably fresh from Africa, were added to the quarter, while others were surely moved around within the families' landholdings.

While most of Bray's enslaved at Utopia were not really in danger of being sold due to an entailment clause in James Bray II's will, it was at Bray's discretion to move laborers among these widely distributed plantations, separating families and friends. Even the entailment restrictions did not prevent James Bray III and his father before him from attempting to circumvent the language and intent of the law. Thomas Bray II sold land and added slaves in the 1730s, some of whom probably were incorporated into the population at Utopia Quarter. Facing action from impatient creditors around 1740, Bray III planned to have the county sheriff seize some of his older, less productive slaves to help pay his debts until he was advised by a lawyer that such a scheme was illegal (cited in Walsh 1997:310). To help alleviate his debts, Bray diversified the activities of his home plantation in the 1740s, expanding into brickmaking, selling meat, wood, and finished lumber, and producing cider and brandy. Bray's financial difficulties would have been no secret in the quarters, and the uncertainty and stress this knowledge generated must have been considerable as the enslaved were faced with the fear of separation from family members and friends.

Upon the death of James Bray III in 1744, his executors sold all of his moveable property at public sale, leaving only his lands and slaves unsold. The enslaved from Utopia came under the ownership of the Burwell family during the final phase of occupation at the Utopia site, a period spanning the third quarter of the eighteenth century. The next sections will analyze the final period at Utopia quarter and a contemporary Burwell quarter known as Kingsmill Quarter.

Utopia Period IV, ca. 1750–1775

With his marriage to Frances Thacker Bray, widow of James Bray III, Lewis Burwell IV consolidated tracts of land along the James River east of Williamsburg into a 2,800-acre estate known as Kingsmill Plantation (James City County, 1768–1769:11). The property remained in the control of Lewis Burwell IV for the next three decades. A fourth Utopia quarter component, dated ca. 1750–1775, was located approximately 600 feet north of the Period III Utopia complex (Figure 3.9). This quarter was probably constructed soon after Lewis Burwell IV came into possession of Utopia in 1745 (Stephenson 1963:19).

After the death of James Bray III, his widow was granted the Utopia property and 29 slaves (Fesler 2004). Most of this group consisted of African-born individuals who had arrived in Virginia during the mid-1730s (Walsh 1997:43), consistent with the Virginia slave population as a whole, where "recent arrivals from Africa comprised 37.8 percent of the black population between 1719–29, 10 percent in 1740–49 and less than 5 percent by the 1750s" (Barden 1993:69).

The probate, which lists the enslaved by name, gender, and status as adult or adolescent, allows some generalizations to be made about the Utopia community. The name of one woman (Ebo) indicated her Igbo origins, while another woman, Mulatta Pat, was the child of a white father and enslaved mother. Mothers' names were listed for some of the children, meaning that these adolescents lived with one or more parents at the quarter. Nanny and

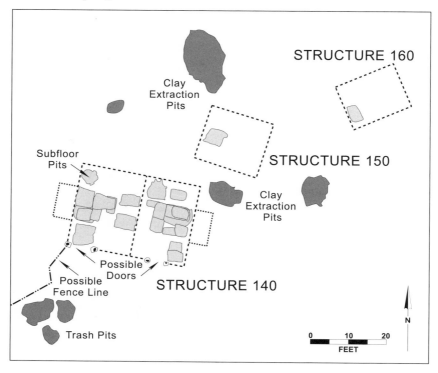

3.9. Utopia Period IV archaeological remains

Jupiter's mothers were at Utopia, and it is possible that Joe Boy and Austin, two older children, had one or more parents there as well. By midcentury, ratios of men to women were more evenly matched at Utopia.

Proportions of African-born slaves in Virginia decreased steadily over the third quarter of the eighteenth century, dropping from 21 percent in 1750 to 5 percent in 1780 (Morgan 1998:61). By the end of this final period at the site, the majority of the resident adults had been in Virginia for a number of years. Unlike recent arrivals from Africa, they probably spoke English relatively well and stood a good chance of marrying and establishing families. Like the earlier Utopia residents, they raised tobacco and grains, with women and children over the age of twelve or thirteen working in the agricultural fields alongside the men (Mullin 1972:48).

Archaeological Evidence at the Site

Three structures, set on ground-laid sills or piers, were present during Period IV at Utopia, with the locations and estimated dimensions of these structures determined by the presence and placement of subfloor pits. One timber-framed structure measured roughly 22 x 32 feet, and two additional smaller structures were in evidence as two isolated subfloor pits that had been set beneath small, single-family ground-sill structures. Several clay extraction pits later reused as trash pits were also found. Analysis of the 19,040 artifacts provided date spans falling within the third quarter of the eighteenth century, with the greatest activity in the 1750s and 1760s (Fesler 2004:152, 182).

Structure 140. The presumed 22-x-32-foot dimensions and alignment of Structure 140 were calculated by examining the locations of the subfloor pits and four remaining piers. Two large multiphase subfloor pit complexes containing ash, charcoal, and daub likely denoted the locations of gable end chimneys, suggesting that this building functioned as a duplex for two families (Figure 3.10). The pier-supported foundation indicates that the building, unlike the earlier Utopia quarters, contained a raised wooden floor.

There appeared to have been three and four phases of repair and redigging, respectively, in the hearth-front complexes in the west and east rooms of Structure 140 (Figure 3.11). In addition to the hearth-front complexes, nine nonhearth subfloor pits were present, with five pits in the east room and four in the west room. Pits stood in each of the building's corners, and the western room also contained two pits located along the partition wall between the two rooms.

Structures 150 and 160. The dimensions of the two additional structures on the site, whose presence was indicated only by the single subfloor pits marking their former locations, were unknown. Given the documentary evidence of families at the site, however, it can be surmised that the two small structures were single-family dwellings. At the Cancer Quarter of Nomini Hall Plantation, one quarter documented in 1789 measured just 8 x 12 feet (cited in Barden 1993:440). Possible pier supports for Structure 150 suggested 16-x-16-foot dimensions, although these features were only vaguely defined (Fesler 2004:252).

The high frequencies of architectural artifacts from the upper zones of subfloor pit fill suggest that they were filled when the overlying structures were destroyed. Fired daub and charred wood from the pits indicated that the structures had stick and mud chimneys.

Archaeological Analysis of Subfloor Pits

Twenty-four subfloor pits were present at the site, with 22 of them cutting through the soil beneath Structure 140 (Table 3.3). Thirteen of these 22 pits were part of hearth-front complexes located at the north and south ends of

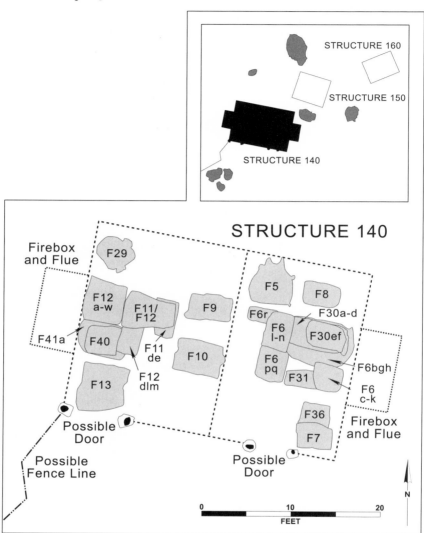

STRUCTURE 140

Firebox and Flue

F29

F12 a-w

F11/ F12

F9

F5

F8

F6r

F30a-d

F41a

F40

F6 l-n

F30ef

F11 de

F10

F6 pq

F31

F6bgh

F12 dlm

F13

F6 c-k

Possible Door

F36

Firebox and Flue

F7

Possible Fence Line

Possible Door

N

0   10   20
FEET

3.10. Utopia Period IV Structure 140 archaeological remains

the structure. Pits were also located in each of the building's corners, and three pits had been cut into the floor along the partition wall. As was evident in the earlier periods at Utopia, there had been sustained efforts to keep the hearth-front pits functional. Pits in other locations were generally constructed, used, and then refilled without attempts at repair.

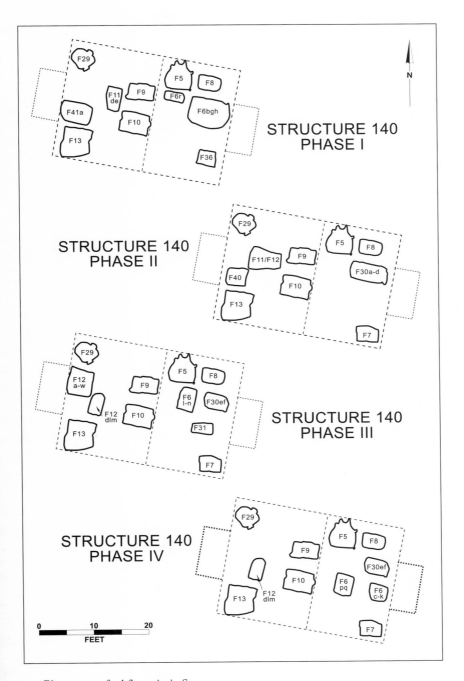

3.11. Phase maps of subfloor pits in Structure 140

Table 3.3 Utopia Quarter Period IV subfloor pits descriptive details

Structure	Feature	Phase	Location	Shape	Cut or repair	Dimensions & depth (in ft.)	Number of artifacts	Artifacts per cubic ft.
140	East Room							
	F6C/E/F/J/K	I	Hearth	Rect.	Multiple	3 x 6.4 x 2	336	8.75
	F6B/H/G	II	Hearth	Rect.	Multiple	7.2 x 4.4 x 1.45	137	3.0
	F6L/M/N	II	Hearth	Rect.	Multiple	2.5 x 3.8 x 1.75	311	18.7
	F6P/Q	III	Hearth	Rect.	Multiple	3.2 x 3.9 x 2	94	3.77
	F30E/F	III	Hearth	Rect.	Multiple	3.8 x 4.2 x 2.2	255	31.95 [c]
	F31	III	Hearth	Rect.	Multiple	2.1 x 3.9 x 1.9	385	24.74
	F30A-D	IV	Hearth	Rect.	Multiple	3.1 x 6.4 x 1.7	745	22.09
	F6R	I	Other	Rect.	Multiple	1.4 x 2.75 x .9	0	0
	F36	I	Corner	Rect.	Multiple	3 x 2 x 1.6	123	12.8
	F7	II	Corner	Rect.	Single	4 x 2.8 x 1.75	203	10.36
	F8	?	Corner	Rect.	Multiple	3.75 x 2.5 x .6	231	41.1
	F5	?	Other	Rect.	Single	3.5 x 4.5 x 3.9	573	9.33
	West Room							
	F11D/E	I	Hearth	Rect.	Multiple	3.8 x 2.3 x 1.0	79	27.2 [c]
	F40	I	Hearth	Square	Multiple	2.1 x 2.5 x 2.3	154	12.7
	F41A	II	Hearth	Square?		3.9 x 4.2 x 1.0	277	16.9
	F11/12 [a]	II	Hearth	Rect.	Multiple	4.9 x 2.9 x 1.8	571	22.3
	F12A/W [b]	III	Hearth	Rect.?	Multiple	4.25 x 4.5 x 2.0	790	20.7
	F12D/E/M/N	III	Hearth	Rect.	Multiple	2.5 x 2.3 x 2.4	380	27.5

	F9	?	Other	Rect.	Single	4.6 x 2.5 x 1.6	376	20.43
	F10	?	Other	Rect.	Multiple	4.5 x 2.9 x 1.0	387	29.66
	F13	?	Corner	Square	Multiple	5 x 5 x 1.5	437	11.65
	F29	?	Corner	Oval	Multiple	2.4 x 4 x 1	70	7.29
150	F4	I	Hearth?	Square	Single	4 x 4 x ?	206	?
160	F19	I	Hearth?	Rect.	Single	6 x 3.8 x ?	322	?

[a] Context numbers for Feature 11/12 are 11A/B/C/F/H & 12C/F/G/J/K.

[b] Context numbers for Feature 12 are 12A/B/V/W/P/Q/S/T/U.

[c] Calculations based on cubic feet of feature fill remaining at the time of excavation, not total original feature cubic footage.

Also in evidence was the continuing practice by the enslaved of relocating new pits in such a way that they fronted on the hearth but cut through the fill of earlier pits as little as possible. Some pits were dug in ways incorporating the walls of earlier features, as well as using boards to stabilize places where new pits cut through earlier backfilled features.

Summary

Analysis of architecture and artifacts from the Utopia IV structures indicates that the three structures at the site housed four family groups (Fesler 2004:403). Structure 140 served as a duplex for two families; Structures 150 and 160 were likely one-room, single-family structures. This pattern of family formation fits the demographic profile of the Virginia slave population during the third quarter of the eighteenth century.

In 1775, Lewis Burwell IV relocated to Mecklenburg County, selling some of his slaves before departing (Walsh 1997:211). Doubtless, some of Utopia's residents were among the enslaved sold. Burwell's son continued to manage Utopia and another family property, Kingsmill, with their reduced labor forces, until the property was offered for sale in 1781. At this point, another property owned by Frances Burwell's husband, Lewis Burwell IV, is considered. Located less than two miles west of Utopia, Kingsmill Plantation and its attendant quarter had been part of the Burwell family holdings for several generations.

Kingsmill Quarter (44JC39), ca. 1750–1780

Lewis Burwell III inherited the Kingsmill estate in 1710 and built an impressive house at the site sometime between 1725 and 1735 (Kelso 1984:42; Walsh 1997:42). The plantation house, which stood on a bluff some 700 yards from the James River, was a Georgian-style, two-story, eight-room brick structure, with two flanking brick dependencies, terraced formal gardens, and a host of farm buildings (Kelso 1984). At his death in 1744, Burwell's property passed to his adult son, Lewis Burwell IV (Wells 1976:22). The son considerably increased his landholdings when he married Frances Bray in 1745, consolidating her Littletown and Utopia tracts with his Kingsmill landholdings (McCartney 1997:170; Walsh 1997:43).

Tobacco, as well as oats and other grain crops, were raised at Kingsmill during the third quarter of the eighteenth century. Importation of laborers from Africa had ceased at Kingsmill by the early 1740s, with most of the Africans enslaved there having arrived in the 1720s and 1730s (Walsh 1997:52). County tax lists for 1768 showed that Burwell paid taxes on 65 tithes, 1,502

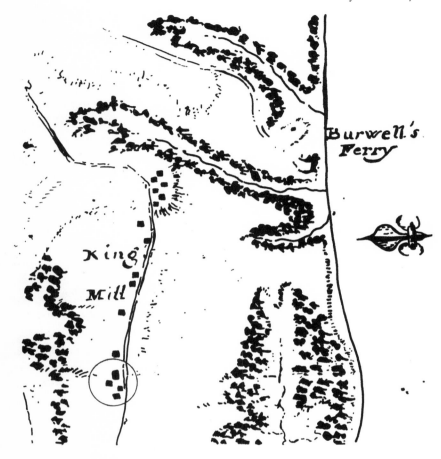

3.12. Detail of the Desandrouins Map (redrawn by author)

acres of land, and one chariot (James City County). These tithables likely represent the number of enslaved laborers on his James City County properties.

Like Utopia, Kingsmill Quarter, dating to the third quarter of the eighteenth century, was one of several outlying quarters associated with Kingsmill Plantation. Kingsmill Quarter, located one-quarter mile from the Burwell mansion, along the ridge road on the south side of a small creek, is depicted on the Desandrouins Map of 1781 (Figure 3.12). The enslaved who lived at Kingsmill Quarter were field workers, performing agricultural tasks associated with raising tobacco and grains.

Archaeological findings from Kingsmill Quarter suggest that occupation of the site ceased around the time Henry Martin purchased the property in 1783, and perhaps as early as 1781, when Lewis Burwell V removed himself and his slaves to the western part of the state. It is also possible that the quarter buildings were demolished right after Martin died in 1786 and the property came under the ownership of Henry Tazewell (McCartney 1997:259). Regardless, the site had been abandoned well before the beginning of the nineteenth century and its location forgotten until the early 1970s, when a five-year archaeological study of the plantation lands preceded planned development. The Virginia Research Center for Archaeology conducted the fieldwork in 1974 under the direction of archaeologist Dr. William Kelso. Artifacts recovered from the site indicate that occupation spanned most of the third quarter of the eighteenth century, with the buildings excavated there falling out of use in the 1780s.

Archaeological Evidence at the Site

Two dwellings for the enslaved community and a small (9-x-9-foot) unheated outbuilding such as a meathouse or granary were defined during archaeological excavation at the site (Figure 3.13). A large irregular depression located just west of the smaller dwelling may have been used for watering livestock and as a garbage dump. Although no well was found during the excavation, a nearby spring provided water for drinking, cooking, and bathing (Kelso 1984).

Structure One. Structure One was a 40-x-18-foot, story and a half frame building, underpinned by a continuous brick foundation. A 12-foot shed addition extended from the north side of the structure (Figure 3.14). An interior brick chimney was centered along the long wall between the addition and the main structure. Since the hearth and chimney brick had been salvaged, the location of the fireplaces was apparent only as an unburned H-shaped configuration surrounded by burned clay (Kelso 1984:120).

Since there was no evidence of a structural footing for the northern addition, this portion of the building rested on a ground-sill or shallow brick foundation. Only the nine subfloor pits contained within its footprint indicated the presence and dimensions of the addition. The configuration of the chimney and hearth, with a fireplace in each of the two 20-x-18-foot rooms, suggests that the structure was used a duplex for two families or groups of enslaved African Americans. Additional individuals could have been housed in the unheated addition which may have received some ambient heat from the chimney stack along the room's south wall.

Twenty subfloor pits were found in Structure One. Most of the pits were rectangular and arranged with their long axes along the walls of the structure. Each room had a pit in front of the hearth. Five subfloor pits contained

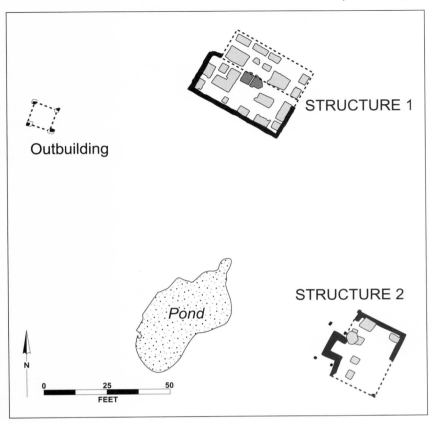

3.13. Kingsmill Quarter (44JC39) archaeological remains

evidence of wooden walls, floors, or partitions, and one pit contained a brick floor. Fired clay patches were evident in the subsoil floors of three pits, suggesting that embers had been used to dry out the pit walls and floors.

Structure Two. The second dwelling, a one-story, 28-x-20-foot frame structure on a continuous brick foundation, contained an exterior end chimney and six subfloor pits (Figure 3.15). Ceramic crossmends between the pits suggests contemporaneous filling of these features.

Archaeological Analysis of Subfloor Pits

Analysis of artifacts from the subfloor pits in Structures One and Two revealed they can be divided into two periods of filling (Kelso 1976). It is highly probable that 18 of the 26 subfloor pits contained artifacts unrelated to the slave occupation of the site (Table 3.4). The remaining eight features, con-

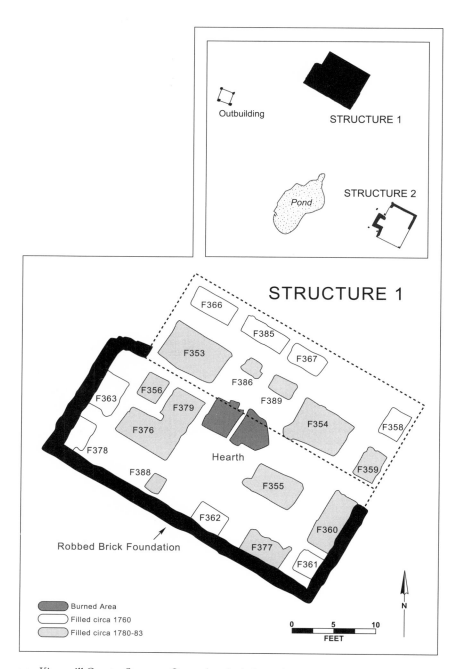

Outbuilding

STRUCTURE 1

Pond

STRUCTURE 2

STRUCTURE 1

F366

F385

F353

F367

F386

F356

F389

F363

F379

F354

F358

F376

Hearth

F378

F359

F388

F355

F362

F360

Robbed Brick Foundation

F377

F361

Burned Area
Filled circa 1760
Filled circa 1780-83

0   5   10
FEET

N

3.14. Kingsmill Quarter Structure One archaeological remains

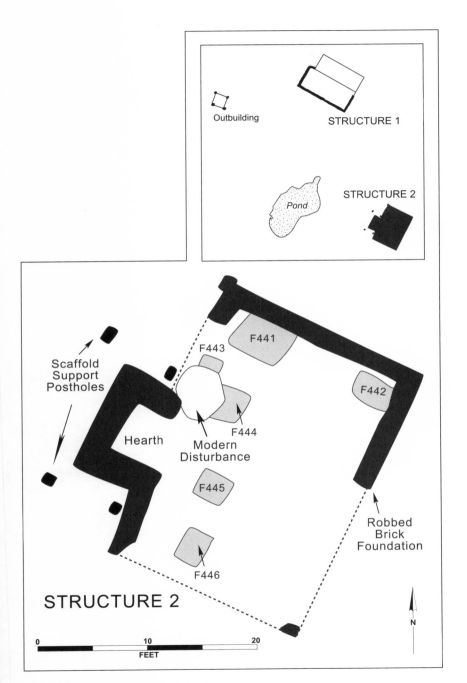

Outbuilding

STRUCTURE 1

Pond

STRUCTURE 2

F441

F443

Scaffold
Support
Postholes

F442

Hearth

F444

Modern
Disturbance

F445

Robbed
Brick
Foundation

F446

STRUCTURE 2

0   10   20
FEET

N

3.15. Kingsmill Quarter Structure Two archaeological remains

Table 3.4 Kingsmill Quarter subfloor pits descriptive details

Structure	Feature	Phase	Location	Shape	Cut or repair	Dimensions & depth (in ft.)	Number of artifacts	Artifacts per cubic ft.
1	KM358	I	Corner	Rect.	Single	3 x 3.2 x 2.8	131	4.9
	KM361	I	Corner	Rect.	Single	2.9 x 4.4 x 2.7	120	3.5
	KM362	I	Other	Rect.	Single	4.8 x 3.1 x 2.1	292	9.3
	KM363	I	Other	Rect.	Single	3.5 x 4.8 x 2.1	668	18.9
	KM366	I	Corner	Rect.	Single	6 x 2.7 x 2	134	4.1
	KM367	I	Other	Rect.	Single	4.7 x 2.9 x 2.3	249	7.9
	KM378	I	Corner	Rect.	Single	2.5 x 4.8 x 3	176	4.9
	KM385	I	Other	Rect.	Single	6.5 x 2.4 x 2.7	18	0.4
	KM353	II	Other	Rect.	Single	7.8 x 5.9 x 3.4	321	2.1
	KM354	II	Other	Rect.	Single	7.1 x 5 x 3.1	3214	29.2
	KM355	II	Hearth	Rect.	Single	7.8 x 3.9 x 3.6	1634	15.0
	KM356	II	Other	Rect.	Single	3.5 x 3.1 x 3.8	1261	30.6
	KM359	II	Other	Rect.	Single	4.3 x 2.9 x 2.1	602	23.0
	KM360	II	Other	Rect.	Single	6 x 3.7 x 3.1	224	3.3
	KM377	II	Other	Rect.	Single	4.4x 4.9 x 3.25	157	2.2
	KM379	II	Hearth	Rect.	Multiple	3.6 x 6.1 x 2.1	1772	38.4
	KM376	II	Hearth	Rect.	Multiple	5.8 x 3.8 x 2.5	Indet.	Indet.
	KM386	II	Other	Rect.	Single	2.5 x 2.9 x .8	Indet.	Indet.
	KM389	II	Other	Rect.	Single	3.3 x 2.0 x 2	109	8.3

2	KM441	II	Corner	Rect.	Single	5.5 x 4 x 1.5	87	2.6
	KM442	II	Corner	Oval	Single	3 x 4.6 x 1.1	166	10.9
	KM443	II	Other	Rect.	Single	2.2 x ? x ?	17	Indet.
	KM444	II	Other	Rect.	Single	3.7 x 2.9 x .5	34	6.3
	KM445	II	Hearth	Rect.	Single	2.5 x 2.9 x .6	7	1.6
	KM446	II	Other	Square	Single	3 x 3.1 x ?	Indet.	Indet.

taining no crossmending ceramics or glass, appeared to have been filled about two decades earlier than the other pits in this building, in the 1760s, based on the presence of creamware and on wine bottle shape.

Numerous crossmending fragments of ceramics and glass show the remaining pits were filled rapidly and simultaneously with garbage from the same source. A military button discarded after 1781 and 23 Virginia halfpennies issued in 1775 indicate a late eighteenth-century filling date for these features. The upper zones of fill contained large quantities of brick and mortar rubble, suggesting that filling occurred when the overlying building was destroyed. The quantities, types, and dating of the artifacts, combined with the history of the property, revealed that these 18 pits were filled with debris from the British occupation of the property during the Revolutionary War. Thus, artifacts from the 18 Phase II subfloor pits in Structures One and Two were not analyzed any further for clues about how the enslaved used these pits.

Since the features were almost certainly created during the slave occupation of the structure, they were included in analysis that examined patterns in pit size, placement, and construction methods. Comparing the Phase I and Phase II subfloor pits in Structure One revealed that the pits filled earlier were more consistent in size and depth than the later pits (Table 3.4). The Phase I features ranged from 8 to 15.8 square feet and varied between 2 and 3 feet in depth below the base of the plowzone. The Phase II pits ranged from 7 to 45 square feet and from less than a foot to almost 4 feet deep. This variation between the two sets of pits may indicate that the original pits were all dug at one time, when the building was first occupied or constructed. The later pits, with their varied dimensions and depths, appear to have been created piecemeal, perhaps as needed in the later years of the building's occupation. The placement of the original pits was systematic, ranged along the exterior walls of the structure, perhaps to be away from foot traffic, while later pit placement was more varied. Some of these pits were also dug against the exterior side walls, while others were placed in the main structure, against the partition wall that divided it from the northern room. Still other pits were in the center of the room, adjacent to the hearths. None of the later pits intruded upon the earlier features, suggesting that some of the original pits were still open, or at least visible, when the later pits were created.

Summary

Financial difficulties and unfavorable political leanings probably factored into Lewis Burwell IV's decision to move west to Mecklenburg County in

1775. His son Lewis Burwell V assumed operation of the plantation, which fared poorly during the American Revolution (Kelso 1984:46). After passing out of the Burwell family in 1781, the land was purchased by Henry Martin in 1783 (Wells 1976:2). A series of short-term owners followed, and the mansion was eventually destroyed by fire in 1844.

By the end of the third quarter of the eighteenth century, the enslaved at Kingsmill Plantation had lived in a fairly stable community for several decades. Most of the individuals under the age of thirty to thirty-five had been born in Virginia and lived at Kingsmill for most, if not all, of their lives. But difficult times for Virginia planters meant difficult times for the enslaved as well. Documented instances of Burwell slave runaways were common in the 1760s and 1770s, as he sold individuals to other planters or moved them to other Burwell plantations in the Piedmont. Fearful of separation from their families and friends, many of Burwell's slaves ran away, either to avoid being sent west or to return to the Tidewater after having been removed from Kingsmill.

The final plantation quarter to be considered is associated with Carter's Grove Plantation, also owned by the Burwell family. This quarter provides an opportunity to analyze slave life at the end of the eighteenth century.

Carter's Grove Quarter (44JC110), ca. 1780–1800

During the last quarter of the eighteenth century, approximately 10 to 15 working adults, their children, and several older individuals lived in a quarter located at the edge of a wooded ravine, within sight of the Carter's Grove plantation house (Figure 3.16). These laborers were responsible for the cultivation of around 125 acres near the house. Although the documentary record does not allow us to place specific individuals on this quarter, Walsh's multigenerational history of the Burwell family slaves provides enough clues to allow a reasonable estimate of the quarter population (Walsh 1997). Because of divisions of the enslaved human property earlier in the eighteenth century, the enslaved at Carter's Grove and Kingsmill shared both real and fictive kinship ties.

Constructed in the 1750s by Carter Burwell, nephew of Kingsmill's Lewis Burwell III, the two-story mansion mirrored his uncle's earlier house in its brick construction, flanking outbuildings, and extensive terraced gardens. As on most other Chesapeake plantations, tobacco, corn, and wheat were the primary crops produced at Carter's Grove, with sales of livestock and meat providing additional sources of revenue.

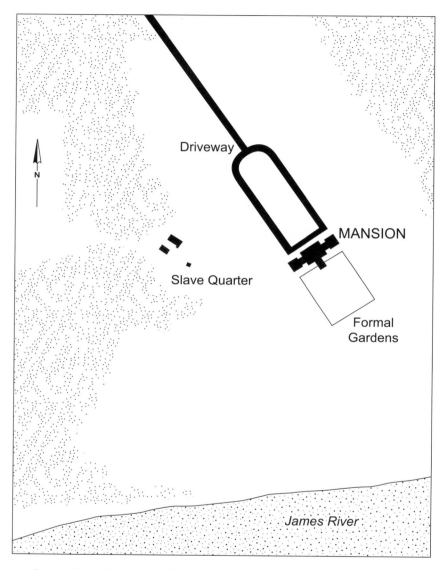

Driveway

MANSION

Slave Quarter

Formal
Gardens

James River

3.16. Carter's Grove Plantation (44JC110)

The quarter at Carter's Grove dates to the last two decades of the eighteenth century, a period when the plantation was under the ownership of Carter Burwell's son, Nathaniel II. Inheriting the farm in 1771, the younger Burwell implemented changes at the home plantation throughout his tenure as owner, with his adjustments reflecting the changing economic and political climate (McCartney 1997; Walsh 1997). In the face of mounting tensions and trade problems with England just prior to the Revolutionary War, Burwell stopped raising tobacco at Carter's Grove, diversifying plantation activities during the war toward the production of goods and supplies needed to sustain the plantation through war-related shortages. The agricultural activities of the enslaved at Carter's Grove became more diversified, as production was expanded to include wheat, oats, barley, peas, and hay that could be used to feed the inhabitants of the plantation and its outlying farms or sold locally (Walsh 1997:125). Other enslaved individuals were skilled in various trades such as carpentry, coopering, weaving, and milling.

Tax lists for 1783 through 1786 show 69 slaves at Carter's Grove, of whom 26 were children (Walsh 1997:131). Approximately one-quarter of the enslaved at Carter's Grove lived at the quarter excavated by the Colonial Williamsburg Foundation.

Archaeological Evidence at the Site

The quarter sat on a marginal piece of land, surrounded on three sides by a wooded ravine. Shielded by woods to the south, the quarters would have been invisible from the river and from visitors arriving at the mansion along the carriage road. While the brick plantation house, ascending two stories above the rise upon which it was built, was visible to the quarter inhabitants, it would have been more difficult for anyone inside the main house to see the low, weathered wooden cabins tucked away in a crescent of forest.

While Burwell's house weathered the passing years, the quarters were more ephemeral, having vanished by the end of the first decade of the nineteenth century. They were rediscovered in 1970 during an archaeological reconnaissance of the Carter's Grove property (Kelso and Frank 1972). Excavation at the site revealed ditches, fencelines, and a series of subfloor pits that appeared to denote the former locations of three structures (Figure 3.17). No traces of subsurface foundations, structural postholes, or chimneys were found, suggesting that these buildings were either of ground-sill log or frame construction with earthen floors, or they sat on very shallow brick piers or foundations that had been removed for reuse or completely plowed away

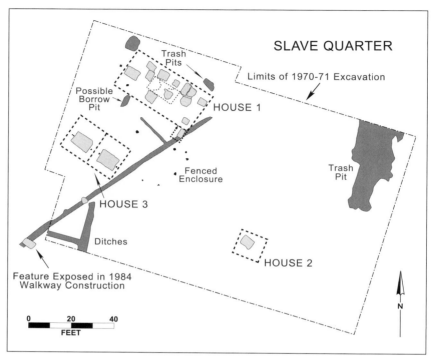

3.17. Carter's Grove Quarter archaeological remains

in the intervening years. Large quantities of nails recovered from the subfloor pits suggest that the buildings were probably of frame, rather than log,
construction.

A well southwest of the quarter and a freshwater spring located in the ravine supplied the quarter inhabitants with drinking water. Despite the slen-
der nature of the structural evidence, it appears that the excavated portions
of the quarter consisted of three dwellings.

House One. The northernmost concentration of subfloor pits indicated
that a building with dimensions at least 42 x 20 feet had rested over 12 pits
(Figure 3.18). Although no archaeological evidence was found to indicate the
location of the building's hearths, the dense scattering of pits over the entire
footprint of the building suggests a central chimney opening into each room.
A lone subfloor pit was located outside the presumed footprint of the building, probably in a small, unheated lean-to addition.

House Two. A subfloor pit located 55 feet southeast of House Three was

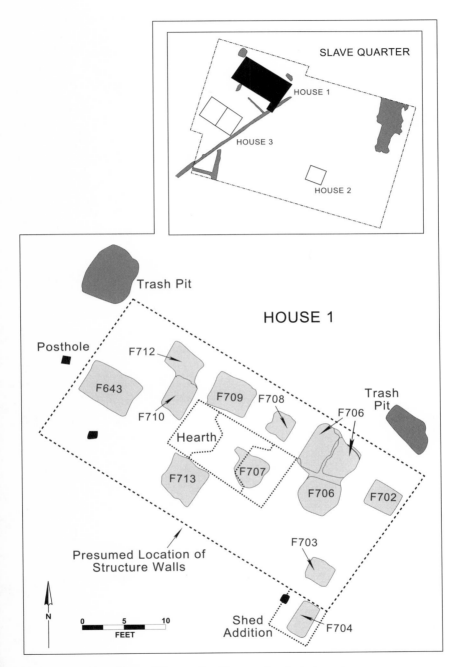

SLAVE QUARTER

HOUSE 1

HOUSE 3

HOUSE 2

Trash Pit

HOUSE 1

Posthole

F712

F643

F710

F709   F708

Hearth

F713   F707

Trash Pit

F706

F706

F702

Presumed Location of
Structure Walls

F703

N

0   5   10
FEET

Shed
Addition

F704

3.18. Carter's Grove Quarter Structure One House archaeological remains interpreted as having been associated with a small single-room dwelling. Other than a small area of scorched earth east of the subfloor pit suggesting the former hearth location, there was no other structural evidence remaining.

House Three. Located 30 feet southwest of Structure One were two identical subfloor pits. These 9-x-6-foot pits, each contained traces of a 6.5-x-4.5-foot wooden box. The dwelling believed to have rested over these two features has been interpreted as a 30-x-12-foot two-room duplex, built to house one family in each of its 15-x-12-foot rooms (Figure 3.19). A fenced enclosure at the eastern end of the duplex, as evidenced by a series of small stake holes, helped form a small courtyard between Structures One and Three. Encircling a garden or forming a poultry pen, this enclosure helped form a visual barrier between the plantation house and the quarter yard.

Archaeological Analysis of Subfloor Pits

Analysis of the subfloor pit fills and artifacts from the three structures revealed that all but several of the pits had been filled at the same time, presumably when the overlying structures were destroyed. The composition of the uppermost fill in these pits was identical, a dark brown loam mixed with wood ash and brick bits, indicating that the features had been filled with material from the same source (Table 3.5).

There was little evidence of the digging and redigging of pits apparent at the other earlier sites. By the end of the eighteenth century, the enslaved had learned to construct pits of sizes and depths not prone to damage from groundwater. The two deepest pits at the site, associated with House Three, contained prefabricated wooden boxes. This construction method would have prevented the collapse of pit walls, a problem that had plagued deeper pits at the earlier Utopia quarters.

A total of 2,530 artifacts was recovered from the Carter's Grove subfloor pits. Since soil was not screened during this excavation, this artifact count, like that at Kingsmill Quarter, is not representative of the complete cultural assemblage from the site. Categories of smaller objects, including some types of faunal remains, buttons, straight pins, and beads are underrepresented in the assemblage. Painted pearlwares provided a *terminus post quem* date of 1775 as the earliest year that the filling could have taken place, with production ranges of the ceramic assemblage suggesting an occupation range of 1780 to 1800. The quarters were likely abandoned when Nathaniel Burwell II removed most of the laborers from Carter's Grove by early 1797.

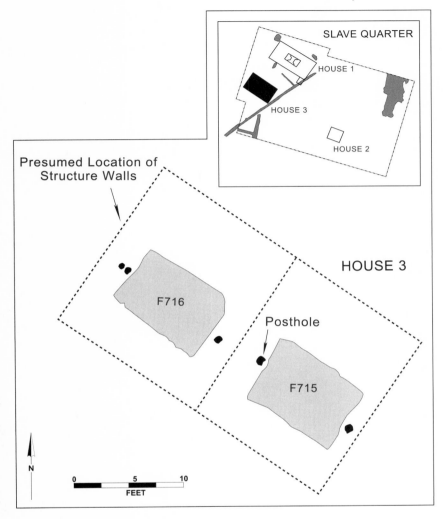

3.19. Carter's Grove Quarter Structure Three archaeological remains

Summary

Although the construction date for the quarter is unknown, it was likely built when Nathaniel Burwell II gained control of the property in 1771. Analysis of the artifacts and fill of the pits suggests that they were filled simultaneously, when the quarter was destroyed at the end of the eighteenth cen-

Table 3.5 Carter's Grove Quarter subfloor pits descriptive details

Structure	Feature	Phase	Location	Shape	Cut or repair	Dimensions & depth (in ft.)	Number of artifacts	Artifacts per cubic ft.
House One	CG643	II	Other	Rect.	Single	6.2 x 4.1 x 1.75	466	10.5
	CG702	II	Corner	Rect.	Single	3.7 x 3 x ?	51	Indet.
	CG703	II	Corner	Square	Single	3 x 3 x .75	38	5.6
	CG704	II	Other	Rect.	Single	2 x 4 x 1	126	15.8
	CG706A/D	I?	Hearth	Rect.	Multiple	5.4 x 6 x ?	424	Indet.
	CG706B/C	II?	Hearth	Rect.	Multiple	3.6 x 4.8 x ?	51	Indet.
	CG707	II	Hearth	Rect.	Single	3 x 3 x 3.3	6	0.2
	CG708	II	Other	Square	Single	2.7 x 2.7 x .33	38	15.8
	CG709	II	Corner	Rect.	Single	5 x 4 x ?	59	Indet.
	CG710	I	Hearth	Rect.	Single	3 x 4 x ?	47	Indet.
	CG712	II	Other	Rect.	Single	4 x 3 x 1.1	29	2.2
	CG713	II	Corner	Square	Single	4.5 x 4 x ?	255	Indet.
House Two	CG721	II	Hearth?	Rect.	Single	5.5 x 4.25 x 2.7	67	1.1
House Three	CG715	II	Hearth	Rect.	Single	6.5 x 4.5 x 3.5	455	4.4
	CG716	II	Hearth	Rect.	Single	6.5 x 4.5 x 3.25	311	3.3

tury. By this time, the buildings would have been almost 30 years old and in shoddy condition.

Nathaniel Burwell II seems to have survived the war with remarkably little hardship to his family or his bondspeople (Walsh 1997:128). After the resumption of trade with the English following the war, he returned to the production of tobacco, although focusing more time and energy on his Virginia Piedmont plantations as the century drew to a close. In late 1796 or early the following year, Burwell removed nearly all of his agricultural workers from Carter's Grove, sending them west to his property in Frederick County (Walsh 1997:217).

Summary

Archaeological findings from these three plantations provide a good opportunity to chart change through time in subfloor pit construction and use, as well as providing a means for examining the material conditions of rural slave life in eighteenth-century Virginia. Each site was occupied for roughly 20 to 30 years, a period corresponding with a single generation of enslaved individuals. Because land transactions and marriages between the Burwell and Bray families brought continuity between the various plantations, there was a corresponding continuity within the slave communities residing in these quarters. Considered together, the sites span the entire eighteenth century—a period of great change within the Virginia economy and slave demographics.

At each site, archaeological excavations revealed a group of buildings that served as slave housing. Each of the quarters was comparable in size, composition, and location within its respective plantation. Each site had been home to a community of male and female adults, as well as young children. The location of these quarters at some distance from the main plantation house and adjacent to arable land suggested that most of the residents were involved in agricultural labor.

While building construction techniques varied between the sites, subfloor pits were present at each location. These sites provided a sample of 103 subfloor pits, with each containing roughly equivalent numbers of pits, between 15 and 26. Of these 103 features, detailed artifact analysis was undertaken on the 81 pits whose contents were associated with the enslaved community. While the artifact assemblages from the remaining 23 features were not analyzed to determine pit function, the pits were not without analytical value. Because enslaved residents originally constructed the pits, these features were considered appropriate for inclusion in analysis of pit size, depth, location, shape, and construction techniques. For example, it became apparent during this descriptive analysis that there were noticeable differences between hearth-front pits and pits in other locations. Hearth pits appeared to have been maintained through repair and recutting to a greater degree than pits in other locations. In Chapter 5, quantitative analysis will be used to explore these variables further to determine if there was significant variation among them.

4
Intersite Comparisons: The Material Lives of the Enslaved

This study examines five sites spanning the full course of the eighteenth century, a period in which Virginia went from being a royal colony to an independent commonwealth within the emerging new nation. It also witnessed the rise of an elite planter class who could afford expansive plantations and large labor forces to work lands green with tobacco. This enslaved labor force was largely African-born in the early part of the century, making the transition as the century progressed into one predominantly Virginia-born. Economic and environmental factors changed the face of agriculture in the second half of the century, as tobacco was edged out by a more diversified economy based in cereal grains and livestock. Westward expansion, accelerating after the Revolutionary War, brought about the relocation of vast numbers of Tidewater Virginia slaves.

The changing demographics of the economy and labor force were writ in the archaeological record, as viewed here through the microcosm of these five sites. Comparing the five quarters within the larger context of Virginia archaeological and historical research reveals changing patterns in architecture, material life, work, and diet, and forms a picture of enslaved life in eighteenth-century Tidewater Virginia.

Architecture and Demographics

All five sites, similar in size, function, and placement at their respective plantations, were outlying quarters that housed slaves whose primary responsibilities were agricultural work and tending livestock. Over the course of the century, changes in construction methods, building sizes, and arrangement on the landscape provided clues to quarter demographics. Some of these changes reflect the transitional nature of the slave population, as the arrival of more women led to the formation of families. Other modifications appear to be related to changing patterns of building technology.

Broad patterns in construction techniques and building size are evident in eighteenth- and nineteenth-century slave quarters excavated in Virginia over the last three decades (Table 4.1). The tradition of earthfast construction, a vernacular building form common throughout seventeenth-century Tidewater Virginia and Maryland, was still in evidence for slave housing prior to 1750. Structures at the two earliest Utopia Quarters were timber-framed buildings constructed around earth-set posts. Roughly riven clapboards, unglazed wooden-shuttered windows, earthen floors, and stick and mud chimneys gave these inexpensively and quickly built structures spartan, rough-hewn appearances inside and out.

By the last occupation at Utopia, beginning around midcentury, earthfast buildings had given way to log or timber-framed structures set on shallow ground sills. Leaving no archaeological traces of foundation walls or supports, placement and estimated dimensions of these structures had to be based solely on the patterns of subfloor pits cut through their earthen floors. This same form of construction, also with stick and mud chimneys, was evident at the late eighteenth-century Carter's Grove Quarter, as well as other contemporary slave dwellings in the Williamsburg area (Franklin 1997). The lower construction costs and the relative speed and ease with which these houses could be built relative to earthfast dwellings helped account for this change in construction methods.

The only permanent architecture at any of the five sites was found at Kingsmill Quarter. This site's two timber-framed structures had been constructed on continuous brick foundations, with wooden floors, glazed windows, and brick chimneys. While these structures may have originally served as an overseer's home and kitchen and were later converted to slave housing, the use of more permanent construction materials and methods as seen archaeologically at Kingsmill and in standing eighteenth-century slave dwellings at Tuckahoe foreshadowed the more substantial slave housing of nineteenth-century Virginia.

In addition to changing construction methods, house size and overall form altered during the course of the century as well. Some of this change can be related to the formation of slave families, which had begun to occur on plantation quarters prior to midcentury. Slave marriage and the establishment of families were generally encouraged by slave owners. While providing a more ordinary course of life for the enslaved, this form of control

Table 4.1. Dimensions of Virginia slave quarters

Site	Site Number	FoundationType	Structure Dimensions	# Rooms	Approximate Date
Atkinson Quarter	44JC648	earthfast	16 x 16		1700–1720
Utopia Period II	44JC32				
Structure 1	44JC32	earthfast	12 x 28	2	1700–1725
Structure 10	44JC32	earthfast	16 x 32	3	1700–1725
			6 x 8.5		
Structure 20	44JC32	earthfast	12 x 28	2	1700–1725
Harbor View	44SK192				1720–1760
Littletown 1	44JC35	earthfast	16 x 20	2	1720–1760
Littletown 2	44JC35	earthfast	20 x 24	2	1720–1760
Tutter's Neck	44JC45	brick	25 x 16		1730–1740s
Utopia Period III	44JC32				
Structure 40	44JC32	earthfast	12 x 16	1	1725–1750
Structure 50	44JC32	earthfast	16 x 24	2	1725–1750
Bray Quarter	44JC34	earthfast	20 x 20	1	1740–1781
Utopia Period IV	44JC32				
Structure 140	44JC32	ground sill	22 x 32	2	1750–1780
Structure 150	44JC32	ground sill	?	1?	1750–1780
Structure 160	44JC32	ground sill	?	1?	1750–1780
Hampton Key	44JC44	earthfast	28 x 24	2	1750–1781
Kingsmill Quarter	44JC39				
Structure 1	44JC39	brick continuous	40 x 18	3	1750–1780
Structure 2	44JC39	brick continuous	28 x 20	1?	1750–1780
Wilton Duplex	44HE493	ground sill	20 x 36	2	1750–1790

Continued on the next page

Table 4.1. Continued

Site	Site Number	FoundationType	Structure Dimensions	# Rooms	Approximate Date
Southall's Quarter	44JC969				
Structure One	44JC969	ground sill	15 x 20	1?	1750–1800
Structure Two	44JC969	earthfast	15 x 20	2	1750–1800
North Quarter	44JC52	brick continuous	25 x 16	2	1775–1781
Rich Neck Quarter St. B	44WB52	ground sill	?	?	1775–1815
Carter's Grove	44JC110				
House One	44JC110	ground sill	20 x 42	2	1780–1800
House Two	44JC110	ground sill	?	2	1780–1800
House Three	44JC110	ground sill	?	1?	1780–1800
Mulberry Row	44AB89				
Quarter O	44AB89	stone	20 x 12		1770–1800
Quarter R	44AB89	stone	12 x 14		1793–1809
Quarter S	44AB89	stone	12 x 14		1793–1820
Quarter T	44AB89	stone	12 x 14		1793–1810
Wilcox	44PG114	brick pier			1840s
Shirley	44CC135	brick pier	20 x 40		1843–1865
Valentine	CWF29F	brick pier	15 x 25		1840–1865
Portici Plantation					
Pohoke Quarter		stone pier	12 x 12		1820–1863
Cellar Quarter		cellar room	12 x 14		1820–1863

Sources: Atkinson: Archer et al. (2006); Kingsmill (North Quarter, Kingsmill Quarter, Hampton Key, Bray, and Littletown Quarter): Kelso (1984); Utopia: Fesler (2004); Southall's Quarter: Pullins et al. (2003); Frank (2003); Wilton: Higgins et al. (2000); Carter's Grove: Kelso and Frank (1972); Monticello: Sanford (1991); Rich Neck: Franklin (1997); Portici: Parker and Hernigle (1990) Valentine: Samford (1999); Shirley: Leavitt (1984); and Wilcox: McKee (1988).

also benefited the planter, as an individual with family ties and obligations
was less likely to run away or cause trouble.

In correspondence and other surviving writings, eighteenth-century Virginia planters differentiated between slave quarters and cabins, suggesting they drew a distinction between single-family dwellings and structures built as barracks to accommodate larger groups of slaves (Morgan 1998:106). Over the course of the century, the occurrence of smaller dwellings increased, corresponding with the formation of family units as the changing demographics of the population allowed (Fesler 2004). These dwellings could be small single-room log or frame cabins or duplexes that would accommodate two families, each living in its own separate room under one roof. Utopia's Period IV Structure 140 was a 704-square-foot duplex set on shallow wooden piers. Some of the earlier and larger barracks-style structures were retrofitted into smaller spaces by adding partition walls and new doorways to accommodate the needs of enslaved families.

Reduction in house size was the most important trend in slave architecture in the second half of the eighteenth century (Fesler 2004:228), illustrating a reevaluation by Virginia planters of slave housing strategies that better fit the emerging family structures of the enslaved population. This transition from group residences to homes for single or extended families occurred as the slave trade diminished in importance and the slave population became self-sustaining. Fesler's analysis of architectural data on 67 Virginia slave quarters determined that housing unit size diminished nearly 60 percent over the course of the eighteenth century (Fesler 2004:258).

Aside from the trend at these sites toward a less permanent and more economical form of construction as the eighteenth century progressed, architectural evidence suggests quarter demographics, as well as slaves' roles in shaping their built environment. In the absence of good documentary evidence on the enslaved communities at these sites, it is impossible to say with certainty how residents were distributed about the quarter or how they used these buildings. The structures themselves offer some clues, however. At Utopia's Period II occupation, only one room in each two-room building was heated, typical of an early English hall and parlor floor plan (Carson et al. 1981). This evidence suggests that all the residents of any given structure had access to both rooms. If this conclusion is correct, then it is possible that the enslaved were using each of the two rooms differently. The floor plan of Structure 50 at Utopia Period III, with its heated central room and small flanking unheated spaces, and that of the unheated addition at Kingsmill Quarter suggest general living and working areas separated from sleeping and storage spaces (Fesler 2004). It is possible that groups of unrelated individuals or even large extended families lived in these structures, with sleeping areas separated by gender or by small groupings within a family. This situation contrasts with the later two-room/two-hearth duplexes at Utopia and Carter's Grove, where a family group presumably inhabited each room.

The limited space (192 square feet) in Structure 40 at Utopia Period III, compared with the other buildings there, may indicate that it served as a single-family dwelling. At Carter's Grove and Utopia Period IV, the presence of several single isolated subfloor pits suggested that small single-family structures had once stood over them. At Carter's Grove and Utopia, several subfloor pits were located adjacent to the houses, suggesting small unheated sheds added as private spaces for individuals.

The U-shaped building arrangement at the earliest Utopia quarter, similar to West African house compounds of that period, suggests that the enslaved had input in the design of quarter structures and communities (Fesler 2004; Sobel 1987). The central courtyard located there and a similar arrangement at the Carter's Grove Quarter formed a communal area largely sheltered from the planter's gaze. Thus situated, the enslaved could expect, as visitor Edward Kimber observed in 1746, to "have a pretty deal of Liberty in their Quarter" (Kimber 1998:148). Assembled around fires that provided a degree of heat in the colder months and kept away the region's hungry mosquitoes in the summer, the residents gathered to socialize, rest, and prepare meals. Charles Janson, traveling in the United States in the 1790s, noted that slaves would "often sit up after their work is done, over a large fire, even in the heat of the summer," talking loudly (Janson 1807:363). Similar to many West African societies, it appeared that numerous activities took place outside the dark and drafty quarters, with these buildings used primarily for sleeping and storage. Although quarters were often built using English building dimensions and floor plans, it appears that the residents used them in African ways. Fesler's (2004) analysis of artifact distributions at Utopia II suggests that the quarter functioned in many respects as an archetypal village compound, with gendered division of space and a communal lifestyle. As Virginia-born slaves began to predominate, quarter layout became less West African in nature. The physical arrangement of the quarters at the later Utopia occupations was more organic than the earlier Utopia settlement, with buildings scattered at various alignments on the landscape.

While the spatial arrangements of some quarters were suggestive of African American influence, slaves may have also been instrumental in choosing the construction techniques used in building their homes. The overall dimensions, post and beam construction, roof framing, small interior spaces, and earthen floors typical of eighteenth- and early nineteenth-century Virginia slave quarters were also common to many West African societies (Sobel 1987; Vlach 1978). Because the enslaved participated in all phases of house construction, they may have been able to create living spaces that conformed to familiar and desirable conceptions of physical space.

While most quarter buildings appeared to have been constructed and used as housing, corncribs, barns, and similar outbuildings were often present at quarters. Livestock enclosures and garden spaces were typical, and the Kingsmill yard appeared to have contained a small pond, probably for watering livestock. Freshwater springs and, less commonly, wells served quarter residents as sources for water. Large trash pits filled with animal bone, shellfish, and other debris stood close enough to the dwellings at each site to have created unpleasant odors for the quarter residents on a warm day, as well as inviting unwanted rodents and other wildlife into the immediate area.

The trend in small single-room structures and duplexes continued into the nineteenth century. Virginia quarters show the influence of that century's plantation reform movement which advocated healthier and cleaner living conditions as well as stricter discipline for slaves (McKee 1992). Buildings were raised off the ground on masonry stone or wooden pier supports to allow a healthy flow of air beneath their wooden floors. Rooms were shielded against the cold by glass-paned windows; substantial chimneys of brick or stone provided heat.

Examining slave housing over the course of the eighteenth century reveals changing architectural form and function reflective of changes in slave importation patterns and Virginia slave demographics. As conditions become more conducive to the formation of families, the building trend moved away from non-kin individuals coresiding in group housing to smaller single-family units. While the total amount of living space allotted to each slave "improved little, if at all, through the eighteenth century" (Morgan 1998:112), perhaps a more important factor in the quality of life for the enslaved came from the greater opportunity to live in relative, albeit cramped, privacy with family members.

Material Life

Eighteenth- and nineteenth-century travelers, particularly visitors from England and Europe, were fascinated with all aspects of North American life and published lengthy travelogues about their journeys. Of particular interest were the lives of enslaved African Americans, and these travelers made it a point to comment on the work, personal habits, and living conditions of the enslaved. These accounts provide interesting glimpses into life in the quarters. The recounting of material possessions generally speaks to the meagerness of material goods owned by the enslaved. Niemcewicz's (1965:100) often-quoted passage about one of George Washington's quarters with its cups and teapot in the midst of little else provides a bleak picture of the level of material comforts experienced by most slaves. Other examples mention wooden beds and straw pallets on the floor, covered with old woolen blankets, and minimal cooking equipment is also often noted, as in the iron and brass kettle, pot racks, iron pot, frying pan, and beer barrel in one Virginia quarter (Morgan 1998:115). These accounts, which focus generally on the absence of furniture, seldom provide the full range of goods found at slave quarters. Archaeological research indicates a range of handcrafted goods, as well as manufactured and imported tablewares, glass, and tools present in the quarters.

 What do the artifacts from the five sites reveal about life at these quarters during the eighteenth century? Generally, the limited range of the artifacts recovered from these features suggested a meager material life for the enslaved throughout the century, with some increase in quantities and varieties of material goods over time. A summary table of the quantities and percentages of subfloor pit artifacts by category for each site is provided in Table 4.2. The increase in material goods coincides with the overall expansion of consumerism throughout colonial American society and the increasing availability of goods for consumers in general. The following pages provide an overview of material life at each of the sites, with a subsequent detailed comparison of several specific categories of material remains: ceramics, dietary evidence, tools, and personal items. The site data are placed within the broader context of slave access to and acquisition of material goods.

While the earliest occupation at Utopia (1700–1730) yielded the largest number of recovered artifacts, it also contained the most limited range of artifact types. Most of the finds were either food or structural remains. Bottle and table glass were nonexistent, and ceramics formed less than 1 percent of the assemblage from the subfloor pits. Food bone, oyster and clam shell, ethnobotanical remains, and eggshell comprised over half (54.5 percent) of the recovered artifacts from Utopia Period II. Nails and other architectural debris made up approximately one-quarter of the artifacts. While ceramics and tools were found in only minimal quantities, their presence shows the incorporation of European-produced goods into the daily lives of the resi-

Table 4.2. Subfloor Pit Artifact type percentages by study site

Artifact type	Utopia II	Utopia III	Utopia IV	Kingsmill Phase One pits	Carter's Grove
Kitchen artifact group					
Ceramics	0.9	4.1	6.3	5.0	21.2
Wine and Case Bottles	0	6.5	6.1	27.3	14.5
Pharmaceutical bottles	0	0.1	0.7	0.7	1.6
Table glass	0	0	0.4	1	0.4
Tableware/Cutlery	0.2	0.2	1.3	1.3	1
Kitchenware	0	0	0.2	0.1	0
Food group					
Animal bone, fish scale	45	46.1	18.9	4	15.4
Oyster and clam shell, crab claws	7.3	4.7	6.9	0	0
Eggshell	2.1	3.1	0	0	0
Ethnobotanical remains	0.1	2.1	0	0	0
Architectural group					
Nails/Spikes	26.6	19.2	37.7	33.6	31.3
Architectural hardware/ window glass	0.2	0.3	0.7	1.8	1.9
Arms group					
Gun or Food- procurement	0	0.1	0.3	0.1	0.1
Clothing group					
Clothing items	0.1	0.3	1.1	1.5	1.6
Sewing implements	0.1	0.9	0.5	2.1	0.3
Personal group					
Jewelry	0.1	0.2	0	0.3	0
Personal	0.1	0.3	0.4	0.3	0.9
Tobacco pipe group					
Tobacco pipes	5.4	1.7	7.2	14.9	7.1
Tools group					
Agricultural tools	0.1	0	0.1	0.5	0.1
Woodworking tools	0.1	0	0.2	0.5	0
Other tools	0	0	0	0	0.1
Horse-related	0	0	0	0.1	0.4

Continued on the next page

Table 4.2. *Continued*

Artifact type	Utopia II	Utopia III	Utopia IV	Kingsmill Phase One pits	Carter's Grove
Miscellaneous group					
Prehistoric artifacts	1.9	2.1	2.9	0.4	0
Fossil shell	5.4	5.8	0.9	0	0.2
Other	0.8	0.3	3.9	0.8	0.9
Indeterminate	1.8	1.6	2.9	3.4	0.9
Total %	98	99.9	99.6	99.8	99.9
Total number of artifacts	13,376	6,054	2,743	1,493	2,483

dents. These items were sparse, however, and other objects such as wooden and gourd bowls and other implements not preserved archaeologically were made by slaves to supplement imported goods. The next two generations at Utopia had greater access to manufactured items than did their predecessors. These later periods reflect an overall increase in the importance of ceramics, glass containers, and tools, as shown in their greater proportions in the site assemblages. In general, however, food-related items and architectural debris remained the categories with the most artifacts.

The increased importance of household goods over time at Utopia was also evident at the two other plantations, with a variety of ceramics, buttons and buckles, agricultural tools, and personal items. Some of the recovered ceramics suggest the residents had some access to discards from the Burwell family.

Ceramics

At the study sites, ceramics were analyzed for what they revealed about slave foodways and about how the enslaved were acquiring material goods. Analysis was performed at the ceramic vessel rather than at the individual sherd level. Minimum numbers of vessels were determined using rims or bases as the initial count, with distinctive vessels added subjectively based on unique decoration or technological attributes. Estimated vessel counts were made based on analysis of the subfloor pit and trash deposits, providing a good idea of ceramic types and vessel forms used by the quarters' residents. Vessel forms were based on examples shown in Beaudry et al. (1983) and

Table 4.3. Vessel forms assigned to vessel function categories

Vessel function	Vessel types
Food preparation/storage	Butterpot, milkpan, milk bowl, baking pan, ceramic bottle, oil jar, pipkin, colander, bowl, storage jar, storage jug
Food consumption/distribution	Plate, porringer, soup plate, serving bowl, charger, dish, salt, tureen, sauceboat, footed dish
Traditional beverage consumption/distribution	Tankard, drinking pot, syllabub pot
New beverage Consumption/distribution	Chocolate, coffee or teapot, milk pitcher, teabowl, saucer, can, punch bowl, sugar dish
Health/hygiene	Chamberpot, drug jar, drug pot, basin

Yentsch (1990). A functional classification of the ceramics was taken, with categories adapted from Yentsch (1990) and defined in Table 4.3.

Ceramics were also classified and grouped, based on their body fabric and glaze, into coarse and refined earthenwares and stonewares, tin enamel earthenwares, colonoware, and porcelain. Table 4.4 lists specific ceramic types from the study sites and the categories to which they were assigned.

A minimum of 18 ceramic vessels was recovered from Utopia Period II and 37 from Utopia Period III. Charting vessel counts shows that ceramic type distributions were very similar for the two periods, but there were differences in vessel functions (Figures 4.1 and 4.2). The vessels present included locally produced as well as English and European wares. Many of the vessels were of inexpensive coarse earthenware and stoneware with high percentages of food storage or preparation forms, such as milk pans, storage jars, and jugs. These vessels may have been used along with wooden bowls, gourds, buckets, bags, or barrels for storing such food rations as cornmeal and salted meat.

Other vessels, such as the tin enamel earthenware teabowl, plate, and punchbowl at Utopia Period II, would have been more appropriate for holding food during meals. At the next Utopia occupation, a wider variety of tea and tablewares was present, including a white salt-glazed stoneware teabowl,

Table 4.4. Ceramic types assigned to ceramic categories

Ceramic category	Ceramic types
Coarse earthenware	Yorktown-type earthenware, Buckley, black glazed redware, Pennsylvania earthenwares, North Devon coarse earthenwares, Iberian coarse earthenware, coarse agateware
Coarse stoneware	Yorktown-type stoneware, Westerwald stoneware, Fulham stoneware, English brown stoneware, American stoneware
Refined earthenware	Creamware, pearlware, Jackfield, North Midlands slipped earthenware, refined agateware, Staffordshire mottled earthenware
Refined stoneware	White salt glaze stoneware, Nottingham stoneware, Staffordshire stoneware
Porcelain	Chinese porcelain, English porcelain

saucer, and bowl, a North Midlands slipped earthenware cup, and coarse stoneware tankards.

The enslaved supplemented imported ceramic vessels with other forms in locally produced colonoware. It is likely that slaves used some of these vessels as cooking pots to prepare stews or cornmeal-based mushes and others as bowls for preparing and consuming food. During the earliest period at Utopia, colonoware fragments comprised 41 percent of the total assemblage of ceramics, decreasing to 13 percent in Period III. Percentages of colonoware fragments decreased through time at the sites, a factor likely linked to the increased availability and lower cost of English and European ceramics later in the century.

The final period at Utopia yielded an enormous variety of ceramics compared with the two earlier occupations, with a minimum of 69 ceramic vessels. Unlike the earlier periods, expensive wares such as enameled white salt-glaze stonewares, overglaze Chinese porcelain, and a refined earthenware known as Jackfield were common in the assemblage. Vessel forms were also quite different from earlier assemblages, including thin-bodied, elaborately decorated teabowls and saucers, and an increasing emphasis on vessels traditionally associated with eating and drinking, such as plates, cups, and small bowls. The presence of Chinese porcelain at the quarters, albeit in

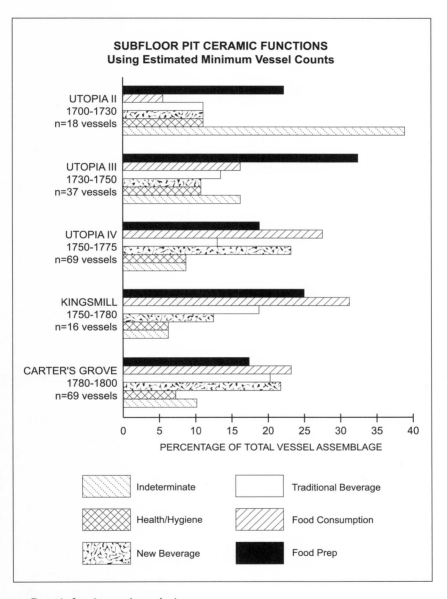

4.1. Ceramic functions at the study sites

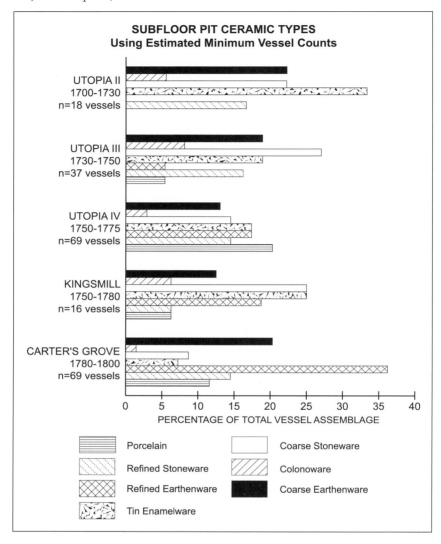

4.2. Ceramic types at study sites

small quantities, was surprising, given the costliness of this ceramic, particularly during the first half of the eighteenth century. Porcelain vessels during the last occupation at Utopia included teabowls and saucers, as well as plates, mugs, and punchbowls. Many of the expensive ceramics from this period, especially the overglaze painted Chinese porcelains, may have originally been part of the Bray and Burwell family tablewares. As they fell out of fashion or components were broken, the pottery may have been passed along to members of the enslaved community. The mismatched nature of the porcelains at the site lends weight to this conclusion, as does the presence of matching ceramic patterns in the plantation house trash pits (Walsh 1997). The enslaved may have also obtained some of their ceramics piecemeal at local stores.

Comparing the three occupations at Utopia revealed that overall numbers of ceramic vessels increased despite the presumed stability in the quarter population size throughout the different periods. The increased use of ceramics may have been related to the greater availability of ceramics overall in colonial society as the ceramic industry in England and Europe expanded during the eighteenth century. Proportions of refined earthenware, stoneware, and porcelain vessel forms manufactured for dining and for partaking of expensive, fashionable beverages rose dramatically in the final period of occupation at Utopia. Although the cost of tea had declined by the end of the eighteenth century, making it economically accessible across a wider range of economic levels, it is unlikely that these vessels were used for serving tea at the quarters. Teabowls and saucers were used in ways that fit with the needs of life at the quarter by holding semiliquid mushes and stews at mealtime.

Although the Utopia quarters assemblages showed increasing quantities and varieties of goods, this experience was not uniform across the remaining two sites. Phase One pits from Kingsmill Quarter, contemporaneous with Utopia Period IV, contained a limited number and range of artifacts. Only 75 ceramic fragments, from a minimum total of 16 vessels, were recovered, with coarse earthenware and stoneware vessels in food preparation and storage forms predominating.

Analysis of subfloor pit artifacts shows fragments from a minimum total of 69 ceramic vessels at Carter's Grove. While the Carter's Grove quarter had the second lowest overall artifact assemblage count of any of the study sites, it had the largest minimum ceramic vessel count, displaying a variety of ceramic types and functions. Almost half (46 percent) of the ceramic vessels were forms originally manufactured for serving and eating food, while another 16 percent were teabowls, saucers, and teapots. The use of these vessels was adapted to African American cuisine, based on a diet of stews and semiliquid foods. Fragments of cast-iron cooking pots were recovered at all of the sites, reflecting this type of diet.

The broad range of ceramic types and mismatched vessels implies that the enslaved were acquiring pottery in a piecemeal fashion, perhaps through acquisitions of cracked, chipped, or out-of-fashion vessels from the planters' tables. Times of prosperity for a planter sometimes resulted in largesse for the slave community. After George Washington purchased a set of cream-ware, the enslaved living in the House for Families received a set of less fashionable white salt-glazed stoneware—presumably recycled from the Washington household (Morgan 1998:115). Tin enameled earthenware plates bearing a peacock design were found both at Burwell's Kingsmill plantation house and at the later-dating Kingsmill Quarter (Kelso 1977). A number of the vessels from the Carter's Grove quarter, including a white salt-glazed stoneware soup plate produced around midcentury, were quite old by the time they found their way into the ground at the end of the eighteenth century. This vessel and others bore heavy scratches and stains that spoke of long periods of use at the quarter.

Some ceramic items may have been obtained through barter or direct purchase at local stores. While it was once believed that slaves had little participation in the market economy, extrapolating from plantation and store accounts suggests otherwise. Plantation account books record the enslaved bartering and selling garden produce, barnyard fowl, and handcrafted items to planters, at local markets, and in stores (Heath 2004; Martin 1997). Plantation tutor Philip Fithian's journal provided a first-hand glimpse into the bartering system that kept goods and services flowing in the internal economy of one Virginia plantation when he received a watermelon from the garden of an elderly enslaved couple in return for writing out a list of their children (Fithian 1968:185). The small truck gardens and fowl tended during the early morning or evening hours were often a family's hedge against hunger and malnutrition, as well as providing an economic means for providing other necessities and amenities.

Diet

To study slave diet at the sites, physical remains from plants and animals were combined with indirect evidence of diet provided by artifacts used in the acquisition and preparation of food. Soil stains delineating traces of garden and animal enclosures, as well as documentary evidence from wills and inventories, help complete the available picture of slave diet at the five sites.

The quarter inhabitants in Period II at Utopia relied heavily on wild food, with the forest, rivers, and marshes around the quarter providing varied resources. The pit assemblages contained evidence of oyster and clam, crab, gar, carp, and catfish, several species of turtle, passenger pigeon, and wild mammals, including squirrel, raccoon, and woodchuck (Fesler 2004). A fish hook, lead shot, and two gunflints were evidence of hunting and fishing by the Utopia inhabitants. Domestic species included cow, pig, and sheep, as well as poultry. Meat from some of the domestic animals would have been planter-provisioned, but the poultry was raised by the enslaved for meat as well as eggs.

Almost half of the artifacts (45 percent) recovered from the Utopia Period II subfloor pits were animal bones and fish scale. While faunal bone also comprised a large component of the assemblages from the later two periods at Utopia, identification of these assemblages has not yet been completed. It is likely that a mixture of domestic mammals, supplemented with wild game, is present in the assemblages. Clam, oyster, fish scale, turtle, crab, and eggshell were all common elements in this period. At Utopia Period III, artifact evidence shows that hunting and fishing continued to be important.

No faunal analysis was available for the slave occupation at Kingsmill Quarter. Faunal bones from the trash deposit at Carter's Grove quarter were primarily from cattle, with some sheep/goat, pig, and raccoon also present (Bowen 1993). Despite this limited range of fauna, the cow and pig body elements present showed that the slaves had access to meatier cuts, as well as what are generally considered the "poorer," less meaty portions such as heads or feet. Like the Utopia residents, the enslaved at Carter's Grove hunted, fished, and gathered food from the nearby river, marshes, and forests.

The small, fragmentary nature of the bones recovered on these sites suggested that meat was used in one-pot meals combining meat, vegetables, and broth. In addition to stretching meat portions, these meals could be left simmering over a fire, requiring less work than roasted meat dishes. Furthermore, West African cuisine is heavily reliant on stewed and other semiliquid foods, favoring cultural preferences as well as economic factors influencing diet. A more extensive discussion of foodways on Virginia quarters is found in Chapter 6.

Analysis of seeds, pollen, and phytoliths recovered at the first two occupations at Utopia provided virtually identical plant evidence (Table 4.5). Charred seeds and nuts recovered from soil screening included corn, beans, walnuts, and peaches. Pollen from several food species, including grapes and legumes, was present. Plants typically considered weeds today, such as dandelion, chicory, pigweed, and amaranth, may have been food sources. Phytoliths and starch granules from cereal grains and sweet potatoes were also recovered.

Coupling the archaeological evidence recovered at these site assemblages with documentary and archaeological evidence from colonial Virginia re-

Table 4.5. Plant food remains from study sites

Plant remains	Botanical name	Utopia II	Utopia III	Utopia IV
Charred seeds				
Bean	Vigna sps.	xx	xx	
Berry, Unidentified	—		xx	
Corn	Zea mays	xx		
Nut (walnut?)	Juglans?	xx	xx	
Peach	Prunus persica	xx	xx	xx
Unidentified	—			xx
Pollen				
Pigweed/Amaranth	Chenopodium sps.	xx	Xx	
Sunflower	Helianthus sps.	xx		
Dandelion, Chicory	Liguliflorae	xx	xx	
Grape	Vitis	Xx	Xx	
Legume	Fabaceae	xx		
Phytoliths				
Cereal grains	—	xx	xx	
Starch				
Cereal grains	—	xx	xx	
Sweet potato	Ipomoea batatas	xx		

veals that slaves relied on a variety of wild and domesticated plant and animal species during the eighteenth century. Provisioned meat was supplemented with game, poultry, and fish. Meat was prepared in stews, along with corn and other vegetables grown in the quarter gardens.

Tools

The tools from the five study sites demonstrate the range of work activities in which slaves were employed on eighteenth-century plantations (Table 4.6). As expected, agricultural tools predominated, with the assemblages showing evidence of the century's changing agricultural economy.

Tobacco, which formed the economic base of the Virginia colony during the seventeenth and early eighteenth centuries, was raised on each of the three plantations. Although timing the planting and cutting of tobacco to ensure a good harvest required close attention to weather and soil con-

Table 4.6. Tools from the study sites

Tools	Utopia II	Utopia III	Utopia IV	Kingsmill	Carter's Grove
Agricultural tools					
Broad & narrow hoes	2	2	16	5	1
Scythes & sickles		1	3	3	2
Woodworking tools					
Axes & hatchets		1	1	1	
Chisels	2		2	1	
Gouge & gimlet			3	1	
Pliers & hammers	1	1	2		
Ruler	2				
Files	4		6	1	2
Adze & lathe			2		
Saw blade			1	2	
Other tools					
Miscellaneous			2	1	1
Sewing tools					
Scissors	1		7		1
Thimble	1	1	4		
Box iron insert			1		

ditions, only a simple tool kit was necessary for raising this crop. Narrow hoes were used to break up soil and create hills for transplanting the seedlings in spring. Slaves plying broad hoes kept the area around the plants free of weeds during the growing season. Hoes were present at all of the study sites and reflect the cultivation of tobacco as well as other crops like corn and wheat. Tobacco lost its economic hold as the eighteenth century progressed, but its production never completely ceased.

Because of fluctuating tobacco prices and declining soil fertility, Virginia planters began to diversify their agricultural production in the 1720s and 1730s. This strategy of raising corn, wheat, and other grains in addition to tobacco helped distribute the economic risks associated with monocropping. Tools used for grain production began to appear in the second quarter of the eighteenth century at Utopia, reflecting the increasing importance of wheat and other cereal grains throughout the century. These tools included scythes and sickles used to cut the ripe grain, as well as sharpening stones for honing knives and other cutting implements. Scythe blades and sickles were also included in the Carter's Grove and Kingsmill assemblages.

While agricultural tasks formed the core of slaves' daily activities at these outlying quarters, the excavated tools also indicate the occurence of both skilled and unskilled woodworking tasks. Axes and hatchets serve as evidence of nonagricultural chores assigned slaves during winter months—cutting firewood and building fences, tobacco barns, corn cribs, and other plantation structures. Saws and hammers were used to fashion timber into a variety of products. Utopia owner James Bray III sold unfinished timber, as well as planking, clapboards, fence rails, barrels, and other finished wood products produced by enslaved laborers (Kelso 1984:40).

Utopia's Period II yielded portions of two rulers, several woodworking chisels, and a hammer suggesting the presence of a skilled carpenter. The rulers indicate an individual possessing a familiarity with the British counting system and possibly the ability to perform at least simple mathematical calculations. The presence of numerous woodworking tools from all the occupations at Utopia, particularly types used in the more skilled tasks of shaping and finishing wood products, may indicate a tradition of cross-generational training at the quarter. Other tools from the quarters expand the range of slave tasks beyond agricultural and woodworking activities to include masonry and shipbuilding.

While agricultural fieldwork would have fallen to both men and women, some tasks appear to have been gender-based. Enslaved women were generally assigned responsibility for the construction and repair of clothing on the plantation. Their sewing equipment was basic; scissors, thimbles, and straight pins were typical. While most of the planter-provisioned slave clothing was probably produced in buildings located near the plantation house, slaves repaired their own clothing at their homes and likely also crafted some new garments made from purchased fabric.

Personal Items

The most prevalent items of personal use at the study sites were kaolin tobacco pipes. The use of tobacco crosscut all segments of Virginia society. Tobacco pipes were inexpensive, easily acquired, and in some instances were even supplied to slaves by the planter. In 1755, Joseph Ball sent to his nephew a number of items from England, including "the foul pipes to be distributed among my Negroes as you think fit" (Ball 1755). Enslaved men and women both smoked, and in Virginia tobacco may have retained aspects of its spiritual significance among some West African cultures, where it was often buried with the dead to speed their journey to the afterlife (Crow 1970 [1830]; Equiano 1987). This practice is also seen archaeologically in the American South. Three of the adults buried in the Utopia cemetery had tobacco pipes placed under their arms (Fesler 1998). In addition, several of the subfloor pit shrines discussed in Chapter 8 contained intact tobacco pipes.

Some items of personal adornment, primarily beads, were found in the pits. At Utopia Period II, these beads included locally produced shell and clay beads, imported European glass beads, and a polished ebony example that may have been brought from Africa. Beads, long associated with African Americans by archaeologists (Stine et al. 1996), are believed to have functioned in several ways for enslaved women. Not only were they objects of adornment, but they may have also reinforced African cultural identities. Other items may have also been used for adornment. Numerous buttons, with several containing paste "jewels," were found in the pits. Buttons could have been used as clothing fasteners or as ornaments. Also notable at the Utopia sites was the presence of fossilized *Glycymeris* shells with naturally occurring worm holes near the shell hinge. These items could have been sewn to clothing as ornamentation or worn on cords around the neck as jewelry.

Other personal items from Period II included handcrafted clay marbles—one marble had been incised with an X, perhaps as a mark of ownership—and mirror glass, bone combs, jaw harps, violin hardware, and several coins.

Summary

Although a comprehensive comparative analysis of eighteenth-century Virginia slave sites has yet to be undertaken, a fuller picture of the physical conditions of life for Virginia's slaves has emerged through archaeology. Housing, as expected, was rudimentary. The small size of most quarters, traces of fenced enclosures, and the spatial groupings of structures denote communal spaces for socializing and cooking, indicating that a substantial portion of free time was spent outside. Like the homes of many middling planters of English descent, quarters generally had dirt floors, and the absence of window glass on most eighteenth-century sites suggests that keeping out cold drafts and insects was virtually impossible. Quarter size ranged from 144 to 704 square feet. While small by modern standards, the majority of colonial Virginian middling plantation owners fared little better in terms of space. A survey taken in Halifax County in 1785 revealed that over 75 percent of the settlers surveyed were living in one-room homes of less than 320 square feet (Nicholls 1989).

Changing plantation management practices in the eighteenth century provided the enslaved greater opportunities to acquire different skills. These new proficiencies could translate into opportunities for economic advancement through the sale of crafted goods or the hiring out of one's labors for cash. The formation of family-based households also allowed families to pool resources (Fesler 2004). Through cooperation and sharing, households were better able to garner and generate material resources, seen archaeologically in the wider array of materials goods on the later dated sites.

The material world of the enslaved, not surprisingly, consisted predominantly of English and European goods and became more standardized throughout the eighteenth century. In some respects, the material conditions at slave communities were tied to the plantation owner. The gentry planters at Utopia, Kingsmill, and Carter's Grove were better positioned to supply their enslaved laborers with necessities than their less wealthy counterparts. The enslaved at Utopia, Kingsmill, and Carter's Grove appeared to benefit from the trickle-down effect created as the consumer revolution of the second half of the eighteenth century made more goods available to a wider segment of the population. Possessing material amenities like Chinese porcelain, however, did not make life any less difficult or the work less arduous for the enslaved at these plantations.

Whether provisioned, handed down by the planter, or acquired by the enslaved through barter or purchase, these goods often bore little similarity to everyday objects from their native cultures. While many of the enslaved in eighteenth-century Virginia had been born here, periods of heavy slave importation during this period brought substantial numbers of newly arrived Africans to the plantations. Nevertheless, the enslaved incorporated these new goods into their lives at the quarters, often no doubt using them in ways that had little to do with their intended function. Teabowls crafted and painted in China to hold a beverage served with elaborate rituals were used instead to hold a hastily eaten meal of cornmeal mush, dipped out with fingers or rough pewter spoons. Scissors that cut fabric to craft a ballgown for the plantation mistress could also be pressed into service as a shrine object whose blades had the power to cut the pain of childbirth or the sharp words of the foreman.

Into this world of manufactured goods, the slaves also introduced locally produced items, such as colonoware pottery, that filled residents' needs.

Many of these items, particularly those fashioned of wood or other plant materials, no longer survive. Some of these items would have been strictly functional, such as furniture, while others would have also been expressions of artistic and spiritual creativity.

Archaeological study of the detritus of daily life can provide a perspective on African American life generally absent in the documents—the perspective of the enslaved themselves, visible through the structural footings of homes, the broken ceramic bowls from which they ate their food, and the objects that gave spiritual meaning to their lives.

Notes

1. Data recovery techniques at Utopia Periods II and III, which included collecting and processing soil from all subfloor pits, account for the higher numbers of artifacts from these two sites.

2. The data presented here have limitations. At the time of this study, partial, unquantified lists of species were the most complete faunal data available. Data recovery techniques prevented comparison of the sites. Because soil was not screened at Carter's Grove and Kingsmill, most small plant and faunal materials went unrecovered, and no shells were retained from these same sites. These two decisions deflate the importance of shellfish and fish in the diet of the sites' residents. No seed, pollen, starch, or phytolith analyses were undertaken at either Kingsmill or Carter's Grove Quarters.

5
Preliminary Analysis and Proposed Functions of Subfloor Pits

One of the most remarkable features of folklore is its adaptability and endurance. Man does not give up the results of his creative acts easily. Instead, he is inclined to change either their form or substance, adapting them into new needs and stresses.

—Abrahams (1968)

Previous chapters demonstrated the association of subfloor pits with African American slave quarters, beginning in the late seventeenth century, with the highest occurrences in the eighteenth century. It has been hypothesized that the enslaved used pits for storage of food and personal possessions, as well as West African–style shrines. This chapter examines the physical characteristics of subfloor pits and provides results of analytical testing on several key characteristics. Through this testing, further refinement of hypotheses about how these pits functioned in Virginia quarters is possible.

The Construction of Subfloor Pits

Subfloor pits are found within the footprints or confines of buildings, although in some cases the impermanence of shallow brick or wooden ground-sill structural footings left no physical traces of walls. In these instances, the locations and limits of the structures were often determined indirectly by the locations of subfloor pits, which had been cut down into the underlying clay subsoil.

Subfloor pits may have originally been dug as sources of clay for chinking log walls and chimneys (Kimmel 1993). Log construction was a common building technique for slave houses in Virginia in the eighteenth and nineteenth centuries, although more typical of upland than of tidewater areas (Herman 1984). Clay would have been a readily available and cost-free material for chinking the interstices between logs, providing some degree of protection from drafts and wind-driven precipitation. A mid-nineteenth-century description of log slave housing in Virginia stated that "the chinks between the logs or boards are filled, entirely or partly, with moss or clay; the chimneys are formed of small sticks and covered with mud" (Sears 1847:488). Clay chinking required frequent replenishing, as noted by a former Georgia slave: "Slaves lived in log cabins what had red mud daubed in the cracks 'twixt them, after a few rains made them shrink, that us could lay in bed and see the stars through the big holes" (Killion and Waller 1972:55).

Stick and mud chimneys remained common features on one- and two-room log and frame houses in Virginia as late as the early twentieth century. Constructing and maintaining these chimneys required substantial amounts of clay, and soil excavated during the creation of subfloor pits was a likely source. An 1850 issue of the *Southern Cultivator* informed planters, "Many persons, in building negro houses, in order to get clay convenient for filling the hearth and for mortar, dig a hole under the floor" (cited in Breeden 1980:121). In light of the construction methods used in Virginia quarters, the explanation that some subfloor pits were originally dug as clay pits for chinking chimneys and walls is plausible. Refashioning clay pits into subfloor units would have obscured any evidence of their original function as clay extraction pits (Kimmel 1993).

Constructing most subfloor pits required little beyond a shovel and a willingness to dig a hole, although a small percentage contained wooden or brick floors or evidence that boards had been fastened with nails to the sides of the pits. In several instances, prefabricated boxes had been placed within these pits. The use of wooden boxes, linings, and floors would have helped in keeping the contents of the pit clean and dry and may have hindered rodent intrusions. Boards fastened to the pit walls or boxes also stabilized the sidewalls and prevented them from collapsing. In structures with raised wooden floors, these boards extended between the top of the cellar and the floor of the house to form a protective skirt or enclosure around the pit. A few pits showed evidence of wooden partitions that may have separated different foodstuffs or created individual storage spaces.

While boards and other building materials would have prolonged the use span of a pit or more fully protected its contents, they were not necessary components. In pit construction, the enslaved used available materials. The relative absence of paving, board floors, or linings in these pits suggests that they generally had limited access to such materials or perhaps chose to use them in other ways, such as the fashioning of furniture or other household goods. The floors and walls of a small percentage of the pits showed evidence of burning, suggesting smoldering coals were placed in the bottoms of newly dug pits to dry out the walls and floors.

How access was gained to these pits has been a matter of debate. In some structures containing multiple pits, the regular spacing of the features reveals they were positioned between floor joists (May and Deetz 1997). At the standing nineteenth-century Bremo Recess quarter in Fluvanna County, Virginia, the floorboards over the hearth-front subfloor pit had been fashioned into a hinged trapdoor allowing easy access to pit contents (Kelso 1984). In other quarters, however, the more random placement of the pits suggests that those buildings contained earthen floors. In these structures, the pits would have been covered with hewn boards that could be lifted away for access to the belowground space. The presence of ledges in some subfloor pits provides evidence for the use of such boards, perhaps set flush with the soil floor. In other instances, boards were simply laid across the open holes to cover them.

The structural stability of pits, particularly in buildings with soil floors, was a challenge. Although most pits had been cut into firm clay, foot traffic across the boards covering the pits would have led to the eventual collapse of the feature walls. Some pits would have been protected from foot traffic by covering them with tables or, in the case of pits along walls, with built-in beds or seating. In 1727, Robert Carter ordered that the cabins for enslaved individuals at his Rappahannock River plantation be constructed so "that their beds may lye a foot and a half from ye ground" (cited in Walsh 1997:90). Not only would these beds have kept the building's inhabitants off the cold and damp ground, they would have also permitted an underlying pit to be created in a location both hidden and out of the way of foot traffic.

While pits beneath houses with wooden floors were protected from damage caused by rain, erosion, and foot traffic, all pits were subject to other types of damage. Rodents tunneled into pits, and rising groundwater undermined and collapsed pit walls. Subfloor pits at the Rich Neck Quarter, located on the outskirts of eighteenth-century Williamsburg, revealed extensive evidence of pit maintenance and repair, partially resulting from groundwater damage (Franklin 1997). Over the 40-year occupation span of this dwelling, pits became smaller and shallower, as residents learned from previous structural failures that large, deep pits were more subject to collapse. New pits were dug into and through older filled pits that had been damaged by groundwater, rodent burrows, and other factors.

Analytical Testing of Physical Variables

What can size, depth, shape, level of repair, and the placement of pit features within the buildings excavated at Utopia, Kingsmill, and Carter's Grove reveal about pit function? Did patterns exist in these physical characteristics

Table 5.1. Categories of analysis and codes for feature variables

Location	Shape	Cuts/repair status
C = pit located in corner of structure or corner of a room within a multi-room structure	Oblong = length > width	S = single cut, a feature with a single period of use and filling. No later features have been cut through its fill
H = in front of hearth or adjacent to hearth opening	Square = length = width	
O = Other, i.e., in center of floor or along wall	Round	M = Multiple cuts, includes pits that have been filled and recut, creating new pits of different dimensions, depths, or spatial alignments. Each pit within a complex is counted separately

that suggested functional differences? At these five sites, general observations of these characteristics seemed to suggest patterning. There appeared to be location-based differences in level of pit repair, with hearth-front pits showing more evidence of maintenance through repair and re-cutting than pits in corners or along walls. Quantitative tests were performed to test the reliability of these observations.

The physical characteristics of 103 subfloor pits from the Utopia, Kingsmill, and Carter's Grove quarters were analyzed, with data collected on pit dimensions, depth, shape, and volume. Pit placement within the structure, the presence of multiple versus single pits within buildings, and whether features showed any signs of repair or reconstruction (characterized as multiple filling and cutting episodes) were also noted. A series of analytical tests were run to ascertain if there were correlations between different physical variables.

Because a visual overview of the study sites suggested high levels of repair for hearth-front pits, pit placements within a room were examined to see if location was correlated with repair or rebuilding. Pit locations were divided into three categories—hearth, corner, and other—and pit repair status was assigned to one of two categories—single and multiple cuts. Table 5.1 defines these location and repair categories.

Examining percentages of repaired versus nonrepaired pits by location

Table 5.2. Repair status of subfloor pits by location

Cut/repair status	Pit location		
	Hearth pits n = 43	Corner pits n = 27	Other pits n = 29
Single	20.9%	66.7%	89.7%
Multiple	79.1%	33.3%	10.3%
Total	100%	100%	100%

(Table 5.2) shows a strong correlation between a pit's location and its repair status, with almost 80 percent of the hearth-front pits having been repaired. These pits were much more likely to be repaired than features that had been constructed in a corner, along a wall, or in the middle of the room. All of the quarter dwellings contained at least one functional pit located in front of each hearth at all times during the lifespan of the building. If the incidence of repair and rebuilding can be taken as an indication of the value placed on a particular location by a structure's occupants, these results suggest hearth fronts were highly valued positions for pits. While only a third of the sample's corner pits showed evidence of repair, they were still three times more likely to be repaired or rebuilt than pits along walls or in the center of the floor. This finding suggests that the enslaved viewed corner pit locations as preferable to these other positions, perhaps because they were the most out-of-the-way locations within a room.

Since pit locations showed patterned differences in repair status, was there similar patterning in other physical variables? Three pit shapes—oblong, square, and round—were recorded, as well as surface area and depth. Oblong pits, encompassing rectangular and oval shapes, accounted for 85 percent of the features. Several factors may account for the predominance of this shape. Oblong pits may simply mirror the shape of the quarters or be a factor of the rectangular arrangement of floor joists in structures containing wooden floors. Because the only wooden-floored structures were at Utopia's Structure 140 and at Kingsmill Quarter, digging pits to fit between floor joists would not therefore have been a consideration at most of the quarters studied here. In structures with earthen floors, it would have also been simpler to construct flush board coverings to fit into earthen ledges on pits with straight corners. Crafting close-fitting covers for round pits would have been considerably more difficult and helps account for the relative scarcity of round pits.

Table 5.3. Percentages of pit shapes by location

Shape	Location		
	Corner N = 27	Hearth N = 44	Other N = 29
Oblong	81.5%	81.8%	93.1%
Round	7.4%	2.3%	0
Square	11.1%	15.9%	6.9%
Total	100%	100%	100%

Table 5.4. Descriptive statistics for subfloor pit surface area by location

Location	Minimum	Maximum	Mean	Median	Sample size
Corner surface area	3.2	25	17.7	12	26
Hearth surface area	3.75	32.4	15.5	15	43
Other surface area	3.2	46	14.7	12.5	27

Even given the overwhelmingly high percentage of oblong pits, however, there was some shape variation by location (Table 5.3). Pits located along walls or in the center of rooms were oblong in 93 percent of the cases. Square pits were more common in front of hearths or in corners. Round pits were slightly more likely to be found in corners than in front of hearths or in other locations.

Quantitative analysis also revealed patterns in dimension and depth variables. Tables 5.4 and 5.5 list the descriptive statistics for these categories, while Figures 5.1 and 5.2 depict box and whisker plots of the same variables. Considered together, these figures reveal several interesting patterns. Hearth and corner pits were more restricted in their depth and size ranges than pits in other locations.

Corner pits showed the least variation for both variables. With a mean depth of 1.2 feet, they averaged half a foot shallower than features in either of the other locations. Corner pits clustered at the lower end of the depth range (Figure 5.1), and they showed the smallest range of variation in surface area, with half of the features clustering between 9.4 and 16.1 square feet.

At an average depth of 1.8 feet, hearth-front pits were nominally deeper than pits designated "Other" (mean = 1.7 feet). Half of the hearth-front pits

Table 5.5. Descriptive statistics for subfloor pit depth by location

Location	Minimum (ft.)	Maximum (ft.)	Mean (ft.)	Median (ft.)	Sample Size
Corner depth	.25	3.0	1.2	1.0	23
Hearth depth	0.5	3.6	1.8	1.8	36
Other depth	0.3	3.9	1.7	1.6	27

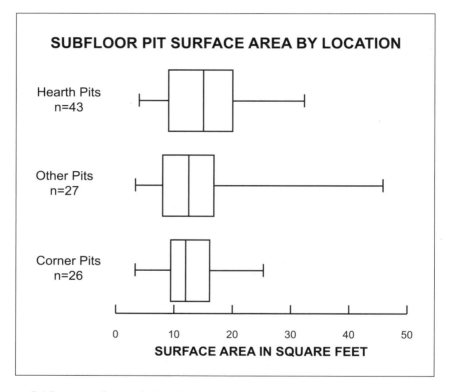

5.1. Subfloor pit surface area by location

ranged between 9 and 20 square feet in surface area, a larger spread than displayed by pits in the other two categories. Similarly, they ranged between .3 and 3.9 feet in depth, with half of the features extending between .9 and 2.7 feet deep. Pits along the wall and in the middle of rooms displayed the largest overall range of variation in depth and size. While half of these features fell within the fairly limited surface area range of 8 to 16.8 square feet,

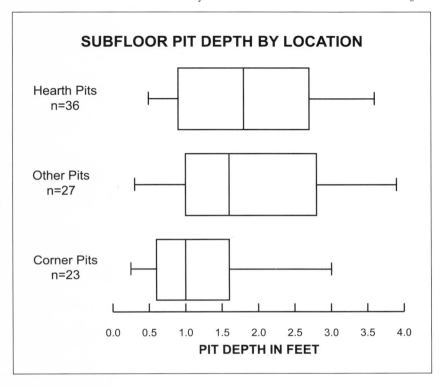

5.2. Subfloor pit depth by location

they showed the largest overall spread of surface area, from 3.2 to 46 square feet.

The restricted area and depth ranges of corner and hearth-front pits suggest pits in these locations served specialized functions that required a specific range of surface area or depth. Pits falling in the "Other" category may have been used for a greater variety of purposes, thus not requiring specific sizes or depths.

Adding pit data from additional sites in Virginia (Table 5.6) provided further support for the patterns visible at Utopia, Kingsmill, and Carter's Grove. While pits appeared in all locations in eighteenth-century quarters, hearth-front locations appeared to be particularly important, comprising around half the pits in any given period. Pits were constructed and maintained in this location throughout the life span of individual structures, and if a structure contained only one pit, it was usually located in front of the hearth. Hearth-front pits were oblong or, less often, square. The few examples of

Table 5.6. Chronological analysis of subfloor pit details

Pit details	1680–1700		1700–1720		1720–1760		1760–1780		1780–1800		1800–1830	
	#	%	#	%	#	%	#	%	#	%	#	%
Location												
Hearth	8	50	7	30	14	45	28	47	7	39	2	67
Corner	3	19	11	48	10	32	10	17	4	22	1	33
Other	5	31	5	22	7	23	21	36	7	39	0	
Total	16		23		31		59		18		3	
Shape												
Oblong	7	44	21	96	22	74	47	79	15	78	1	
Square	2	12			4	13	9	15	4	22		
Round	7	44	1	4	4	13	2	3				
Irregular	0						1	2				
Total	16		22		30		59		19		3	
Cut/Repair												
Single cut	6	37	12	52	15	48	39	66	17	89	2	67
Multiple cut	10	63	11	48	16	52	20	34	2	11	1	33
Total	16		23		31		59		19		3	

See Table 1.3 for sites represented in this table.

round or other shaped pits were only found in other locations within rooms. The data suggest that a standard pit shape became established within the first several decades of intense slave importation in the Virginia colony. Between 1680 and 1700, there was an equal distribution of oblong and round subfloor pits, with each shape comprising 44 percent of the total number of pits. For the remainder of the eighteenth century, oblong pits predominated, with square pits present but in much smaller proportions. Round pits virtually disappeared over the course of the century. It appears that newly arrived Africans at the end of the seventeenth century and early eighteenth century were experimenting with different pit shapes, settling very quickly on an oblong shape.

Part of this narrowing of shape options may have been functional. A rectangular pit may have been better suited for a hearth-front feature's intended use. Oriented properly, this shape would have taken advantage of the greatest frontage on the hearth, thus providing the most access to ambient heat and less humidity. As discussed in detail in Chapter 6, both conditions were favorable for the storage of sweet potatoes, a common component of the Virginia slave diet.

There was also evidence of extensive repair and redigging of pits in most of the structures in the expanded data sample. Consistent with the study sites findings, analysis showed more evidence of repair and redigging of hearth-front pits than features positioned along building walls or in corners. While there appeared to be no standard rules for the sequencing of hearth-front pit construction and repair, an interesting trend was evident at the study sites. When newer hearth-front pits were cut through filled older pits, the orientation of the newer pits was often changed, with shorter dimensions of the pits rotated 90 degrees. In this fashion, hearth frontage would still be a consideration, but with the new pits cutting through as little of the older pit fill as possible. When newer pits cut older pits, there was often evidence that clay facings or wood were used to stabilize loose fill and reinforce pit walls. Changes in pit patterning through time revealed what quarter residents learned through trial and error and from one another about successful methods of subfloor pit construction.

The one site analyzed in this study that did not reveal extensive pit cutting and repair was Kingsmill Quarter. The main structure at this site, while containing one of the highest numbers of pits (20), also had the lowest incidence of pit recutting. The primary difference between this structure and other quarters analyzed was the presence of a suspended wooden floor. This finding suggests that it was easier for the enslaved to use space more effectively under a wooden floor, with less incidence of damage from the collapse of pit walls.

Differences revealed in the physical characteristics of subfloor pits appeared to be linked to their location within a room. Hearth-front features were the deepest pits on average and usually showed evidence of repair or rebuilding. Corner pits were the shallowest and had the smallest range of variation in surface area and the largest diversity in shape. Approximately one-third of the corner pits showed evidence of repair. Pits whose locations fit the "Other" designation showed the largest range of variation in surface area and depth and were almost never repaired. These results suggest that pit location was possibly correlated with pit function. Guided by and used in conjunction with the results of the preceding quantitative spatial analysis, can analysis of artifact assemblages aid in determining how pits were used?

Analysis of Subfloor Pit Functions

To construct ways to test the functions of subfloor pits, several assumptions were made. First, it was suspected that most of the subfloor pits were filled when the overlying structures were moved to another location or destroyed. Thus, the pits were most likely filled with debris largely unrelated to the feature function. Architectural debris from a building's destruction, such as nails and brick fragments, can be considered primary refuse, that is, debris deposited at the location of its use (Schiffer 1987:18). Soil strata containing fragmented debris from daily life, such as pottery and food bone, were created by the deposition of organic matter and trash swept up from the yards or floors of the quarters. This discard of debris in a place away from the place of use defines it as secondary, or casual, refuse (Schiffer 1987). If these assumptions are accurate, the original functions of most of the pits will be obscured because they were emptied of their useful contents before their final use as trash pits.

Physical evidence associated with original pit function should be evident in some cases, however, and this study assumes that when this evidence is present, pit function can be defined. The assumption is made that physical traces of the food and other plant remains stored in pits functioning as root cellars will be evident in soil samples as ecofacts like pollen, starch granules, seeds, and phytoliths. Given the proposed function of pits as root cellars, it is unlikely that analysis of more traditional artifacts, like ceramics and glass, would aid in determining this function.

Determining if a subfloor pit had been used as personal storage or in a religious function would be evident if a cache of artifacts had been left behind in the pit. Shrine objects or stored goods would be characterized as de facto refuse, a deposit of useable materials "left behind when an activity area is abandoned" (Schiffer 1987:89). Artifacts from secondary and de facto refuse display distinct size differences (Schiffer 1983:679, 1987). Secondary refuse, such as yard scatter, has generally been trampled and broken into smaller fragments than objects that have been discarded directly into a trash pit. Based on the assumptions made in the preceding paragraph, this study hypothesizes that artifacts from most of the pits' strata would be characterized by attributes that marked them as secondary fill. These attributes include (a) small, highly fragmented pieces of pottery and glass, (b) small percentages of ceramic and glass mends within and between subfloor pits, and (c) small percentages of reconstructable ceramic and glass vessels.

It is hypothesized that artifacts from secondary refuse will measure less than 1.5 in. in diameter and be less than 10 percent complete. To determine whether pits had been filled with secondary refuse, the overall size of easily breakable artifacts (ceramics, earthenware tobacco pipes, glass, bone, and shell) from each assemblage was examined. Artifacts from each pit were examined by distinct strata and grouped by overall dimensions, using 1.5-in. diameter intervals as units of measurement. Data were also recorded on the relative completeness of each object.

It is hypothesized that shrine objects or stored goods would display different physical attributes than artifacts discarded as secondary refuse. Cached goods were more likely to be unbroken or nearly complete serviceable objects. For the purposes of this study, any item that was greater than 75 percent intact was defined as a complete object. These caches would likely be found either resting directly on the floors of the pits or in layers directly overlying pit floors. Analysis revealed that soil layers directly above the pit floors were more likely to contain larger and more complete objects, presumably associated with the primary use of the pit rather than trash discarded as secondary refuse. If artifacts came to rest in a pit through discard as trash, artifacts of all sizes should be randomly distributed throughout the pit, with upper soil layers and floor layers containing the same proportions of complete versus incomplete objects. Concentrations of complete objects should delineate de facto deposited caches that can provide clues to pit function.

The next stages of analysis required a two-step process for recognizing caches and determining cache functions. The first step was to identify and isolate caches within subfloor pits, particularly when caches were not recognized and recorded in the field during excavation. Once caches were isolated,

Table 5.7 Average size of artifacts from hearth and nonhearth pits

Pit type	0–1.5″	1.6–3.0″	3.1–4.5″	4.6–6.0″	>6.0″	Total artifacts
Nonhearth	77.64	17.95	2.41	1.41	0.54	3105
Hearth	82.15	14.66	2.88	0.27	0.09	10,804

could spiritual caches be distinguished from nonspiritual caches? Caches were isolated by analyzing artifact size and completeness within pit assemblages, coupled with close reading of excavation field notes. After the caches are isolated, detailed analysis of the objects in context with one another and in relation to ethnohistoric, ethnographic, and archaeological data allowed the separation of spiritual and nonspiritual caches.

The subfloor pits were separated initially into hearth and nonhearth pits, since pit location is presumably linked to original function. The overwhelming majority of the artifacts in both hearth and nonhearth pits were under 1.5 in. in diameter, averaging 77.64 percent of the artifact assemblage in nonhearth pits and 82.15 percent in hearth pits (Table 5.7). Most artifacts (over 95 percent) measured less than 3.0. in. In no instance did any of the pits contain more than 5 percent of its artifacts measuring over 4.5 in. in the categories analyzed. This finding suggests that subfloor pits contained predominantly secondary refuse, which would not provide clues to original pit function. While it had been anticipated that artifact size analysis would be successful at revealing instances where individual pits contained higher than average percentages of large (>4.5 in. diameter) objects, indicating the probable location of de facto caches, this analysis proved largely ineffective. Only in several instances did significantly higher percentages (>10 percent) of objects measuring over 4.5 in. in diameter appear: Utopia Feature 44 with 23 percent and Kingsmill Quarter Feature KM362 with 18.1 percent. In each case, further analysis did reveal de facto caches, and these features are discussed in Chapters 7 and 8. Interestingly, none of the hearth-front pits, believed to have functioned as root storage areas, contained significantly high percentages of larger artifacts.

Based on the failure of the size analysis to provide useable results, the decision was made to add additional artifact categories to analysis of the completeness of pit artifacts. Hearth-front pits were excluded from this phase of analysis because the size results had shown no potential caches. The decision was made to include all metal artifacts (with the exception of nails) because metal items, particularly iron objects, have special significance on Igbo and other West African shrines.

Examining the relative completeness of artifacts by layer from nonhearth pits revealed that the majority of the artifacts were less than 25 percent complete, reinforcing the earlier conclusion that secondary refuse predominantly filled these pits. Furthermore, very few artifacts were between 26 and 75 percent complete; if they were not highly fragmented, they were likely to be unbroken. For analytical purposes, any soil layers that contained over 15 percent complete artifacts were deemed worthy of further analysis for the presence of a cache.

Twenty-one features met this criterion, and of these features six examples showed definite evidence of artifact caches. These six features (Utopia Features 9 and 44, Kingsmill Features KM362 and KM363, and Carter's Grove Features CG643 and CG715) are discussed in Chapters 7 and 8. In several instances, such as Utopia Feature 8, contextual information in the field notes and maps led to further analysis of these features, despite the lower than designated percentages of complete objects. These features were also analyzed more thoroughly and are discussed in the following chapters.

Summary

A subfloor pit on a Virginia quarter may have gone through a complex use life, from being originally dug as a clay source, to serving as a storage pit, and then ending its use span as a convenient disposal place for garbage. Prior to these rather ignominious endings, however, how did the African Americans, who went to the trouble to create these features, use them? The analytical evidence of artifact size was deemed largely inappropriate for isolating caches, although it did demonstrate that pits were filled largely with secondary refuse.

Quantitative analysis indicates that pit location and function were related on Virginia quarters. Hearth-front pits are hypothesized to have served as root cellars for food storage, likely of sweet potatoes. Pollen and phytolith testing of soil layers deposited during the use of the pit will be key in testing this hypothesis. Pits found in other parts of the structure, such as in corners, along walls, and in the center of floors, are believed to have been used as personal storage spaces or as West African–style shrines. Analysis of artifact size and completeness revealed that 21 pits appeared to contain de facto deposits, or caches, probably associated with the original use of the feature.

Using information on West African shrine groupings and spiritual objects, the subfloor pit artifacts were analyzed contextually to determine if they represented spiritual caches or simply household items left in storage.

In the next three chapters, subfloor pits features will be analyzed individually by hypothesized function. The archaeological data will be combined with ethnohistoric and documentary evidence to determine original pit function. Chapter 6 examines subfloor pits as root cellars. Thirteen pits containing what are believed to be cached goods are analyzed in Chapters 7 and 8. Nine pits showed evidence that they were used as shrines, and four contained evidence of personal storage. Eleven features that earlier analysis had isolated as containing high percentages of complete artifacts failed to show clear-cut evidence of an original pit function.

Notes

1. Since many quarter sites were farmed and plowed after site abandonment, the upper portions of the subfloor pits had been truncated, destroying any evidence of ledges.

2. The quality of the field notes from the Utopia project was consistently high and allowed the determination of caches in several instances. The assessment of these caches was double-checked using quantitative analysis. At Carter's Grove, field notes were missing. The overall site plan included several pit profiles, and stratigraphy of the other pits was reconstructed using information on the artifact bag labels. The Kingsmill Quarter field notes did not allow easy determinations of caches.

6
Subfloor Pits as Root Cellars

Setting: Debb's Quarter, Bray Plantation, October 1723

The weather was unexpectedly warm and sunny for a late October day along the river. Debb paused in her work, straightening up from the half-filled split oak basket and squinting into the sun. About twenty yards away, she could make out the figures of the two children, giggling as they cut handfuls of the grass that grew tall at the side of the clearing that defined the quarter. She smiled to herself. Although Martin and Daniel were spending a fair amount of time chasing each other, clutching the late season grasshoppers they found clinging to the stalks, they were managing to accumulate quite a tidy bundle of grass. They would spread the grass in fragrant layers on the old quilt placed in the sun near the door of her house, where it would dry over the course of the afternoon.

Pretending to admonish the children sternly to continue with their task, she turned back to her own work. As she picked up each sweet potato from the ground surface where it had been drying for three days to toughen the outer skin, Debb carefully brushed away the sandy soil. Examining each potato carefully, she set aside any that had been nicked by the hoe. These potatoes they would eat over the next few weeks; only the undamaged potatoes would be packed carefully away into the hearth-front pit. Cushioned by the dried grasses, the potatoes would last out the winter, kept from freezing by the warmth of the hearth. The rains and the sun had come at the right times this year, she reflected—the potato harvest was good and would feed the community through the winter.

Debb's mouth watered at the thought of the roasted potatoes they would enjoy tonight. She still remembered from her youth in the homeland the taste of the yams that her mother grew along the forest margins of their village. The potatoes she held in her hands were not as tasty as the white-fleshed yams of her childhood, but they made an adequate substitute. Perhaps tonight, she thought, I will try to use these potatoes to prepare her mother's special *foo-foo* to go with the stewed salt pork and greens she had simmering over a low fire in back of her cabin. Although the flavor of these potatoes was sweeter than the yams from home, they cooked up in the same way. She smiled as she thought of later in the evening, when she would teach Daniel and Martin how to form small balls from the mashed potatoes, using their thumbs to press an indentation that would be used to scoop up the greens. It was important for the children not to forget about the old ways of their ancestors. As the head of the quarter, she would ensure that these traditions were not forgotten.

Root Cellars

In the eras before the advent of refrigeration and commercial canning, the ability to preserve the bounty of the summer harvest for the approaching days of winter was crucial to a family's survival. Salting, smoking, drying, pickling, and fermenting have been used for centuries as means of preserving fruits, vegetables, and meats to make them available all year round. In addition to methods that alter the composition of the food as a means of preservation, storage of fruits, vegetables, and grains in environmentally controlled conditions presents another way to lengthen the useful life of foodstuffs. Granaries, corn cribs, potato mounds, and root cellars are storage strategies that function by keeping the foods in conditions conducive to their preservation.

One of the most often cited functions of subfloor pits is that of root cellar (Franklin 1997; Kelso 1984). The term "root cellar" evokes memories of rows of canned vegetables and bushel baskets of earth-scented potatoes and turnips stacked in a dim corner of a basement. Root cellars are generally defined as underground pits created for the storage of root vegetables, such as potatoes, carrots, and turnips. In recent terminology, root cellaring has come to encompass a variety of food storage methods, including subterranean pits, small rooms set aside in unheated basements or attics, and earth-covered mounds of straw and potatoes. Whatever their design or placement, however, root cellars need to meet conditions that allow for the successful storage of food.

The use of subterranean food storage is a cross-cultural phenomenon with a long past. Included in the cultures using food storage pits are several of the groups who populated the American Southeast just prior to and during the colonial period. A number of sources from the seventeenth through the nineteenth centuries, including garden manuals and personal reminiscences, suggest the use of subterranean food storage in Virginia. Archaeological and ethnohistoric evidence suggests Native American use of storage pits in eastern North America in the centuries prior to and following European settlement to conceal food in seasonally abandoned settlements (DeBoer 1988; Stewart 1977). A 1705 reference to Native American pits from Robert Beverley lists sweet potatoes as one of the plants "our Natives had originally amongst them" and that "they are so tender, that it is very difficult to preserve them in the Winter; for the least Frost coming at them, rots and destroys them; and therefore People bury em under Ground, near the Fire-Hearth, all the Winter, until the Time comes, that their Seedings are to be set" (Beverley 1947 [1705]:145).

Neolithic and Iron Age subterranean storage pits used in Britain primarily for the storage of cereal grains, such as spelt, barley, and oats, set a cultural precedent for their use by English colonists in Virginia (Fowler 1983; Reynolds 1974). Later, gardening manuals written in Great Britain and in the American colonies advocated storing vegetables underground (Miller 1733; Worlidge 1675). Most of these references, however, are to subterranean trenches dug in the garden, similar to examples discussed by eighteenth-century Virginia gardener John Randolph (1924). A slightly later manual written by New Yorker John Nicholson (1820) recommended storing turnips in an insulated storage cellar underneath a building constructed for storing hay.

Three written accounts of interior subfloor pits used as root cellars in homes in the American South are attributed to enslaved African Americans. Frederick Douglass remembered such a feature in an 1830s Maryland context: "The old cabin, with . . . its clay floor downstairs, and its dirt chimney . . . and that most curious piece of workmanship dug in front of the fireplace, beneath which grandmammy placed the sweet potatoes to keep them from the frost, was MY HOME" (Douglass 1855:34). Booker T. Washington lived with his mother in the plantation kitchen as a young child in Virginia in the years directly preceding Emancipation. He remembered that "there was no wooden floor in our cabin, the naked earth being used as a floor. In the centre of the earthen floor there was a large, deep opening covered with boards, which was used as a place to store sweet potatoes during the winter" (Washington 1965:2).

Both of these accounts reference the clay floors of the structures, a feature consistent with findings on earlier Virginia quarters. William Henry Singleton, enslaved near New Bern in eastern North Carolina, spent three years in the early 1850s hiding in a root cellar underneath the floor of his mother's house. He explained that "it was not exactly a cellar, but a hole dug to keep potatoes and things out of the way" (Singleton 1999 [1922]:39).

One of Thomas Jefferson's African American gardeners apparently used subfloor pits as temporary storage for foodstuffs purloined from Jefferson's garden. The plantation's white gardener complained that "Nace takes every thing out of the garden and carries them to his cabin and burys them in the ground and says they are for the use of the house. . . . The people tells me that he makes market of them" (quoted in Heath 1994:40).

Each of these four references shows subfloor pits serving in food storage capacities. Given these references, how plausible is the root cellar explanation for subfloor pit construction on African American sites? In the following pages, three types of evidence are considered to answer this question. The ethnohistoric and archaeological evidence of slave diet and food production is considered in greater depth to determine the range of foods eaten by slaves. This evidence is followed by a discussion of whether subterranean pits would have served as an effective form of storage for foods that typically formed an Afro-Virginian diet. And, last, paleobotanical evidence of plants from pits on other Virginia sites is considered.

Afro-Virginian Slave Foodways

While Nace, enslaved at Monticello, used a subfloor pit for short-term storage of stolen food, the other references to underground food storage were specifically about the long-term storage of sweet potatoes. Was underground storage particularly suited to preserving sweet potatoes? What other types of foods were commonly found in Afro-Virginian diets, and were they suited to similar storage conditions? The enslaved acquired their plant foods through planter provisioning, by cultivation of small garden patches at the quarters, through gathering wild foods, and through trade or purchase at markets or stores.

The variety of foods provisioned to the enslaved was limited and appeared to consist mainly of cornmeal and small quantities of meat. Fairly typical was Thomas Jefferson's weekly provisioning for each adult slave at Monticello: a peck of cornmeal, a pound of beef or pork, a gill of molasses, and four salt herring (Kelso 1986:32). Other planters provided meat only on special occasions or during slaughtering times. Corn, described by naturalist Mark Catesby as "the properest food for Negro slaves," was a provisioning mainstay in Virginia (as cited in Moore 1989:72; Walsh 1997:101). This grain could be cooked in a number of ways, although cornbread, hominy, and mush were undoubtedly the most common means of preparation.

The enslaved supplemented their provisioned rations in a number of ways, both to ensure adequate food for survival and to vary the limited range of supplied food. Michel noted during his 1702 visit that slaves added turtles to their diet, and faunal remains from eighteenth-century Virginia quarters suggest that nocturnally active animals such as opossum and raccoon were consumed (Franklin 2001; Michel 1916 [1702]:42). Since work schedules for the enslaved prohibited their abilities to hunt species active during daylight hours, night hunting, as well as the trapping of small game, such as squirrel and rabbit, enabled them to incorporate varied species into their diets. The nearby creeks and rivers of the tidewater provided opportunities for fishing and gathering shellfish such as oysters, crabs, and mussels. Raising domestic fowl provided eggs and meat, as well as the option of selling or bartering the eggs.

Plantation account books and travelers' journals reveal that enslaved Virginians had personal gardens, described in 1732 as "little Platts for potatoes peas and cymlins, which they do on Sundays or at night" (Stiverson and Butler 1977:32). Hugh Jones wrote in 1724 that Virginia slaves ate pork, Indian corn, white and red (sweet) potatoes, as well as "roots and pulse [peas and beans]" (Jones 1956 [1724]:78). In 1774, Philip Fithian noted the enslaved "digging up their small Lots of ground . . . for Potatoes, peas &c.," and Jefferson wrote of the enslaved at Monticello growing sweet potatoes (Fithian 1968:128; Hatch 2001). Archaeological excavations around quarters have revealed traces of small fenced or ditched enclosures adjacent to the houses, where chickens were kept or gardens planted (Fesler 2004).

In these gardens, the enslaved grew a number of species, many of them West African cultigens, including black-eyed peas or cowpeas (*Vigna unguiulata*), okra (*Hibiscus esculentum*), and watermelon (*Cucumis lanatus*). Also present were peanuts (*Arachis hypogaea*), sweet potatoes (*Ipomoea batatas*), squash (*Cucurbita melopipo*), and pumpkins (*Curcubita pepo*)—all plants indigenous to the Americas that had been incorporated by the early to midseventeenth century into the diet of Igbos in West Africa as a result of trade (Chambers 2005:168). Thus, enslaved people of Igbo descent in Virginia were able to reconstruct a diet that contained familiar ingredients and flavors. Other plants available in Virginia, such as West Indian pigeon peas

(*Cajanus indicus*) and the Windsor or horse bean (*Faba vulgaris*), were similar in taste or texture to West African cultigens and were incorporated into Afro-Virginians' culinary palette.

Ethnobotanical analysis from Virginia quarter sites provides evidence of foods eaten at these quarters. At Williamsburg's Rich Neck Quarter, eighteen types of charred seeds, including cowpeas, squash, lima beans, corn, peanuts, and melons were found in the household refuse filling the subfloor pits in the quarter (Franklin 2001). Monticello's Mulberry Row assemblages included seeds from melon, beans, peach, and chestnut (DAACS 2006). Other Virginia excavations have yielded evidence of wheat, sunflower, pumpkin, persimmon, watermelon, beans, peaches, cherry, huckleberry, corn, and peas (McKnight 2000, 2003; Pogue and White 1991; Raymer 1996). Wild plant components of slave diets were generally small, but traces of walnuts, grapes, blackberries, and hickory nuts have been found.

Although the "tool kit" of ingredients available for Afro-Virginians differed in some respects from that used in West Africa, the repertoire of food preparation techniques remained essentially West African in nature. Low-maintenance one-pot meals of stewed starches and vegetables supplemented with protein both suited the work schedules of Afro-Virginians and mirrored African foodways (Franklin 2001:97). Like typical West African meals, the Afro-Virginia diet was heavy in starch and fat and light on meat, which was used primarily as a flavor enhancer for stewed dishes. Cayenne pepper (*Capsicum annuum*) added seasoning to the blandness of starch-heavy dishes and was a taste familiar to West African palates. Ground cornmeal, mixed with water, made an unleavened bread which was served with these vegetable and meat stews.

Afro-Virginian foodways are an example of the ways the enslaved crafted cultural identities in the first half of the eighteenth century, as African-born and creoles created lives for themselves on the plantations of Tidewater Virginia (Franklin 2001; Moore 1989). Archaeologically recovered food remains from the Rich Neck plantation quarter showed that the enslaved were experimenting with the wide variety of wild and domesticated foods available to them in the woods and fields of Tidewater Virginia. Earlier components on the site (1740–1765) contained a wider array of foods than later decades (1765–1778), a finding attributed to the enslaved determining their food preferences after an initial period of experimentation with available foods.

Anthropologist Sidney W. Mintz asserts the complex place that food holds within societies: "The foods eaten have histories associated with the pasts of those who eat them; the techniques employed to find, process, prepare, serve, and consume the foods are all culturally variable, with histories of their own. Nor is the food ever simply eaten; its consumption is always conditioned by meaning" (1996:7). The foods that newly enslaved Africans and the following generations incorporated into their diets in Virginia were influenced by both cultural and environmental factors. While some of the foods available in this new environment were familiar to them from West Africa, others were entirely new. Some West African culinary traditions were continued in Virginia, and others were adapted to the local environment and the restrictions of enslavement. In attempting to reconstruct in Virginia flavors remembered from West Africa, the enslaved were forging collective identities.

The Effectiveness of Virginia Subfloor Pits as Root Cellars

The diversity of plant species represented archaeologically on slave sites and in the documents contradicts the notion that slave diets were as restricted and monotonous as previously believed, but were these plants the types that could be successfully stored in subterranean pits? A small body of modern literature (Bacon 1991; Bubel and Bubel 1979; Thomas 1995) on the construction and maintenance of root cellars was invaluable in this regard. Given their recommendations, does physical evidence from the pits themselves suggest that these features were used for food storage?

Root cellars work by providing a controlled environment conducive to the preservation of fruits and vegetables, with temperature and humidity ranges the most critical variables in determining a root cellar's success. Optimal temperature and humidity storage requirements of different vegetables from modern root cellaring manuals are used to make hypotheses about food storage in eighteenth-century Virginia. Cold temperatures decrease the rates of metabolism in fruits and vegetables, slowing decomposition, while high humidity prevents shriveling. A humidity level ranging between 60 and 75 percent must be maintained (Bacon 1991:57), since higher levels of moisture cause condensation to form on the cellar walls and the produce, promoting spoilage. Elevated temperatures, coupled with high humidity rates, encourage the growth of mold and fungus. Humidity levels can be manipulated in a number of ways. Setting pans of water inside the cellars or packing vegetables in moist sawdust or peat moss can raise the humidity in a dry cellar. An earthen floor and gaps in the boards that form the walls and ceilings of some cellars can also assist in maintaining proper humidity levels (Bubel and Bubel 1979).

Temperature ranges for root cellars are also very specific; in order to preserve food successfully, a range of 32–40°F must be maintained (Bacon 1991: 57). Proper placement and construction methods can help assure that temperature levels remain constant. In addition, the deeper the hole is excavated, the more stable the temperature will be. A cellar set at a depth of 10 feet usually provides complete temperature stability (Bubel and Bubel 1979).

Different varieties of vegetables require slightly different combinations of temperature and humidity for successful storage. For example, white potatoes, turnips, beets, parsnips, radishes, collards, and leeks stay fresh longer under cold (32–40°F) and very moist (90–95 percent humidity) conditions (Bubel and Bubel 1979:138). Apples, pears, cabbages, and cauliflowers prefer slightly less humidity, while pumpkins, sweet potatoes, green tomatoes, and winter squash like relatively dry (60–70 percent humidity) and warm (50–60°F) conditions (Bubel and Bubel 1979:4; Thomas 1995:44).

To be successful, the interiors of root cellars need to maintain restricted ranges of temperature and humidity. Optimally, the vegetables should be harvested during a cold spell, with initial packing of the pit occurring after nighttime temperatures are consistently cold. The experiences of modern gardeners suggest that the southeastern states may not be the best geographical locale for underground food storage (Bubel and Bubel 1979). Studies of climate in colonial Virginia suggest solid parallels between current and eighteenth-century temperature and precipitation levels (Linebaugh 1994). The temperature range in Virginia is erratic, particularly in the early winter. With highs topping the 60°F range and lows sometimes falling into the single digits, it would be difficult to maintain the limited range of temperatures necessary for a truly successful food storage area. Since none of the cellars found on enslaved sites extended beyond a depth of 3.9 feet, it is unlikely that temperature stability could have been maintained. Given these findings, it is unlikely that optimal storage conditions could have been met with a subterranean pit.

Other variables affect the success of a root cellar. Fruits and vegetables emit gases that are conducive to sprouting or spoiling, so gas levels need to be kept low by maintaining temperatures below 45°F and through the use of vents and other means to assure adequate ventilation (Bubel and Bubel 1979:151). Virginia subfloor pits show no evidence of any venting systems, but it is possible that boards covering the pit openings would have provided adequate spaces for ventilation as well as keeping light, which encourages sprouting, from entering the cellar.

Just as critical as the proper planning and construction of a cellar is the manner in which fruits and vegetables are stored. Only vegetables in perfect or near perfect condition should be placed in the cellar, since bruising encourages spoilage. They should be packed in moss, sawdust, wood shavings, or damp sand and checked regularly for signs of spoilage (Bacon 1991:4, 59). One source recommends laying a 2–3-inch base of dry sand in the bottom of the cellar, on top of which the vegetables are placed. The vegetable layer should be no more than one foot thick and should be followed with a layer of sand, then leaves, and finished off with more soil (Bubel and Bubel 1979:127).

The limited documentary evidence available from early nineteenth-century Virginia suggests that sweet potatoes were the primary food stored in hearth-front pits. The sweet potato was adopted in Virginia and other parts of the upper South as a dietary staple by the enslaved. A native of South America, the sweet potato (*Ipomoea batatas)* was brought to Europe by explorers and was a part of the English diet by the late sixteenth century (Gerard 1597). They were commonly recognized by the British in Virginia by the seventeenth century, and the Swiss traveler Francis Michel noted "potatoes in great quantities" during his 1702 visit to the Virginia Tidewater (Ewan and Ewan 1970; Michel 1916 [1702]). Well suited to the sandy soils of the tidewater, they came to form an important component of the Afro-Virginian diet.

Chambers (1996:366) argues that the use of subfloor pits in Virginia is a cultural adaptation that can be traced to the prevalence in Virginia of people of Igbo descent and their dietary preferences. Olaudah Equiano described eighteenth-century Igbo foodways: "Bullocks, goats, and poultry, supply the greatest part of their food. . . . The flesh is usually stewed in a pan; to make it savory we sometime use also pepper, and other spices. . . . Our vegetables are mostly plaintains, eadas, yams, beans, and Indian corn" (1987:15).

Yams (*Dioscorea rotundata*), the main staple crop in Igboland, are very similar to the American sweet potato. In Igboland, yams are boiled, pounded into a stiff, doughy consistency, and rolled into small balls (*foofoo* or *fufu*) which were eaten with vegetables and meat. *Foofoo* could also be made with sweet potatoes, plantains, and cassava. In the American South, *foofoo* evolved in a number of ways, most recognizably as hoecakes made of cornmeal and water.

In Virginia, the enslaved substituted sweet potatoes for yams, incorporating these tubers as a staple in their diet. Since American sweet potatoes became a cultivar in West Africa during the colonial period (Moore 1989:75), they would have already been familiar to enslaved West Africans. The naturalist Mark Catesby wrote in the 1730s that sweet potatoes were "a great support to the Negroes" with planters raising this crop "in proportion to the number of his slaves" (as cited in Moore 1989:74). Sweet potatoes continued their importance in the Chesapeake slaves' diet, with William Tatham noting potatoes, pumpkins, and melons among the crops planted by the enslaved at the turn of the nineteenth century (Tatham 1800:55).

To be stored successfully, sweet potatoes require conditions with higher temperatures and less humidity than most vegetables. The optimal temperature range for sweet potato storage is 50–60°F.; colder temperatures increase spoilage by rot and warmer temperatures encourage sprouting. Other foods with storage conditions similar to sweet potatoes are pumpkins, winter squash, and green tomatoes, foods that do not appear to have played a significant role in the diet of the enslaved in Virginia.

Virginia subfloor pits do not begin to approach the 10-foot depth required for the complete temperature stability needed for optimal storage conditions. If, however, radiant heat rather than temperature stability was needed to protect stored food from frost damage, a hearth-front location would have been well suited for this purpose. Any ambient heat from the fire would have been more beneficial for sweet potato storage than vegetables such as white potatoes, turnips, or apples, which require cooler temperatures and greater humidity. Earlier quantitative analysis revealed that hearth-front pits were deeper than pits located in other parts of slave quarters. Perhaps these greater pit depths were related to the storage requirements of the produce, either in the need to create more interior space for adequate levels of food storage or as a temperature-related matter.

What was clearly obvious from the archaeological data, however, was the continued use of hearth-front pits throughout the life of quarter buildings. Like the slipshod structures that stood over them, subfloor pits had relatively short use spans, as rising groundwater, burrowing rodents, and collapsing walls made it necessary for residents to replace pits frequently. If the hearth front was an optimal location for sweet potato storage, as suggested by documents, then the quarter's inhabitants would need to rebuild pits in the same location throughout the lifespan of the overlying structure. Evidence from Virginia quarters supports this hypothesis. At Utopia II's Structure 50, occupied between 1725 and 1750, archaeologists found five phases of pit construction, with eleven separate pits in the immediate hearth vicinity. Multiple phases of hearth-front pit construction were also evident at Rich Neck and Governor's Land.

Hearth-front Pits: Storage for Sweet Potatoes?

Converging lines of evidence—slave diet, food storage requirements, and slave trade demographics—combined with evidence of repairs on hearth pits suggest that hearth-front pits were used as food storage for sweet potatoes. Does the physical evidence support this hypothesis?

Most plant remains recovered from subfloor pits in Virginia have been from secondary refuse unrelated to the primary function of the feature. The recovered seeds were charred, indicating their disposal was connected with cooking or discard into the hearth fires rather than storage. Thus, it is problematic to conclude a food storage function based on this evidence. If food storage occurred in subfloor pits, however, pollen, phytoliths, and starches from foods stored there should be present in soil layers created through storage activities, such as sand used to layer vegetables or fruits, or in organic layers created by the decomposition of stored produce or plant-packing materials.

A number of Virginia subfloor pits contained layers of sand that could have functioned as a base for food storage, but paleobotanical analysis has thus far been limited. Analysis of a hearth-front pit in a planter's dwelling at a late seventeenth-century Virginia farmstead site revealed a layer of sand near the base of the feature. High concentrations of phytoliths from introduced European grasses (of the Pooidae subfamily, which includes wheat, barley, rye, and bluegrass) suggested that the sand was mixed with straw to provide aeration (Archer et al. 2006:92).

The following analysis of hearth-front pits focuses on soil strata resting directly above pit floors. Before becoming a repository for household garbage, the pits would have been emptied of any useable contents, including food. Only spoiled food and packing materials would have remained in the bottom of the feature. These bottom layers are thus believed to be the most likely locations for recovering any plant remains associated with the use of these features as root cellars.

Paleobotanical evidence performed in determining whether hearth-front pits served as root cellars included the identification of pollen, phytoliths, and starches in the soil strata. No seed analysis was performed, since seeds are generally preserved only under circumstances unrelated to food storage. Since Kingsmill and Carter's Grove were excavated before the systematic retrieval of soil samples became common, pits from these sites could not be included in the paleobotanical analysis. To determine which features from the

Utopia Quarter were chosen for analysis, field notes documenting the excavation of hearth-front pits were carefully examined. Features containing thin bands of organic soil or sand along the floors of the pits were chosen as the features most likely to contain paleobotanical evidence of food storage. The soil strata tested included these lower layers, which may have served as packing strata or contained physical evidence created by the decomposition of plant material in the feature.

Three soil samples from two hearth-front pits at the Utopia Quarter were analyzed for microfloral remains. For comparative purposes, analysis was also completed on two additional Utopia pits (Features 9 and 44). These corner pits, which analysis later demonstrated had been used in spiritual fashions, contained different paleobotanical profiles than the hearth-front pits. A detailed discussion of the paleobotanical analysis for these two corner pits and how these results relate to their spiritual functions is provided in Chapter 8.

Results of Paleobotanical Analysis at Utopia Quarter

Analysis was performed on three soil samples from two hearth-front subfloor pits at Utopia Quarter. One pit (Feature 36) was from the earliest occupation at the Utopia Quarter, dating to the first quarter of the eighteenth century. The other pit (Feature 53) had been constructed in a structure built and used during the second quarter of the century. Pollen preservation ranged from good to poor in the Utopia Quarter samples. The results of this testing are summarized and discussed below (Cummings and Moutoux 1999).

Feature 36

Feature 36, located in Structure 10, was a hearth-front subfloor pit complex with at least two periods of construction and repair. Analysis of the fill and artifacts showed that this pit contained a prefabricated wooden box 4.5 feet square with a hinged and locked top. Toward the end of the site occupation, probably in the 1720s, the top of the box collapsed into the pit, and the feature was subsequently abandoned. Hinges, a lock, and a metal keyhole surround were all found resting in the bottom of the feature, atop a thin layer of brown sandy loam that accumulated during the use of the pit.

The two soil layers of the pit floor analyzed for plant remains appeared to have accumulated during the use of the wooden box. Layer 36J was a .2-foot-thick brown sandy loam that sealed a light brown sandy loam (36L), the earliest deposited strata within the wooden box. Pollen analysis was performed on Layer 36J; Layer 36L underwent phytolith analysis.

Testing these two layers revealed aggregates of grass pollen (Poaceae family). The presence of aggregates, or clumps of a single type of pollen, often indicates that portions of a plant were deposited into the archaeological setting (Cummings and Moutoux 1999). Of particular interest were the food remains from the samples. Pollen from the Cerealia family, representing an unidentified grain, was present, as was grape (*Vitis*) pollen. Starch granules, some of a form common in sweet potato (*Ipomoea batatas*) tubers and corn (*Zea mays*) were also identified during analysis. Phytolith analysis of Layer 36L showed elevated levels of festucoid forms. These results suggest that the plant remains in the pit were cool-season grasses, a finding that would be consistent with autumn storage. Cereal grains, whose phytoliths display an elongated form, were not present in substantial quantities in the bottom of the pit.

Taken together, these results suggest that sweet potatoes or corn were stored in the pit, with grasses used as a lining or packing material for the food. An account of a 1737 Virginia quarter fire noted that the enslaved residents had lost "their Bed cloathes and Peas and Potatoes" (Carter Family Papers 1737), which suggests that these crops were stored in the house, most likely out of the way in subfloor pits. While the storage of corn could not be ruled out based on the evidence, sweet potatoes were more likely to have been stored in a subfloor pit. Cornmeal was generally a planter-provisioned food in colonial Virginia. Having access to a regular supply of cornmeal made it less likely that the enslaved would chose to use their limited personal garden space growing corn or their even more limited underground space storing it. Documents from eighteenth-century Virginia often indicate that aboveground structures called cribs were located at slave quarters for the long-term storage of communal corn. While the presence of a crib and the provisioning of corn products would not preclude the storage of corn or cornmeal underground, it does make it less likely that the subfloor pits would have been used in this fashion.

Feature 53

Feature 53 was a rectangular hearth-front pit located in Structure 50, occupied during the second quarter of the eighteenth century. The bottom soil layer (Feature 53X), a medium-brown organic loam, was analyzed for pollen, phytoliths, and starches.

The results of this testing provided less conclusive evidence of food storage than analysis indicated for Feature 36. The sample contained high levels of pollen from oak and pine trees, with smaller quantities of alder, hickory or pecan, beech, and elm. These arboreal pollens, along with the pollen from weedy plants such as ragweed and pigweed, were likely deposited as wind-borne pollen. Elevated levels of grass pollen again suggested that vegetables stored in the pit may have been wrapped or cushioned with grass. Starch granules recovered from this feature showed characteristics indicating the presence of cereal grains like wheat, barley, or rye, while forms typical of sweet potatoes and corn were absent.

Analysis was performed on soil samples from two nonhearth pits in order to provide a basis of comparison with the hearth-front features. While the results of pollen and phytolith testing on the hearth-front pits were less con-clusive of food storage than anticipated, differences in the paleobotanical profiles of hearth and nonhearth pits support the conclusion that pits near the fireplace had been used for food storage.

While each of the four Utopia Quarter pits contained moderate quanti-ties of pollen from trees and weedy species that are indicative of the local en-vironment rather than of the original function of the feature, there are some distinct differences between hearth and nonhearth pits. These differences appear to be related to the original functions of the features. Starch gran-ules and evidence of cereal grains are absent from the two corner pits but are present in small quantities in each of the hearth-front pits. In addition, levels of grass (Poaceae) pollen are noticeably higher in the hearth-front pits (36 and 53), perhaps indicating that grass was used as a lining or packing mate-rial for stored food. Pollen grains from grapes (*Vitis*) or a grape product such as wine or raisins were present in small quantities in each of the hearth-front pits but in elevated quantities in one of the corner pits (Feature 44). This un-usual result is discussed in detail in an upcoming chapter.

Summary

Based on the results of paleobotanical analysis from the study sites, a strong case can be made for additional pollen, phytolith, and starch testing of sub-floor pit strata at future excavations. A critical consideration in gathering more data to support the root cellar interpretation of hearth-front pits would be to test strata believed to have accumulated during the use span of the fea-ture. Testing of secondary deposits associated with trash disposal at the site would provide evidence of the quarter residents' diet and of the local envi-ronment but would not indicate whether the pit had originally functioned as a root cellar. The identification at Utopia Quarter of starch granules with a form characteristic of sweet potatoes holds promise. Excavation at the Wilton Quarter (1750–1790) in Henrico County, Virginia, revealed the unusual discovery of noncarbonized fragments of sweet potato from a subfloor pit (McKnight 2000). While the recovery of noncarbonized plant remains is extremely rare, this finding lends further support to the Utopia starch evidence that sweet potatoes were stored in hearth-front pits. Better pollen preservation, coupled with ethnobotanical analysis of soils from subfloor pits on future quarter projects, may lead to additional evidence of sweet potato storage in hearth-front subfloor pits.

Sweet potatoes played a substantial role in the diet of enslaved Virginians, who created subterranean pits suitable for the long-term storage of this critical staple through the winter and early spring. The connection in Virginia between peoples of Igbo descent, the use of subfloor pits, and the importance of sweet potatoes coincides in a manner that points to hearth-front pits being used to store this important dietary staple. Significantly, only in those areas of the American South where descendants of the Igbo comprised a large percentage of the enslaved population did sweet potatoes form an important part of the diet. In addition, subfloor pits are not found in association with slave quarters in parts of the American South where other dietary staples, such as rice and corn, prevailed.

The old adage "given a choice, man tends to eat what his ancestors ate before him" is a fitting maxim for examining the development of Afro-Virginian foodways in the colonial period. Food, with its power to confer identity, remains one of the realms of life most resistant to change. The enslaved in Virginia made deliberate food choices based on their ideas of what constituted an appropriate diet. Many of those choices had their origins in their West African ancestry. In Virginia, West African foods, grains, and spices, as well as new foods encountered there by the enslaved, helped them fashion a collective cultural identity as well as a regionally distinct cuisine. These foods and methods of preparation became part of southern cuisine, adopted by white planters and still important in southern cooking today.

Note

1. Cummings and Moutoux (1999) give an alternate identification to the *Vitis* pollen from Features 36 and 44 as *Ceanothus*, commonly known as New Jersey tea. Leaves from this ornamental shrub were used as a substitute for tea during the American Revolution.

7
Subfloor Pits as Personal Storage Areas

Carter's Grove Plantation. Early evening in midsummer, 1750

Marcellus stepped inside the dwelling, setting the broad hoe just inside the doorway. After waiting a few seconds for his eyes to adjust to the low light, he moved toward the center of the room. As he approached the small space along the far wall that he called his own, he noticed something amiss.

Tossing aside a small cloth sack containing a gourd dipper and a jaw harp, Marcellus knelt beside his cornshuck pallet. The cotton blanket, which he carefully folded every morning, was not the way he had left it earlier. Grasping the thin mattress, he folded it back toward the wall, revealing rough boards covering a rectangular hole in the ground beneath the bed. Removing the boards, he looked anxiously into the depths of the hole. As his eyes adjusted to the darkness, he saw that everything appeared in place—the extra shirt and breeches, knife and fork, and the broken cup holding his small treasures: a gunflint, straight pins, and the small, curious earthen pipe he had found in the field by the river. Then he noticed—the short length of red ribbon, bartered last week for the oak market basket he had crafted, was missing. That ribbon was to have been a gift to planter Burwell's cook Molly, a woman Marcellus admired.

As the sounds of the other returning men filled the structure, Marcellus thought. In all of his five winters here, never had anything been taken from this place. Everyone in the quarter knew that these hidey holes were private and not to be violated. Who would risk the anger and alienation of the group for such a small trinket? Marcellus silently assessed everyone who had access to the building. He suspected Lot, the carpenter hired in earlier in the month, who had a wife on Foace's quarter. Assigned a temporary space here in this quarter, he started his day's work at least an hour after the other men had gone to the field. He had nothing to lose, since he would soon be done with his work here and gone. But how was he to determine if Lot was really the thief? "What should I do?" thought Marcellus, as he remembered with frustration and anger the hours he had spent making the basket.

Storage Spaces

One of the most obvious uses of subfloor pits by the enslaved would have been as storage spaces. Living in cramped quarters, often with virtual strangers during the early decades of heavy importation from West and Central Africa, the enslaved would have needed places to store personal possessions and rationed food supplies. Although storage spaces were limited within the confines of slave quarters, several options were available. Second-story lofts, either completely or partially floored, were used for storage as well as additional sleeping space. Wooden chests or trunks also served as storage containers. In 1754, planter Josiah Ball sent Aron, his enslaved personal assistant, to live on his Virginia plantation. Arriving with Aron and holding his personal belongings were an 80-gallon barrel, a small chest, and a box. Ball took special care to instruct the plantation manager that Aron was allowed to have these containers in his new cabin (Ball 1754).

Subfloor pits would have served the same storage functions as barrels, boxes, and chests. North Carolina resident William Henry Singleton remembered that the subfloor pit in his mother's home was used not only to store potatoes but also to "keep . . . things out of the way" (Singleton 1999 [1922]:39). Finding ways to keep items from cluttering floor space in the small confines of quarters was critical. Although most cooking and socializing took place outside around the quarters, interior space was at a premium in most quarters, where evenings often found the floor crowded with people sleeping. Trunks and other containers that took up valuable floor space were found in minimal numbers in these buildings. Thus, subfloor pits solved storage needs without diminishing useable floor space. There, the enslaved could stow extra clothing, items of personal adornment, eating utensils, food and drink, or items they had crafted to barter or sell.

Not only might subfloor pits be used to store personal possessions, but they could be used also for concealment of ill-gained items. One of the few known references to slaves and subfloor pits involved stolen produce hidden in a subfloor pit, illustrating one strategy of slave resistance to planter control. Theft of food, alcohol, poultry, livestock, clothing, and household supplies was an ever-present problem for planters, as the enslaved took supplies for their own use or to sell. Evidence from the eighteenth- and nineteenth-century American South suggests that subfloor pits did sometimes serve as places to conceal stolen goods. Ex-slave Charles Grandy related in an early twentieth-century interview how he would hide stolen chickens under a trap door cut through the floor of the house (Perdue et al. 1976:116). At Kingsmill Plantation in Virginia, one subterranean pit yielded several unbroken wine bottles bearing the seal of planter Carter Burwell, suggesting perhaps an illicit acquisition (Kelso 1984).

While some pits may have been used to hide stolen goods, the difficulty with relying on subfloor pits for such concealment was that they were not always a secret from slaveholders. Virginia planters Thomas Jefferson and Landon Carter both acknowledged the presence of subfloor pits and their use as repositories for stolen goods (Carter 1965:495; Heath 1994:40). Fraser Neiman (1997, 2004) has argued that subfloor pits made inadequate hiding places for several reasons. These pits, covered with boards and thus easily visible cutting through the dirt floors of the cabins, would have been the easiest and most obvious place to search for missing goods. Because each pit could be associated with a particular individual or group of individuals living in the cabin, blame for any theft could easily be assigned and punishment administered. Instead, Neiman argues that subfloor pits were "good tricks": a design solution employed by the enslaved not to hide stolen property but to protect their own possessions from theft by fellow slaves.

Neiman asserts that the use of subfloor pits and their spatial and temporal distributions on Virginia slave sites can be explained by the changing demographics of Chesapeake slavery during the eighteenth century. During the seventeenth and early eighteenth centuries, the importation of slaves directly from Africa was heavy, with the enslaved population of Chesapeake plantations comprised predominantly of males. Plantation demographics shifted as more females began arriving in Virginia and the enslaved began to form families.

Archaeological evidence in the Chesapeake indicates that non-kin groups of males imported directly from Africa were generally housed in larger, barracks-style structures, as evident at Utopia's Structure 50 and at Carter's Grove House One. Later, as the enslaved began forming family units, smaller buildings consisting of one-room cabins or two-room duplexes became prevalent, with each family assigned a single-room living space. Because these families could be considered cooperative units where sharing resources was in the group's best interest, personal possessions were not at

risk of theft from other household residents. In the larger structures housing nonrelated individuals, however, the need for distinct personal storage
areas was greater than in a structure occupied by a cooperative kin group. In
the larger barracks structures, these subfloor pits thus served as "safe-deposit
boxes" where each individual could store his or her belongings. Because the
ownership of each pit would be known by all residents of the structure, they
were thus relatively protected from thievery (Neiman 1997, 2004). Boards
covering the pits made them more difficult to access quickly, increasing the
chance that an unauthorized entry into a pit would be witnessed by another
resident.

As "safe-deposit boxes," subterranean pits can thus be viewed as an adaptation to conditions of enslavement, as individuals devised new ways to assert private property rights under less than ideal group living conditions.
The need to assert ownership of personal property within their quarter communities continued to be a matter of concern for the enslaved in the antebellum period. Many former slaves reported keeping their personal property outside in plain view, where it was visible to all and ownership publicly
acknowledged (Penningroth 2003). Such open acknowledgment made successful theft within the community more difficult. In those instances when
certain types of possessions, such as food supplies or clothing, needed to be
stored inside buildings, spatial segregation of goods within a room was employed as a means of tracking ownership. In eighteenth-century Virginia,
subfloor pits served the same functions as these antebellum strategies of
public display and interior segregation of possessions. All individuals living in a quarter would know the ownership of each pit; thus, the visible display was created by the pit itself. The number of subfloor pits in Virginia
slave dwellings decreased with the passage of time in response to the formation and increase in family groups among enslaved Virginians and the practice of using single-room dwellings for the family units (Neiman 1997). This
finding fits the hypothesis that subfloor pits served as secure storage spaces
within structures occupied by non-kin groups.

Archaeological evidence from Virginia on pit patterning and distribution
supports the hypothesis that the enslaved were using pits as personal storage and as safe deposit boxes. Was there West African cultural precedent for
underground storage that would aid in determining why this strategy was
adopted by enslaved Virginians? During a visit to the imperial Igbo capital
at Bonny, sea captain Hugh Crow described a form of storage used by the
people there. In his 1830 account, he wrote that "most of the hard articles
such as lead and iron bars, chests of beads, and marcelas (a kind of coin), they

bury under the floors of their houses. Much valuable property is secreted in that way" (Crow 1970 [1830]:251). How widespread this form of storage was among the Igbo is unclear, but an architectural survey of traditional Igbo architecture done in the 1950s and 1960s showed that the storage of valuables had by then largely been consigned to small, strong wooden chests placed in inaccessible storerooms (Dmochowski 1990:27).

Although the correlations between distributions of pits through time and the development of kin-based households support their use for storage, can artifact analysis serve as an analytical means of reinforcing this conclusion? Evidence of storage would be provided by the presence of curated items remaining in the bottoms of pits. These items could include pottery, bottles, agricultural tools, cutlery, buttons, and buckles. The description of the goods lost during a fire by slave Charles Cox in 1783 serves as an example of the types of items that could have been stored in subfloor pits (Sprinkle 1991). The account of the Maryland fire stated that Cox kept his clothing, razors, shoe buckles, sleeve buttons, coins, sewing needles, two pulleys, and some gun hardware in a wooden chest in the mill house where he lived and worked.

The likelihood of finding goods abandoned in subterranean storage units is highly improbable, however. If they were considered valuable enough to store, their owners surely would have removed these items when a quarter was moved or abandoned or if the resident moved on. Exceptions might occur under unusual circumstances, such as if the overlying structure had been destroyed by fire. If residents had no time to remove belongings before the building was consumed by flame, these objects would remain to be retrieved by archaeologists.

Thus, the very nature of using a subfloor pit for storage of personal possessions hinders the ability of archaeologists to definitively assign this function through artifact analysis in most instances. It should be possible, however, to detect those uncommon instances where stored goods remained intact in pits. During careful excavations, it is often possible for archaeologists to identify groups of objects left in situ. These items, in this case resting on the floors of features, comprise evidence of what archaeologists term de facto deposition. De facto refuse consists of "the tools, facilities, structures, and other cultural materials that, although still usable (or reusable), are left behind when an activity area is abandoned" (Schiffer 1987:89).

Archaeologists attempting to find evidence of storage would need to look for assemblages that contained complete or useable items resting on or near the floors of the pits. On some of the study sites, the quality of the field notes prevented determining the presence of caches from using the notes alone. An analytical tool using artifact size and completeness to locate de facto deposits within the pits was thus devised. Discussed more thoroughly in Chapter 5, this tool analyzed the completeness of individual artifacts within the subfloor pit assemblages in order to pinpoint possible instances of de facto or primary refuse. For analytical purposes, any soil layers whose assemblage contained over 15 percent complete artifacts were deemed worthy of further analysis.

Subfloor Pits as Storage Areas

Four subfloor pits contained caches of items that appeared to have been personal goods either stored or hidden underground. These pits were notable in their lack of similarity in shape, location, or content, reflecting the individuality of each pit's owner. The features are discussed here in chronological order.

Kingsmill Quarter, ca. 1750–1780, Feature KM363

This rectangular pit was located along the exterior wall of the western room in the quarter and contained 13 unbroken wine bottles, an unbroken German Pyrmont mineral water bottle, and another 6 bottles that were over 80 percent complete. Excavation photographs show they were contained within the last few inches of fill above the floor of the feature (Figure 7.2). The shapes of the bottles date their manufacture to the 1730s. At the time of excavation, the bottles were lying on their sides along the floor of the feature, and some of the others appear to have been broken in place, perhaps by other debris and soil being tossed in on top of them. The placements suggest these bottles had been stored on the floor of the pit.

Numerous explanations are possible for the presence of so many bottles in this feature. It is feasible, although not likely, that wine or brandy was stored at one time in the pit. Store and plantation records show that enslaved individuals were allowed to purchase small quantities of alcoholic beverages on some plantations. Slaves typically purchased pints and half pints from Phillip Moore's Mount Tizrah Plantation store in early nineteenth-century North Carolina (Moore Papers), although it is unknown whether amounts were restricted by some agreement Moore had with area planters or if cost of the alcohol was a limiting factor for the enslaved. Nevertheless, it is unlikely

7.1. Excavation of Kingsmill Quarter Feature KM363 (Virginia's Division of Historic Resources)

that an enslaved individual or family would store such large quantities of alcohol at one time, unless the cache represented entrepreneurial activity—selling alcohol to residents at the quarter and neighboring plantations.

Since bottles were hand-blown during this period, and thus expensive to produce, they were recycled, often for years. Bottles could be returned for refilling or exchanged for a small sum of money. In 1810, an enslaved man named Joe received a small sum of money for returning "1 black Bottle" to

Phillip Moore (Moore Papers). It is unlikely that the complete bottles from this feature had been discarded. The feature's bottles, even if they originally contained alcohol, were probably reused to hold other liquids. The person with access to this pit may have been a conjurer, midwife, or healer who needed the bottles for the preparation and storage of herbal and root remedies. The subfloor pit in this instance would have been used as a storage place for these homemade remedies and tonics.

Carter's Grove Quarter, ca. 1780–1800, Features CG643, CG715, CG716

The two pits in House Three (CG715 and CG716) and one in House One (CG643) contained items associated with their original functions as storage pits. Feature CG643 was located at the western end of the barracks-style structure and contained 467 artifacts within its two levels of fill. The uppermost zone of fill contained 402 artifacts, including numerous nails and window glass fragments, suggesting this fill was associated with the destruction of the quarter. Sealed by the destruction fill was a brown, ashy loam containing 65 artifacts. While fewer than 1 percent of the items from the upper stratum were unbroken objects, 16 percent of the artifacts from the lower zone were complete, suggesting that some of the objects in this zone were placed there deliberately during the life span of the building. The absence of detailed field notes from this site made it impossible to determine if these complete objects rested on the floor level of the pit.

The complete items included an early seventeenth-century kaolin pipebowl, two two-tined forks, a table knife, a pewter spoon, an iron shoe buckle, a copper alloy button, a set of sleeve links, a straight pin, a gunflint, and a quartzite flake. The pipebowl, ca. 1620–1660, was likely a found and curated item from the earlier Martin's Hundred settlement located between the quarter and the river. The base and partial body of an American salt-glazed stoneware mug (approximately 40 percent of the vessel) did not appear to be functional as a drinking utensil but could have been used to hold small personal items. If examined as a group, these items look strikingly like personal gear: clothing, dining equipment, the gunflint for hunting or making sparks to start a fire, and the flake used for cutting or scraping.

Some of the complete items from Zone A correspond with items from the lower zone. A shoe buckle matching the example found in the lower zone of soil and similar buttons in various sizes were also included in the zone. It is possible that some of these items were found at the intersection between Zones A and B. If this conclusion is correct, then it would appear that items of clothing, including a pair of shoes, a jacket or some similar item with buttons, cutlery, and other personal items were left abandoned on the floor of the pit. By the late eighteenth century, most enslaved individuals owned a second set of clothing, usually reserved for Sunday use (Walsh 1997:191). The nature of the clothing remains—the shoe buckles, the copper alloy buttons, and the sleeve links inlaid with opaque blue colored glass—suggest that these items were not from a set of work clothes. While most clothing was seasonally apportioned by the planter, additional attire could have been purchased or bartered by the enslaved or received as planter castoffs.

The incomplete spoons from the subfloor pit were modified in ways that suggest they may have served as some form of tool. Both sides of the bowl ends of two spoons had been cut on the diagonal, forming a pointed end to each bowl. A third partial spoon bowl, which had been flattened by hammering, had been cut into an irregular shape with a pointed end. Both the interior and exterior of the spoon bowl were heavily scratched. Another pewter spoon handle was bent at a 45° angle midway along the handle length. These partial spoons may have been used in some form of craft activity, such as basket making. Basket makers in coastal South Carolina use modified spoon handles as awls called "sewing bones" to hold the grass basket coils apart for ease in attaching the adjacent coil (Rosengarten 1986:13). In Virginia, baskets constructed of split white oak in the European tradition were more commonly produced. Bone awls and bladelike metal implements are often used as "rapping irons" to level the rows of woven splints and to insert handles and finish basket borders (Wright 1983). Whatever their use, the spoons from this feature had been modified for use other than as implements for eating.

In Structure Three, features CG715 and CG716 showed evidence of storage. A number of items rested directly on the floorboards of the prefabricated wooden boxes in the duplex, in a dark organic loam generated by the decay of the wooden floors (Figure 7.1). In CG715, these items included a complete iron padlock, a key, a scythe, a gridiron handle, 60 percent of a wine bottle, and an iron saddle tree. The padlock and key suggested that the contents of the wooden box had been locked away from prying hands and eyes. If, as the evidence seems to suggest, a saddle had been stored in this box, the residents of the house would have been wise to protect it from theft and probable resale. While the larger tools appear to have been deliberately placed on the floor of the pit for storage, other items, such as the small fragments of ceramics, faunal bone, tobacco pipes, and bottle glass, probably fell in through the floorboards during the life of the building. An iron broad hoe

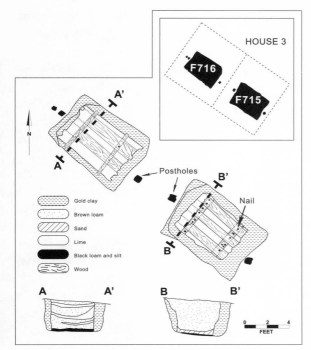

7.2. Plan and profile of Carter's Grove Features CG715 and CG716

and nine wrought iron spikes were stored on the floor of the pit on the opposite side of the duplex (CG716).

Summary

In the cramped environs of eighteenth-century quarters, subterranean pits provided effective storage units—not only were they an efficient use of the limited floor space, but they were also relatively secure from unauthorized entry and theft. Pits along the walls of the buildings could be covered with bedding, creating personal spaces within the quarter, where spare clothing, tools, extra food supplies, and other items could be stored. With these pits, it is possible to see the enslaved transforming their living spaces, with the patterning and distribution of these subfloor pits reflecting changing social organization on the quarters. These subfloor pits are symbols of individual and collective agency on the part of the enslaved, as they resisted the domination of slave owners and the conditions that, in the early decades in bondage in Tidewater Virginia, forced them to reside in nonfamily group settings. In asserting individual property rights and establishing ways to protect that property, the enslaved took control over an aspect of life legally denied them—that of owning their own property, however negligible.

Perhaps not surprisingly, only a few of the analyzed subfloor pits showed evidence of use as personal storage units. The very nature of this function would preclude physical evidence of storage, since personal possessions would be removed before the pit was decommissioned and filled with soil and garbage. In light of the earlier conclusion that the need for individual storage would diminish as the eighteenth century progressed, it is surprising that all but one of the pits showing evidence of personal caches or the concealment of items dated to the second half of the century, a period when cooperative family units began to share living spaces. The variation in shape, location, and contents of the subfloor pits characterized as storage spaces is not surprising. While root cellars might have narrowly defined size, shape, location, and depth requirements that affected their success as food storage units, personal storage pits could be as individual as the persons creating them. The same factor holds true for the final presumed use for subfloor pits—that of shrines.

8
Subfloor Pits as Shrines

The woman named Ebo knelt in the southeastern corner of the darkened cabin. She had long waited for this moment, but now the time was here. She carefully maneuvered the cork from the mouth of the brandy bottle on the floor beside her. It had taken months to save the money needed to purchase this brandy. The few eggs her scrawny chickens had managed to lay could have gone to feed her two daughters but had instead been sold to Mistress Bray for small change. Before she could purchase the brandy, there had been even harder work, coming home dead tired from the tobacco fields to sew by the light of the fire, stitching a Sunday apron for Daniel to give to his future wife. In exchange, he had been able to procure for her the seven fossil scallop shells that he removed from the river embankment on one of his boat trips carrying loads of lumber upriver for Master Bray.

She brought the bottle to her lips, carefully took in a mouthful and held it there a moment before leaning over and spitting the brandy into the rectangular hole she had cut through the earthen floor of the cabin. Although the hole was in shadow, she knew what rested on the slight mound of earth built up on the bottom of the hole. There, in addition to the seven shells representing water and Idemili, the female deity of water, she had arranged the bones of cows—sacred to the Igbo people of her homeland—and the white clay tobacco pipes representing an offering to Idemili. She took another mouth of brandy, leaned over, and spit into the hole again. This action she would repeat for six more nights. The seven shells and the seven nights of prayers and offerings were critical, since seven was the number of continuity and cyclical movements of life for her ancestors. After the seven days, she would carefully fill the hole, sealing the shell, pipes, and bones so that no one could disturb these sacred items. And at the end of that time, if Idemili looked favorably upon her actions, she would grant Ebo's request that her husband, now residing on another plantation, would be allowed to come and live with her here at Deb's Quarter.

Finishing her prayer, Ebo glanced at her two small children, Patience and Sukey, asleep on the pallet near the fire that barely kept the April evening's chill at bay. She got slowly to her feet and, with a tired sigh, moved toward her own blankets, for dawn and another day's work would come early.

Shrines in West Africa

Our daughters are headed for a World they call *New*. And we, their ancestor mothers, are alive in their blood. They are not alone, the ones who cross over. They take us along.

—Sandra Jackson-Opoku 1997:2

The men, women, and children arriving in the Virginia colony in the eighteenth century had been uprooted from, but not knowledge-deprived of, their birthright cultures. Beliefs about individual worth, the importance of family and kinship, gender and age-related roles, and spirituality traveled with them across the Atlantic and helped Africans forge lives under the new and trying circumstances in which they found themselves. Particularly critical in guiding their actions were spiritual beliefs, especially sacred beliefs that fostered kinship ties.

The final hypothesized function for subfloor pits has its basis in the religions of the Igbo and other cultures whose members were enslaved in the Virginia colony. This explanation is derived from strongly held spiritual beliefs and practices that the enslaved transformed into altered, but still recognizably African, forms. Based on a combination of archaeological evidence and West African religious practices, it appears that some of the subfloor pits functioned as shrines. Some of the pits contained groups of unbroken or nearly complete items, such as bottles, pottery, and agricultural tools, resting on their floor surfaces. Since even wealthy planters reused bottles, it is unlikely that individuals with more limited access to consumer goods would have accidentally left behind these still functional objects. Were these cached artifacts actually ritual objects left intentionally as shrine goods?

Shrines are important household components in many West African societies, where they serve as places for the living to negotiate daily with the spirits of deceased ancestors for guidance and benevolence (Offiong 1991:11; Uchendu 1976:283). Ancestor veneration is one of the ways West Africans used ritual performance to gain control over aspects of their lives. The following pages outline the historical and contemporary importance of such shrines in West African, and more specifically Igbo, cultures. Ethnographic, archaeological, and historical sources reveal how these shrines were used and what types of material objects they included. Based on these sources, questions were formulated for testing whether subfloor pits were used as shrines in Virginia. What follows are the results of this testing and analysis, as well as the implications these results hold for the study of slave culture and identity in Virginia.

Religion can be understood as a cultural institution of beliefs and practices that allows groups and individuals to understand and contend with life's experiences and uncertainties. Encompassing emotional, expressive, cognitive, and symbolic dimensions, religion generally involves interaction between humans and supernatural entities. In order to examine how specific African spiritual traditions were transformed on Virginia's plantations, it was necessary to determine the religious beliefs of the cultures whose members and, later, descendants were enslaved there. Given the prevalence of Igbo-descent peoples in Virginia, the focus is on Igbo spiritual traditions, embedded within a larger corpus of spiritual beliefs common to West Africa as a whole. Because of these overarching similarities, it is argued that enslaved individuals from different West African cultures developed creolized spiritual practices recognizable to other enslaved West Africans.

The key to understanding the West African worldview lies in spiritual beliefs that provide their followers structured approaches to balanced, purposeful, and successful living (Oramaisonwu 1994:56). The West Africans and their descendants enslaved in Virginia brought with them these rich traditions of spiritual beliefs, which shared enough basic elements to allow the formation of beliefs and practices that were recognizably African (Mintz and Price 1992:9, 45; Quarcoopome 1987). These elements included belief in a sovereign creator and ruler of the universe, belief in divinities and ancestors who acted as intermediaries between humans and God, and reliance on practices of magic and medicine to influence events and people (Quarcoopome 1987:12, 40–43).

West Africans generally view religion as an instrument for facing the anxieties and uncertainties of life and as a means to attain important goals (Offiong 1991:18). West African cultures also share a holistic worldview, in which there is no distinct separation between the sacred and the secular or the world of the living and that of the dead. Emphasis is placed on the unity and interrelationships among all aspects of the world. European concepts that stress individualism and self-sufficiency are alien in West African philosophy; each person's identity is instead linked with community identity and in the social and historical contexts within which an individual and the community are embedded. Deceased ancestors play a critical and active role in the lives of individuals on earth and in the ongoing life of the community.

Belief in ancestors, as well as other spirit forces and deities, is particularly prevalent among small-scale stateless African societies, where political and social controls are descent-based (Ray 1976:140). The Igbo and Ibibio, among the groups enslaved in Virginia, were stateless societies during the period of the Atlantic slave trade. In such societies, ancestors remain one of the most powerful spiritual forces, generally acting as intermediaries balancing relations between the living and the higher deities (Offiong 1991:11; Ray 1976:140). Olaudah Equiano's narrative of eighteenth-century Igbo life attests to the importance of ancestor spirits: "Those spirits . . . such as their dear friends and relations, they believe always attend them, and guard them from the bad spirits, or their foes" (Equiano 1987:19). Equiano, when first taken aboard the slaving vessel, believed that his English captors were *mo ndjo,* or evil spirits, who meant him great harm (1987:33).

Ancestral blessings can help assure individual health and achievements, as well as community well-being and agricultural plenty (Bockie 1993:18). Although honoring the spirits of the founding fathers, the living are not passive recipients of their benevolence or wrath; instead, they are actively engaged in strategic negotiations to enhance their own well-being. In cultures where ancestors are honored, continual contact is maintained through the construction of shrines and activities centered on these sacred places (McCall 1995; Offiong 1991:8; Thompson 1993). Shrines—places where people can commemorate or commune with ancestral spirits and deities—include a vast repertoire of living and nonliving articles, including sacred medicine packets, trees, waterfalls, and bonfires. Shrines can be subsumed under a more general category of Igbo spiritual items and practices (*ju-ju*) consisting of medicines or spiritual powers used for petitioning the spirits (*a-juju*). These practices also include the creation of personal ritual objects like *ikenga, ofo,* and community shrines like *mbari. Juju* objects are imbued with sacred power (Chambers 1996:99).

Shrines are visible and tangible places upon which to place a gift made to an invisible and intangible deity (Awolalu 1979:117; Onwuejeogwu 1981:

39). Ancestor-honoring activities include making offerings of food and animals and pouring libations of palm wine or other liquids on the ground to ease communication with the founding fathers (Bockie 1993:19; Okehie-Offoha 1996:64). Historical and current sources are similar in their instructions on appropriate offerings, suggesting continuity in this practice across at least several centuries. Eighteenth-century Igbo "always before eating . . . put some small portions of the meat, and pour some of the drink, on the ground for them" (Equiano 1987:19). This practice continued into the twentieth century, with Major Arthur Leonard, a British colonial administrator, observing, "It is customary, as a mark of esteem, gratitude, and fear to their ancestors, but especially to the protector and daily giver of food, to offer up a short prayer or petition, in addition to a certain amount of food and libations of water or liquor, in accordance with what they may happen to be drinking at the time" (Leonard 1906:434). Prayers are offered to the ancestors every morning, with the breaking of kola nuts and the drinking of wine prerequisite for any critical conversation betwen the living and the ancestors (Metuh 1985:155). No elaborate sacrifices are made to the ancestors—just portions of food eaten in the home and some wine and water were considered sufficient (Uchendu 1965:102). Neglect of a shrine would have negative consequences on an individual's life.

Modern-day shrines and Nigerian archaeological findings reveal objects of spiritual significance in Igbo culture. Archaeological examples of spiritual objects recovered from a tenth-century A.D. burial vault, Igbo Richard, included iron tools, copper and bronze jewelry, pottery, beads, waterworn pebbles, shell, and ferruginous stone (Onwuejeogwu 1981:57; Shaw 1977). Excavations at the Igbo Isaiah revealed a complete shrine group dated around a thousand years ago. The objects on this shrine had been arranged on a low rectangular platform, probably enclosed within a light structure (Shaw 1970:236). The shrine's goods, which included earthenware pottery, beads, iron knives, and bowls, pots, and shells cast in bronze had been left untouched by vandals, perhaps because the objects were imbued with spiritual power that made it too dangerous to risk the consequences of theft. This example and another shrine from the tenth-century burial site, Igbo Richard, provide not only time depth to analysis of Igbo shrines but also evidence for what objects were considered spiritually significant. Similarly decorated bronze items from the fifteenth century demonstrate continuity of iconographic motifs over the centuries (Hartle 1967).

Some of the items included on these early shrines were accorded great value in later periods. The presence of shrines was of great interest to English and European travelers in Nigeria, who often noted them in their writings. Visitors to New Calabar in 1699 noted that residents there offered sacrifices to idols and ritual objects called *juju* (Barbot 1732:462). These objects, including iron tools, iron and copper bars, pottery, beads, waterworn pebbles, and shells, were located both in private homes and on public view along the streets (Chambers 1996:275; Onwuejeogwu 1981:57). Visitors in the 1840s noted that many of the outdoor shrines had offerings of water and food placed near them, as well as European pottery, glass bottles, cowrie shells, and copper or iron ingots (Allen 1848:242). In the 1850s, a missionary noted a roadside shrine whose components included a flat calabash gourd containing an earthenware pot and a sacred wooden stick called an *ofo*, a round gourd holding an earthenware pot decorated with pebbles and white clay, a stone marked with chalk, and a pottery vessel containing feathers, pebbles, eggshells, and soil (Taylor 1968 [1859]:338–339).

Ethnographers working among the Igbo at the turn of the century noted that rounded pebbles, earthenware pots, cones of chalk or kaolin, and pieces of wood were commonly used as sacred objects. Colonial administrators writing about the Igbo and Ibibio in early twentieth-century Nigeria (Talbot 1969:20–21) and current ethnographies (McCall 1995:260) also stress the importance of pottery: its placement on shrines, use in rituals, and placement in graves. Modern-day Igbo ancestral shrine goods include carved wooden figures, metal or wooden dumbbell-shaped objects called *okponsi,* and hollow vessels containing various objects, such as chalk, pierced coins, and kola nuts (Onwuejeogwu 1981:50). Metuh's (1985:14) list of items kept as part of the ancestral shrine (*Irummo*) in the reception hut (*Obi*) of each household included wooden ritual objects called *ikenga* (a personal spirit) and *ofo*, as well as food offerings on a wooden platter. What is apparent from these descriptions is that these shrines were not elaborately constructed or adorned but rather were created using everyday items and materials.

Subfloor Pits as West African–Style Shrines

Since it is likely that subfloor pits served a multitude of purposes, with functions possibly linked to size, depth, and placement of the features, it may be possible to use physical characteristics to predict which features might have served as shrines. The assumption is made that complete and useable objects would not have been forgotten or intentionally discarded by the enslaved. Very few descriptions of the interiors of slave houses are known, but those examples document the sparseness of material possessions. A visitor to a late eighteenth-century quarter at Mount Vernon described its rudimentary furnishings: "We entered one of the huts of the Blacks. . . . They are more miserable than the most miserable of the cottages of our peasants. The husband and wife sleep on a mean pallet, the children on the ground; a very bad fireplace, [and] some utensils for cooking" (Niemcewicz 1965:100). Other Virginia travelers noted slave houses that contained "no convenience, no furniture, no comfort" (Smyth 1784:75–76). Given historical evidence of the meager material conditions of eighteenth-century slave life in Virginia, it seems unlikely that complete bottles, dishes, scissors, and agricultural tools were left behind when quarters were moved or torn down. A more likely explanation is that these items were shrine goods, sacred to an individual or family and thus left in place in the pits for spiritual reasons.

How can these spiritual expressions on Virginia archaeological sites be recognized? To increase the likelihood of recognizing material expressions of slave spirituality, this research used contextual analysis to make relevant cultural connections across time and space (Beaudry et al. 1991; Hodder 1987). A contextual framework was created within which to analyze Virginia archaeological and historical data using ethnohistoric, archaeological, and ethnographic data from the Igbo culture and, in particular, Igbo shrines and the range of religious practices associated with their use. The symbolic meanings of artifact assemblages are inferred by examining them contextually, both within a system of colonialism and power and also from within the historical context of precolonial to postcolonial Igboland. Although Igbo culture has undergone enormous changes over the centuries, long-term continuities in core beliefs are visible archaeologically in ritual iconography (Ray 1987).

This contextual approach has been used successfully by archaeologists studying the spiritual traditions of enslaved peoples. In the late 1980s, Texas archaeologists digging in a former slave quarter at Jordan Plantation discovered a group of artifacts left in a corner after its occupants had been abruptly evicted (Brown and Cooper 1990). Unremarkable as single objects, the seashells, beads, doll parts, chalk, bird skulls, bottles, and bases of cast iron cooking pots gained significance when analyzed contextually as related items. These artifacts, virtually identical to those used by modern-day Yoruba diviners for healing and other rituals, were components in a creolized West African–style conjurer's kit showing both Yoruba and BiKongo traditions (Brown 2001; Brown and Cooper 1990).

The Jordan Plantation discovery is important in several respects. There, in an abandoned quarter, were the tangible expressions of creolized West

African spiritual traditions, surviving under the harsh conditions of enforced labor. These objects had been used in culturally significant actions, demonstrating that objects, viewed contextually, can shed light on those intangible aspects of culture. Several caches of objects recovered from Maryland and Virginia contain items clearly traceable to West African–based spiritual traditions (Leone and Fry 2001; Logan et al. 1992; Pullins et al. 2003; Ruppel et al. 2003). Similar items have been recovered from slave quarters in Kentucky (Young 1996) and Louisiana (Wilkie 1995). Late nineteenth-century discoveries in Delaware (De Cunzo 2004) and North Carolina (Jones 2001) also attest to the strength and longevity of these practices.

Determining which subfloor pits served spiritual functions was a multistep process. All pits were examined and compared as a group, and features with the highest percentages of complete items were considered as possibly containing de facto deposits. Additional analysis then determined if the cached items were possibly spiritual in nature. An interpretive analysis, by which the symbolic meanings of artifacts were recovered through analysis of historical and cultural contexts, was used in order to make this determination. To demonstrate how objects found in subfloor pits were shrine groupings required that artifacts be viewed within the context of West African spiritual practices. In doing so, several key points became clear.

First, Igbo peoples in Africa, after initial contact with Europeans, readily incorporated European manufactured items into their corpus of shrine goods. This evidence is important for this study in several ways. The functional objects of daily Virginia life, used in plantation and household work and recreation, may have acquired spiritual connotations for Igbo peoples and other Africans prior to their arrival in Virginia and would thus have been easily incorporated into spiritual practices once there. Tobacco pipes and trade goods such as hoes and mirrors are good examples. The enslaved could also be expected to introduce additional formerly nonspiritual items into service as sacred objects. As suggested in Chapter 7, it was not always easy to assign a specific meaning to an artifact cache. The complete bottles in the Kingsmill Quarter pit may have simply represented a collection of bottles waiting to be recycled for cash; they may have been part of a healer's medicines; or they might have formed the core of a shrine grouping. A large part of the challenge rested on the fact that regular household objects were often used in a spiritual fashion in West Africa. How then can the nonspiritual, manufactured uses of these objects, such as bottles and iron tools, be distinguished from any spiritual significance they might have acquired?

While ethnohistoric and documentary evidence suggests a basic corpus of West African shrine goods (bottles, iron tools, copper items, pottery, wooden objects, polished stones, chalk), individual freedom is allowed in shrine assembly, making it impossible to define a set formula for the delineating shrine goods. A successful approach for defining shrines archaeologically takes into consideration the flexibility and individuality that characterize spiritual expression. Several strategies aid in this approach, including examining artifact materials. The materials from which shrine goods were made are often a more critical consideration than the form taken by the object (B. Campbell, personal communication, 1998). Also important will be the physical relationship of objects to one another, artifact colors, patterns, and the presence of themes or similarities within the artifact assemblages. The close links between iron and the Yoruba deity Ogun (Thompson 1993) make nails, axes, and other iron objects potential items for honoring that deity.

Given this challenge, it was often difficult to assign a spiritual function to a subfloor pit with certainty. Even so, four instances were found at the study sites where contextual evidence strongly supported the interpretation that the pits served a spiritual function. These four examples were all from Utopia. Analysis also revealed three other possible shrines. Spiritual attribution is less certain for these features, although the artifacts support these interpretations.

Feature 9 Structure 10, Utopia Quarter Period II, ca. 1700–1730

Only one of the features from the earliest Utopia quarter contained an artifact cache that suggested it had been used for as a shrine. Feature 9 was located in the southwestern corner of the eastern room and contained a dark brown sandy loam. This zone had been excavated in two-centimeter levels, with artifacts from the north and south halves of the feature separated, thus making it possible to re-create the locations of excavated objects with some accuracy. A thin lense of brown loam overlay the clay base of the feature, and several objects comprising a shrine grouping were placed on this layer. In the northeast corner of the pit was an agricultural hoe of iron, whose significance in West African cultures has already been noted. Located slightly to the south and toward the center of the feature was a wine bottle. Its neck and upper shoulder were missing, but inside the intact body were fragments of bone and eggshell, interpreted as food offerings. Eggs, symbolizing fertility, are used in current Igbo spiritual practices, and an egg pendant among the Igbo-Ukwu assemblage symbolizes their importance in the past (Cole and Aniakor 1984; Shaw 1970). A paving brick, a waterworn black cobblestone, a kaolin pipestem, and a raccoon mandible were in close proximity to the bottle and hoe. These symbolically important objects appear to form a shrine grouping.

Feature 44 Structure 50, Utopia Period III, ca. 1730–1750

Feature 44, a 4-x-3-foot rectangular pit, was located in the southeastern corner of Structure 50. A .4-foot platform of soil had been built up in the center of the feature's clay floor. Arranged on the platform's surface were seven complete fossil scallop shells, three large cow bones, two kaolin tobacco pipebowls, and a pipestem. A single deposit of brown sand filled the pit, sealing the artifact-covered platform (Figure 8.1).

This assemblage's parallels with past and present Igbo and other West African shrines are striking. The placement of the shell and bone on the platform is reminiscent of elevated earthen platforms on early twentieth-century Igbo shrines, as well as Mande ancestral shrines of the upper Niger Delta (Jones 1931; Thompson 1993:117). The composition of the assemblage bears a remarkable resemblance to objects associated with Igbo spiritual traditions. Water, symbolized by the fossil shells, is where the souls of the dead find temporary abode while awaiting reincarnation (Oramasionwu 1994:123–124). Fossil scallops like the Utopia examples are common finds along the James and York Rivers that border the study area, where they have eroded from the 3.5-million-year-old Yorktown formation. The fossil deposit nearest to the Utopia Quarter is located five miles away (Walsh 1997:200), however, meaning that considerable effort went into obtaining these shells.

The other objects placed on the platform were also spiritually significant. Olaudah Equiano, an Igbo enslaved in eighteenth-century Virginia, noted that pipes and tobacco were placed in the graves of departed Igbo spiritual leaders (Equiano 1987). The animal bones—a pelvis, humerus, and femur from at least two different cows—were also significant. Bulls were considered a sacred animal by at least some groups of precolonial Igbo and continue to be held sacred today (Ifesieh 1986:68). Grazilhier, an associate of James Barbot, noted in 1699 that "they worship bulls . . . and it is not less than death to kill them" (Barbot 1732:462).

The artifacts on the platform's surface were largely unbroken, and two of the bones (the pelvis and femur) appeared to have been arranged to encircle the top of one of the shells. In addition, all of the artifacts on the platform surface were white. Sacrifices to *Onishe,* an Igbo river spirit, are always white (Isichei 1978:182). Among the Igbo, as well as many other West African cultures, white is a sacred color, associated with the spirit world and symboliz-

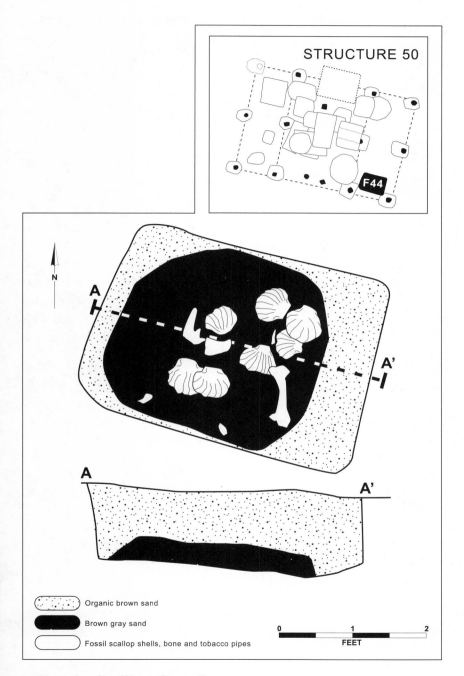

STRUCTURE 50

F44

N

A

A'

A   A'

Organic brown sand

Brown gray sand

Fossil scallop shells, bone and tobacco pipes

0   1   2
FEET

8.1. Plan and profile of Utopia Quarter Feature 44

ing purity, moral ideals, and the Supreme Being (Cole and Aniakor 1984:216; Metuh 1985:113). White stones were used in West African ancestor shrines, and such stones and ceramic fragments have been found with spiritual assemblages in Maryland (Leone and Fry 2001; Talbot 1967:128), as well as in subfloor pits in the Virginia Tidewater. The number of objects also appears significant. There were seven scallop shells on the platform—a number that often occurs in Igbo rituals, indicating continuity and the cyclical movement of life (Cole and Aniakor 1984:18).

Perhaps the most compelling evidence that this feature served as a shrine came from pollen analysis of soil from the earthen platform. Most of the pollen from the sample was from native or cultivated grapes (Cummings and Moutoux 1999). Although pollen analysis cannot distinguish between the presence of grapes or a processed grape product like wine, grape pollen has been recovered from baked goods containing raisins (Dimbleby 1985:140), suggesting that pollen is present on the skins of grapes. Thus, it would be reasonable for pollen to be present in wine, whose manufacturing process includes the crushing of whole grapes. The large quantity of grape pollen from Feature 44 suggests that the Igbo practice of pouring libations of wine onto shrines as offerings continued in Virginia. This practice has also been documented in the colonial Southeast. Bristoe, an enslaved man living in Johnston County, North Carolina, was brought to trial as a conjurer in 1779. One of his alleged wrongdoings consisted of pouring brandy into a hole in the earth as part of a ritual undertaken on behalf of another enslaved man (cited in Crow et al. 1992:21). A detailed discussion of this court case and its implications for the durability of such beliefs is provided in Chapter 9.

Eighteenth-century plantation and store accounts record alcoholic beverages as a common slave purchases (Martin 1997). In addition to medicinal and recreational purposes, the presence of grape pollen in Feature 44 suggests that the enslaved were using alcohol in a spiritual capacity. Elevated levels of hickory/pecan (*carya*) pollen in the soil sealing the shrine suggest that the pit was filled in the spring, when these trees were pollinating (Cummings and Moutoux 1999).

This feature is spiritually sophisticated when compared with other shrine groupings found at these sites and appears to commemorate a specific tutelary deity (*alusi*). The considerable effort that went into the creation of this shrine—digging the pit, constructing the earthen platform, and gathering very specific shrine materials, some from a distance—indicates that this pit was perhaps created for a particular purpose. Deities associated with water, such as Idemili, were vital in Igbo culture, and each had its own priest and cult objects (Cole and Aniakor 1984). The combination of white and water-related objects arranged on the earthen mound suggests that this pit may have contained a shrine that venerated Idemili, one of the Igbo water spirits. Idemili, the daughter of the Almighty God, came to earth in a pillar of water that rose from a sacred lake (Achebe 1987:93). As Igbo peoples spread throughout modern-day Nigeria and into the Diaspora, well away from the sacred waters, they continued to create shrines to Idemili. These shrines were often simple and relatively plain, consisting of a stream, or a mound of earth, a stone, or an earthen bowl with seven pieces of chalk (Achebe 1987:94–95). Only women can make requests of Idemili; thus, this feature appears to denote a female spiritual expression. Created during a period of heavy Igbo importation into the Virginia Tidewater, this feature appears to have been created by someone with direct knowledge of Igbo spiritual traditions.

Shrines to Idemili are located near water, and the Utopia shrine was placed in the structure corner closest to the James River, which was visible from the building. The mound of soil upon which the shells rested represented the pillar of water "fusing earth to heaven at the navel of the black lake" (Achebe 1987:94), with the seven shells mirroring the seven chalk sticks in Achebe's novel, *Anthills of the Savannah*. While it was not possible for the enslaved to re-create exact Igbo spiritual configurations in Virginia, this shrine shows sophisticated spiritual knowledge in use.

Feature 10 Structure 140, Utopia Quarter Period IV, ca. 1750–1780

Feature 10, filled with brown sandy loam, contained a concentration of complete iron and copper objects (Figure 8.2). Iron tools, including two scythes, one of which was crossed over an adze and the other over an iron hitch, were in the northeastern quadrant of the feature. An iron padlock and key were present in the southeastern quadrant. A brass candlestick and cufflinks lay in the southwestern quadrant, and a bone-handled knife, clay marble, and an iron hook and file were found in the northwestern portion of the feature.

The objects as well as the segregation of the objects by material in the various compass quadrants of the feature arrangement are reminiscent of Igbo shrine groupings. The two copper alloy objects were placed in the southwestern quadrant, items containing natural materials (bone and clay) were adjacent to one another, and most of the iron objects were present in the eastern half of the feature. The material composition of shrine goods is just as critical as the forms and functions of the objects themselves (B. Campbell, personal communication, 1998), so the segregation of the objects by materials is significant.

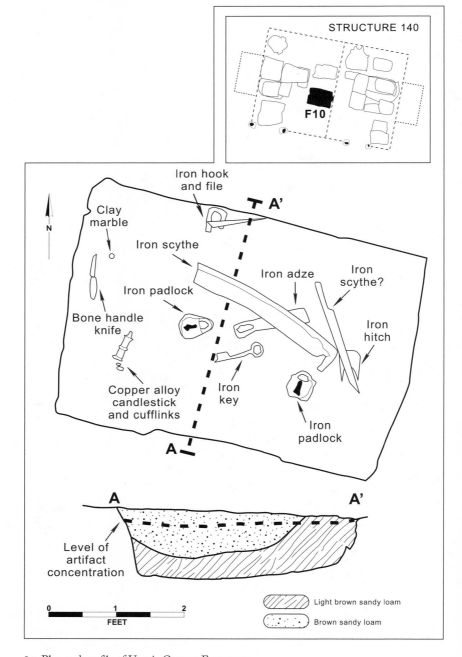

STRUCTURE 140

F10

Iron hook
and file

A'

Clay
marble

Iron scythe

N

Iron adze

Iron
scythe?

Iron padlock

Bone handle
knife

Iron
hitch

Copper alloy
candlestick
and cufflinks

Iron
key

Iron
padlock

A

A

A'

Level of
artifact
concentration

0   1   2
FEET

Light brown sandy loam

Brown sandy loam

8.2. Plan and profile of Utopia Quarter Feature 10

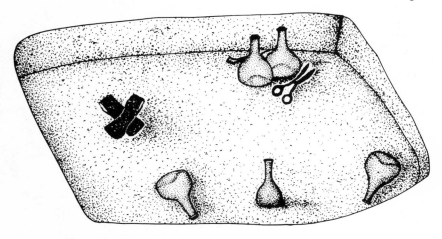

8.3. Shrine objects arranged on the floor of Eden House Feature 3 (drawn by Kim Kelley-Wagner)

Artifacts in this feature bear a strong resemblance to a group of finds from a 1730s subfloor pit at the Eden House site (31BR52) west of Edenton, North Carolina (Lautzenheiser et al. 1998). The North Carolina Tidewater, originally settled by Virginians, was also a tobacco-producing region with many similarities to Virginia's economic and social history. At an earthfast structure, likely housing for the enslaved, one of four subfloor pits contained an array of objects arranged on the feature floor (Figure 8.3). A pair of iron scissors and a serviceable kaolin pipe were placed on either side of two complete wine bottles in the northeastern quadrant of the pit, forming an X-shaped configuration. In the southwest corner were two iron axe heads, crossed one over another, also in an X-shape. In the center of the pit was a complete leaded glass decanter and two additional complete wine bottles.

The types of artifacts and their placements on the floor of the pit are significant and suggestive of West African shrines. The wine bottle grouping was placed in the northeastern portion of the feature, paralleling findings from a number of other slave-related sites in Virginia and Maryland, and it may be related to the northeastern quadrant of the Bakongo cosmogram, which corresponds with birth and life (Thompson 1983:108–116). Igbo ancestors are given libations of palm wine or other spirits daily, and the grouping of the tobacco pipe with the wine bottles links two types of artifacts with significance for ancestor veneration. The axe heads and scissors, with their cutting edges in the southwest corner of the pit, could signify the protective powers of iron (Thompson 1993).

Feature 10 also bears strong resemblance to a subfloor pit shrine assemblage from the similarly dated Southall's Quarter, outside Williamsburg (Pullins et al. 2003). Wine bottles, a tobacco pipe, scissors, a wig curler, shell, a knife blade, and animal bone had been placed on a raised soil platform.

Feature 8 Structure 140, Utopia Quarter Period IV, ca. 1750–1780

Feature 8 was located in the northeast corner of Structure 140. Contained within the only level of fill was a copper frying pan, 12 inches in diameter, containing a French wine bottle. The pan also contained fragments of animal bone, one of only two cowrie shells found at the site, wood, and three kaolin tobacco pipe fragments. The configuration of objects inside a shallow pan is similar to Igbo ancestral and divination shrines (Figure 8.4). The spiritual importance of tobacco-related items and their role as Igbo grave goods has been addressed, with the animal bone and the bottle, which may have contained wine or some other alcoholic beverage, representing spiritual offerings. Cowrie shells were used as currency and as divination tools throughout Igboland and in many parts of West Africa. This shell had its top surface cut away, a modification typical for use in divination. With the convex surface thus removed, the cowrie would have an equal chance of landing on either of its sides when tossed onto the ground during divination. By reading the patterns created when the shells were cast, a diviner could counsel his client (Cole and Aniakor 1984:73). The presence of deteriorated wood fragments, which may have been part of a carved figure or some similar ritual object, is also consistent with shrine goods.

Possible Shrines

Several subfloor pits from the study sites contained artifact assemblages suggestive of shrine groupings. Because excavation strategies were not designed to address questions about pits functioning as shrines, it was not possible to state with certainty that these assemblages represented shrine goods.

Feature 39A Structure 50, Utopia Period III, ca. 1730–1750

Feature 39A was located in the northwest corner of Structure 50. Artifacts recovered from the floor fill hint at the feature's original use and included a cowrie, modified for use as a divination tool. Also present was a complete tobacco pipebowl, 5 complete oyster shells, and almost 50 fragments of fossil-

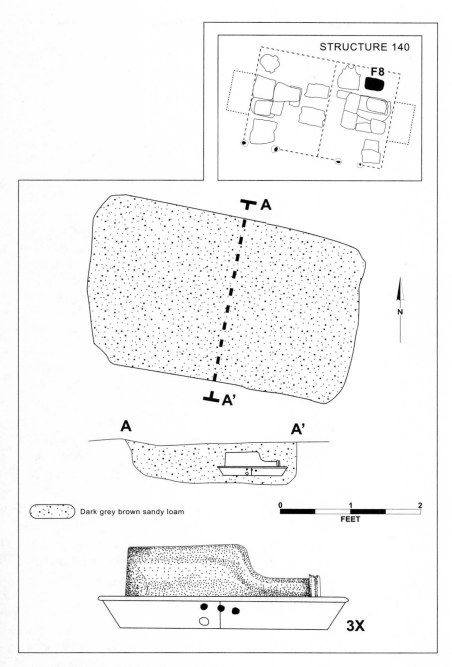

STRUCTURE 140

F8

A

A'

A   A'

Dark grey brown sandy loam

0   1   2
FEET

3X

8.4. Plan and profile of Utopia Quarter Feature 8

ized scallop shell, paralleling the previously discussed and contemporaneous Feature 44. These features, located in opposing corners of Structure 50, were both rectangular and similar in size. It is uncertain whether the items in Feature 39 were ever part of a shrine grouping, but the composition of the assemblage suggests a spiritual function for the artifacts.

Feature 9 Structure 140, Utopia Quarter Period IV, ca. 1750–1780

Another subfloor pit, located along the partition wall in the western room, displayed characteristics suggesting a spiritual function. Feature 9 had a small mound of brick and broken brick bats built up on the clay floor in the northwestern corner of the feature floor and a single tapered brick (Figure 8.5). Mounded objects frequently form the main components of shrines in West African cultures: for the Yoruba, a mound of iron signifies Ogun, and Lobi ancestral shrines are pillars of earth (Thompson 1993:114, 150). The general assemblage of artifacts from the single layer of fill in this feature was typical, but artifacts with possible spiritual significance included a piece of fossil coral emblematic of water, a mirror fragment, worked flint, and two knives. Since no artifact locations were noted, it is impossible to conclude that they had a spiritual function.

KM362 Structure One, Kingsmill Quarter, ca. 1750–1780

KM362 was located along the southern wall in the main portion of Structure One. The lowest zone of fill, a dark brown loam, contained 116 objects, among them a collection of complete items. These unbroken items included a saw and a chisel, four complete and one partial tobacco pipe bowls, three complete wine bottles, large fragments of faunal bone, a finished block of white marble, a copper alloy cooking pot handle, a seventeenth-century faceted pipestem, and several nails. This feature also shares some significant similarities with Utopia Feature 10 and the Eden House example. Both pits contain complete wine bottles and pipebowls, as well as iron objects with sharpened cutting edges. Unfortunately, it was impossible to determine from the field notes whether the artifacts in the Kingsmill Quarter feature were grouped on the feature floor in a fashion similar to the North Carolina pit.

Objects with Spiritual Significance

Archaeological findings in Virginia and other parts of the American South also confirm that the enslaved were continuing to practice at least some African-based spiritual beliefs, including the use of protective charms and

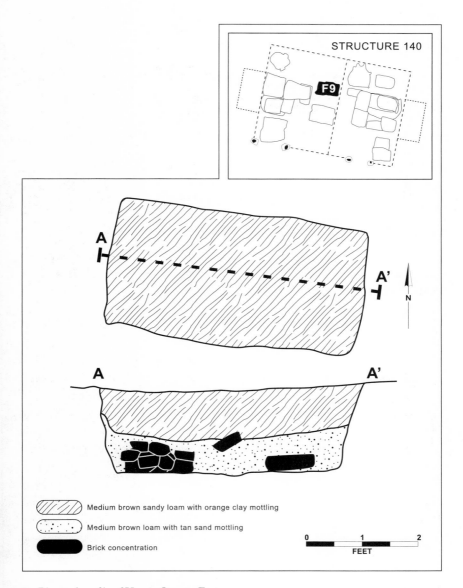

STRUCTURE 140

F9

A — A'

N

A — A'

Medium brown sandy loam with orange clay mottling

Medium brown loam with tan sand mottling

Brick concentration

0   1   2
FEET

8.5. Plan and profile of Utopia Quarter Feature 9

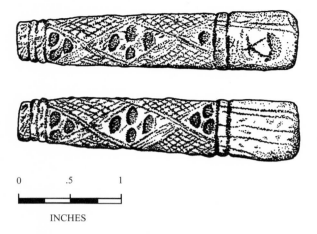

0   .5   1

INCHES

8.6. Carved bone container from Utopia Quarter Feature 3 (drawn by author)

medicine bundles (Franklin 1997; Young 1996). Incised markings on the bases of colonoware vessels suggest that some of these pots were used in African-based spiritual practices (Ferguson 1992). Other objects of spiritual significance recovered by archaeologists include glass beads and pierced coins (Young 1996) worn as charms, protective devices, and adornment (Stine et al. 1996; Yentsch 1994). Caches of objects discovered in slaves' living quarters and resembling Central African *minkisi* suggest evidence of a more fully developed aggregate of spiritual beliefs and practices than previously believed (Brown and Cooper 1990; Logan et al. 1992). Virginia pits yielded not only evidence of shrines but also other objects of potential spiritual significance. These objects, comprising either items crafted by the enslaved or modified manufactured goods, displayed iconographic motifs that had spiritual significance for the Igbo and other West African cultures.

Among these items was a carved bone implement from the 1700–1730 occupation at Utopia. This implement had been crafted from a hollow limb bone of a medium-sized mammal such as a deer or sheep, tapering slightly along its 2 7/8–inch length. The larger end had been plugged with a small carved disk of bone inscribed with a carved "X." Elaborate carvings decorated the entire surface of the bone, with a series of geometric, crosshatched patterns (Figure 8.6).

While this object has been interpreted as a bone handle for a knife or some other piece of cutlery (Walsh 1997), its physical characteristics suggest otherwise. Cutlery handles were typically constructed from a solid slab of bone split lengthwise, with the flat iron tang of the knife or fork sandwiched between the pieces of bone, which were then riveted together. The hollow interior of this implement would not have provided a secure fit for a cutlery tang. This object was created to serve another function, as a needle case, or for a sacred function, like holding ritual medicines. Since one end of the bone was plugged, it was probably created to serve as a container of some kind, with the smaller end stopped with a cork or a plug of fabric or leather.

The decorative carvings have sacred meanings in Igbo culture. The pattern of alternating plain and crosshatched diamonds and triangles is similar to the Igbo "eyes of God" motif. Alternating zones of decorated and undecorated space recalling the dualist cosmology so critical to Igbo culture are a style of surface treatment particularly common on objects from Igbo-Ukwu and seen continuing in Igbo art today (Cole and Aniakor 1984) and on other items found at the study sites. The bowl of a kaolin tobacco pipe from Utopia's Feature 41 and a spoon handle from Kingsmill had been incised with a similar cross-hatched pattern.

The Utopia bone container bore other details of Igbo cultural significance. Elongated ovals were carved into the nonhatched portions of the container. One triangle contains one oval, three triangles have three, and each of the two diamonds contains four ovals. Numbers have important sacred meanings for the Igbo: one is the symbol for *Chukwu*, the Supreme Creator, three symbolizes the *chi*, which provides an individual with the power to affect change in one's life, and four is the number of completeness, symbolizing *Chukwu's* home. What appears to be a boat is carved along one side of the object's base. This design could symbolize either the boat that brought the enslaved to Virginia or a vessel to return them to the homeland. Another oval, carved over the boat symbol, again refers to *Chukwu*, perhaps indicating a desire that appeals to the spiritual world would bring about a return trip, either in this life or in the afterlife.

Particularly interesting are a group of 30 cast pewter spoon handles from the mid-to-late eighteenth-century context at the Kingsmill Quarter (Figure 8.7). Ethnohistoric and ethnographic evidence suggests the spoon handles from Kingsmill and several other Virginia sites were used as divination tools. Most of these handles were found in the fill of subfloor pits in the quarter. The handles had been deliberately broken away from the spoon bowls, and in some instances the broken end had been shaped into a point. Proportions of handles to spoon bowls was very pronounced (4 to 1), and 60 percent of

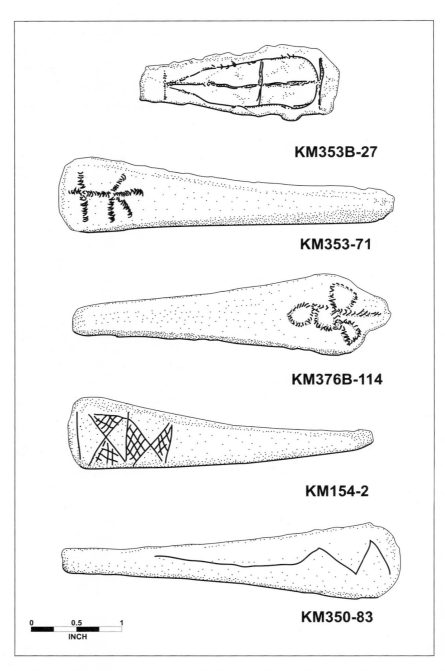

KM353B-27

KM353-71

KM376B-114

KM154-2

0   0.5   1
INCH

KM350-83

8.7. Carved designs on pewter spoon handles (drawn by Tamera Myer-Mams)

the handles had been decorated with engraving that postdated the original manufacturing process. Most of the decorated spoons had been incised with linear zigzag patterns produced by a hand-held metal-working tool known as a graver. Other examples were etched with straight lines that could have been produced with any sharp implement.

The engraved motifs on the spoon handles bear strong resemblance to Igbo decorative motifs. The use of running lines of V-shaped decorative elements has precedent among cast bronze bells and other Igbo ritual objects (Neaher 1976; Shaw 1970), some dating back as far as the tenth century. Several of the Kingsmill handles display decorative elements also used on personal ritual objects called *ofos,* while other handles have designs resembling Igbo body cicatrization motifs (Bentor 1988). Body scarification serves multiple functions for the Igbo—the scars can be symbols of rank, clan, tribe, social or marital status and sometimes are done for medicinal or protective reasons (Adepegba 1976; Cole and Aniakor 1984). While the Kingsmill Quarter has the largest assemblage of engraved spoon handles, there were three similarly incised spoons recovered from the Rich Neck Quarter (Franklin 2004:121).

While owning such objects would contribute to an individual's sense of self and well-being, the real power was in their creation (Cole and Aniakor 1984; Nooter 1993). Woodcarving is the favored Igbo medium in which to craft spiritual objects (Cole and Aniakor 1984:1). Because wood does not survive well archaeologically, the presence of some important categories of spiritual items, such as carved wooden ritual objects called *ikenga* or *okposi,* would be lost. Wood fragments found in Feature 8's copper pan at Utopia may have been remnants of similar objects. The poor preservation of wood obscures the degree to which it played a role in the spiritual lives of Virginia's enslaved. The carved bone implement from Utopia's Structure One, however, establishes that the carving tradition lived on in eighteenth-century Virginia.

Archaeological Determination of Subfloor Pit Functions

As seen in the analyses of subfloor pits from the five sites, data recovery methods, level of record keeping, and the thoughtful sampling of subfloor pit soils make a critical difference in the ability to determine original pit function. In the case of hearth-front pits, the only means of determining whether food storage actually occurred in them is through analysis of microfloral remains. The sample used in this study, although small, suggests that food storage did occur in these features, but additional samples need to be studied to create a larger database. These results should be compared with similar analysis on nonhearth pits either to strengthen further or to undermine the argument that hearth-front pits were used primarily for food storage.

In the case of caches of de facto artifacts, denoting personal storage or spiritual areas, it was generally much more difficult to identify and isolate caches when the locations of artifacts were not noted during the actual excavation. In this study, the strongest arguments for spiritual functions could be made when extensive mapping or photography of the feature and its objects had occurred during fieldwork. In the case of shrines as well, soil analysis strengthened the spiritual interpretation in one case. Because there was a high degree of crossover between spiritual objects and items used in everyday life, it is only through viewing objects in relation to one another that insight will be gained into their functions and meanings.

The value of this recommendation has been clearly proven at archaeological excavations in Texas, South Carolina, and Maryland. At the Levi Jordan Plantation in Brazoria, Texas, and Frogmore Manor in South Carolina, careful excavation and detailed recording revealed extensive evidence of creolized West African–based spiritual practices (Brown 2001; Brown and Cooper 1990). At Levi Jordan, a conjurer's kit, a BiKongo-style *nkisi* curing kit, and several other deposits formed a BiKongo cosmogram on the floor of the former slave quarter. One of these deposits, an arrangement of nested cast iron cooking pots wrapped in an iron chain, is identical to Yoruba shrines to Ogun, the deity of war, ironworking, and hunting (Thompson 1983). The Levi Jordan Plantation deposits were created using spiritual elements from the BiKongo and Yoruba cultures—evidence of the intersection of different West African cultures enslaved in the American South. Another series of distinct subfloor features at one of the antebellum Frogmore Manor quarters also formed a cosmogram (Brown 2001).

Objects symbolic of status and power in West Africa allow the examination of the structure of the slave community and the ways in which slaves could enrich their lives with articles of deep spiritual and cultural significance. Analysis at the study sites showed parallels between assemblage configurations in pits believed to contain shrines. Only through careful excavation, with sensitivity to and knowledge of African American spiritual beliefs, will additional spiritual caches such as the examples in Texas, South Carolina, Maryland, and at the study sites be recovered.

Notes

1. Medicine (*ogwu*) can be defined as "useful things charged with powers which man can exploit" (Arinze 1970:21).

2. A cosmogram is a visual representation of the worldview of the peoples of the Kongo. It consists of a cross enclosed within a circle, with the top half of the circle representing the world of the living and the bottom half the world of the dead (Thompson 1993:53).

9
Subfloor Pits and Slavery
in Colonial Virginia

In an age of political infidelity, of mean passions, and petty thoughts, I
would have impressed upon the rising race not to despair, but to seek in a
right understanding of the history of their country . . . it is the past alone
that can explain the present.

—Benjamin Disraeli (1845)

Enslavement and Subfloor Pits

In the preceding chapters, archaeological evidence for five enslaved communities on three eighteenth-century Tidewater Virginia plantations has
been examined. In all cases, these communities were linked to one another
through family ties and, in the case of the three phases of occupation at the
Utopia sites, probably formed successive generations of the same community. This analysis made it possible to look at changes over the course of the
eighteenth century in material conditions of life and in subfloor pit patterning in a fashion that controlled for physical location and community continuity.

One of the goals of this study was to determine how these pits were used
by the enslaved. Hypotheses included the enslaved using the pits as sources
for clay chinking, as food storage, as personal storage units, and as sacred
spaces. Since the pits could have been used as a clay source and then modified for other uses, it is impossible to state with certainty whether they functioned in this capacity.

Clear-cut functions for most of the subfloor pits were difficult to determine because the features had been predominantly filled with soil and garbage not directly associated with the original use of the features. Analysis of
artifact size and completeness provided clues as to how and why pits were
filled. When a pit was taken out of service and filled with soil while the
building was still occupied, there was a low ratio of artifacts to cubic feet of
fill. This finding suggested that pits were generally emptied of their original
contents before being filled with relatively clean and garbage-free fill. The
extensive use of organic materials such as kitchen or household waste as fill

was probably avoided as much as possible when pits were filled in buildings still in use. As the garbage decayed, it would have created foul odors in the dwelling. Residents would also need to add fill as the organic matter decomposed and settled. It appeared that quarter residents were gathering up soil containing sheet midden from the yard or nearby for filling decommissioned pits. The presence in some Utopia pits of artifacts dating from the seventeenth century supports this conclusion. Most pits were filled rapidly with one deposit of soil containing secondary refuse. A smaller number of pits appear to have been filled with soil dug from the construction of new adjacent subfloor pits.

Pits whose use span had been cut short by the collapse of a wall or some other damage were generally filled with a combination of primary and secondary refuse. The primary fill was characterized by organic soil strata containing large quantities of animal bone, complete oyster shell, and large fragments of ceramic and glass, suggesting these layers were the product of dumping daily quarter garbage. These strata were generally mixed with layers of cleaner, less organic fill containing highly fragmented secondary debris. The mixed fill typical of these damaged pits suggests the enslaved needed to fill them rapidly in order to replace them with other pits. Since later pits often appeared adjacent to or even cutting earlier pits, filling the damaged pits provided more structural stability for the new features. Any debris that was handy, including generally shunned smelly household garbage and hearth ash, as well as yard sweepings, was called into service. Later-phase pits in the quarters generally contained higher percentages of architectural artifacts, suggesting that pits in use at the end of a building's life were filled after the overlying building was destroyed or removed.

During the first half of the eighteenth century, the inhabitants were experimenting and making modifications in pit construction, particularly pit orientations and depths on hearth-front pits. The complex in Utopia's Structure 50 provided an example. Perhaps remembering the hearth-front pit collapse in Structure 10, the residents of Structure 50 chose to place their pit (Feature 56) some six feet away from the hearth, well back from the busiest foot traffic area. Later in the life span of the building, a pit of similar size and alignment (Feature 53) was placed much closer to the hearth, at a distance of less than two feet. The reason the earlier pit was abandoned is unclear. If gaining the effects of radiant heat from the fire for food preservation was indeed a consideration in locating hearth-front pits, it is possible that Feature 56 was simply located at too great a distance from the hearth to be beneficial.

Later, during the final phase of pit construction, the orientation of the hearth-front pits was changed, as the residents dug three pits with their short axes facing the hearth (Features 55, 57, 58). By the time these three pits were constructed, large areas of the floor around the hearth had been disturbed by earlier pit construction. This final phase of construction apparently represented an attempt by the structure's residents to access the warmer areas in front of the hearth, while at the same time locating the pits where they cut through the greatest area of undisturbed soils that would provide the sturdiest pit walls.

The residents were also experimenting with pit depth, particularly for hearth-front pits. When pits were too deep, as in Feature 53 at Utopia, erosional undercutting from rising groundwater was evident. The enslaved had to balance the need for adequate food storage space with the threat to food preservation from groundwater. Later in the eighteenth century, pit depths seemed to stabilize between 1.5 and 1.75 feet deep, presumably out of groundwater range but adequate for storage needs.

The level of repair and reconstruction on hearth-front pits was far greater than in any other location. In several cases, the residents at the sites attempted to strengthen pit walls when they cut through earlier back-filled pits by using clay sheathing and wooden linings. Despite the apparent difficulties and extra work involved in maintaining hearth-front pits in good repair, it was evident by the continuing use and upkeep of these pits that the location was viewed as important. The extra work needed to maintain the hearth-front pits in soil-floored structures may have been a function of greater foot traffic around and over these features. The hearth would be one of the areas with the highest level of foot traffic in the house, as people warmed themselves at the fire, prepared meals in inclement weather, or used its light for sewing or other tasks. Activity around and over the pit covering may have accelerated the collapse of the clay walls. If the hearth-front pits were more likely to be used for food storage than were pits in other locations, frequent access to the pits for adding or removing food may have also put more stress on the feature walls as boards were moved away from the openings. The walls and floors of food storage pits would have also been more prone to damage from tunneling creatures, such as rats or moles, in search of a meal. Finally, radiant heat from the hearths may have also dried and baked the clay side walls, causing soil to shear away from the pit walls.

What this location potentially offered that other spots did not was access to ambient heat from the hearth. Based on all lines of evidence—nineteenth-century slave narratives, dietary preferences of Virginia's enslaved, storage needs for sweet potatoes, and the results from limited paleobotanical evidence—hearth-front pits served primarily as food storage. These pits exhibited greater standardization of shapes and sizes, suggesting a specific use with communal implications, as opposed to individually created pits in other locations. The hearth was perceived as a communal space within a dwelling, and pits located there best served communal functions such as food storage.

Evidence for the use of pits for storage of personal items was limited, since personal goods would presumably be removed prior to the abandonment and filling of a pit. If, however, fire or disaster destroyed a building, personal objects might still be present in the bottoms of pits if residents had no chance to rescue them. Pits whose assemblages suggested their use for personal storage were more typical in non-kin coresidential dwellings rather than family-based households. Cooperation within family units helped account for the decreased number of pits present in later slave quarters, where family groups shared single-room living spaces.

African Traditions: Subfloor Pits as Shrines

Some of the sites' subfloor pits were used in African-based spiritual practices. In light of these findings, the idea of sacred spaces is explored more fully in the following pages. Archaeological evidence of similar spiritual practices has not been found on seventeenth-century sites. Berlin (1998:33) has suggested that there was a greater tendency for seventeenth-century Africans in the colonies to adopt English ways without feeling they were capitulating to a greater power. Also, while seventeenth-century living and working conditions were poor for black and white laborers alike, slavery had not yet been institutionalized before the end of the century, and acts of resistance may have been less typical than they were later. With the huge influx of Africans at end of the century and the beginning of the next, however, and their increasing mental and physical separation from whites, it is not surprising that there is archaeological evidence for African-based traditions.

Planters and others in the New World on occasion noted practices within their enslaved labor communities that can be traced to African origins. Travelers recorded African polygynous marital practices among the eighteenth-century Maryland enslaved communities (Kimber 1998). Music and dance were other practices that had African roots. An early eighteenth-century Virginia-made drum now in the collection of the British Museum is similar in design to Akan instruments (Sobel 1987:29). Andrew Burnaby, a visitor to Virginia in 1759 and 1760, wrote that the enslaved danced "without any method or regularity" (1960 [1775]:26). To the Western eye, the arhythmic movements of the enslaved appeared odd and perhaps even distasteful, but they carried deep spiritual meaning for the dancers and African American spectators.

How does the archaeological evidence of these shrines fit with what is known about enslaved Virginians and their African forebears? The past experiences of the individuals newly enslaved in eighteenth-century Virginia were West African, and in many cases Igbo. While self-awareness—a sense of agency and differentiation from others—comprises crucial elements of an Igbo sense of self, critical differences separate Western and Igbo definitions of identity. For an Igbo, identity and personal achievement are communally based (Njoku 1990) and linked with what Chambers (1996:336) calls "honorance"—ideas about proper righteous behavior that include dignified conduct, respecting elders, and protecting the weak. Igbo men strive to achieve personal honor and wealth within their communities, enabling them to support multiple wives and children and take community titles. Through hard work, an individual can rise from a low status within the community to a position of great honor and esteem (Madubuike 1974). An individual's achievements, however, are intricately bound to those of the community, both living and dead.

Igbo beliefs about the nature of the universe and how identity and individuality correspond with ancestor veneration made individual and family-based spiritual practices an effective means of resistance. The veneration of ancestors and deities are expressions of the living's relationship with the transcendent. The Igbo believe in one supreme god (*Chukwu*), the creator of all things, who is the designer of human destinies. Upon conception, each individual is granted a decreed-upon destiny entrusted to the personal spiritual guardian (*chi*) that oversees his or her life (Metuh 1985). Although one's destiny is largely predetermined from birth, appropriate actions taken by an individual in his or her lifetime, including constant petitioning and veneration of ancestors, can change one's fate in a favorable fashion. Conversely, ignoring the spiritual forces and taking inappropriate actions can negatively alter one's destiny.

Thus, the living are locked in a continuous cycle of birth, life, death, and rebirth, with their actions on earth determining their fate here and in the afterworld. In Igbo religion, the ultimate goal of every individual is to join his or her ancestors after death and enjoy the veneration of descendants before eventually being reincarnated back to the land of the living (Madubuike

1974:12; Metuh 1985:106). Joining the ancestors after death was viewed by the enslaved as their only means of returning to Africa. Jamaican planter Matthew Lewis noted in the first decades of the nineteenth century that to his Igbo slaves, "nothing is more firmly impressed upon the mind of the African, than that after death they shall go back to Africa, and pass an eternity in reveling and feasting with their ancestors" (Lewis 1834:344–345). If one did not honor the ancestors and *chi* with the proper respect and actions, he would not be rewarded in death by becoming an ancestor. So it became doubly important in Virginia to honor the ancestors and personal spirits, not only to effect positive change in their lives on earth but also to ensure a return to the homeland. Honoring activities included the construction and maintenance of shrines, as well as masquerades, music, dances, and the creation of art objects. The Igbo make shrines honoring various deities or personal spirits, and these sacred spaces take many forms, including family ancestral shrines, shrines to specific deities, and personal shrines.

It is hardly surprising therefore that the enslaved in Virginia continued to construct shrines for petitioning ancestors and deities or as representations of personal identity. Since historical sources did not suggest that elaborate West African political and social structures survived in Virginia, shrines there were probably limited to sacred spaces with family or personal connotations. Ancestors receive more attention than the Supreme Being or deities in daily worship (Metuh 1985:106). The following pages provide an in-depth look at the West African (particularly Igbo) ethnohistoric and ethnographic record with a view toward pits used as shrines.

Placement of a shrine below ground must be considered within the context of Igbo traditional religion and Virginia slavery. Igbo ancestral and personal shrines are located in a private part of the home, away from the prying eyes of visitors. In other parts of West Africa and throughout the African Diaspora, modern household shrines are often hidden in the backs of closets or disguised as laundry bins (Thompson 1993:61). In the cramped space of a quarter, a hole cut into the earth under the house may have been the most private place within the building. Ethnohistorical evidence from the nineteenth century indicates that the Igbo used underground storage pits (Yentsch 1991), so the use of such pits had a cultural precedent.

In addition, the underground location would have been dark. In some parts of Igboland, family shrines are constructed in small mud and thatch structures that are kept locked and dark (Starkweather 1968). So, too, the subfloor pits found on Virginia sites were sheltered from unwanted attention, either from the planter or from other members of the enslaved community. Privacy does not equate to secrecy, however. The contrast between an earthen floor and a board-covered hole would have made these pits noticeable to cabin visitors, even if the planks were covered with sand. Subfloor pits were a common enough feature of slave housing, and there is ample evidence that white planters knew about them. The knowledge of a shrine's presence was not a secret, but having improper eyes looking upon it did present a problem.

Moreover, in his discussion of sacred places of the Yoruba, another West African culture whose members were enslaved, although largely in other parts of the American South, J. Omosade Awolalu (1979:117) reveals, "whatever form a sacred place takes, what is most important is the belief that such a place constitutes a break in the homogeneity of space; this break is symbolised by an opening by which passage from one cosmic region to another is made possible" (from heaven to earth and vice versa, from earth to the underworld).

Virginia subfloor pit shrines may have represented the break between heaven and earth, the regions of the living and the dead. Only very rarely in African religions were the dead believed to reside in the sky; instead they were thought to live on or in the earth (Sobel 1987:174). In the novel *Things Fall Apart*, the noted Igbo author Chinua Achebe discusses a ritual in which the spirits of the ancestors let their presence be known. During the ritual, "Evil Forest . . . thrust the pointed end of his rattling staff into the earth. And it began to shake and rattle, like something agitating with a metallic life" (Achebe 1994:89). The Ibibio and the Bakongo of the present day pour libations onto the ground to call upon and venerate the ancestors (Bockie 1993:19, Offiong 1991:39). Today, Igbo in the Ohafia region of Nigeria pour palm wine into small holes cut into the earthen floors of their homes, sending this libation directly into the mouths of their ancestors (Lieber 1971:30; McCall 1995). These actions recall the brandy or wine poured onto the shell-covered shrine from Utopia.

Perhaps more important than the hole in the earth representing a break is its connection with the deity *Ala*. Also known as *Ani* or Mother Earth, *Ala* keeps in close communication with the spirits of departed Igbo ancestors (Ndubuike 1994). Igbo elders will caution children "*Toonti n'ani*" (listen to the earth), for it is there that the wisdom of the departed ancestors resides (Oramasionwu 1994:155). Another Igbo proverb states "*Ogba oso anaghi agba ghara ihu ala.*" Translated literally, this proverb says that "wherever you run, there is nowhere you don't touch the ground," meaning that the ancestors and the sacred ground (*Ala*) know whatever one does (Ogbalu 1965:118).

The earth is one of the most important sacred places in Igbo traditional religion, serving as the "sacred seat of all sacred things" (Ifesieh 1986:59). By creating shrines that were cut into the earth, enslaved African Americans further strengthened the connection between themselves, their ancestors, and *Ala*. Small balls of earth or mud also represent *chi*, or each individual's deceased ancestor reborn in the living, in special Igbo worship services (Isichei 1978:183). To the Ibibio as well, the earth (*Isong*) is sacred, and protective charms are buried in earthenware pots in compounds to prevent harm to the family (Offiong 1991:5, 46–47).

The Igbo have shrines that consist of earthenware pots buried in the ground, including shrines that women construct by embedding pottery vessels in the hearths of the women's houses (McCall 1995). Igbo women place yams in their female pottery shrines (*ududu*) and sprinkle them with wine to honor ancestresses (McCall 1995:260). Archaeological findings in several slave work areas in Virginia and Maryland appear to have been a derivation of a female personal shrine (Samford 2004). Excavation at Williamsburg's Brush-Everard House revealed an eighteenth-century tin-enameled earthenware drug jar buried in a narrow foot-deep hole cut through the clay floor of the kitchen (Frank 1967). It is quite likely that this vessel was used as a woman's personal shrine, particularly since it was found in a work area associated with female activities.

A mid-twentieth-century survey of traditional Igbo architecture reveals interesting parallels between subfloor pits in Virginia and Igbo houses (Dmochowski 1990; Moughtin 1988). Clay is an essential component in constructing traditional Igbo buildings, with many structures built with mud walls or mud covering a stick framework. Much of the furniture inside the homes, including platform beds and seating, is also built of clay, as are altars and shrines. In the home of Chief Akumwafor Ogbua, the altar was placed in a rectangular recess or niche in the clay wall; in other structures, shrines had been constructed from platforms of baked or hardened clay (Moughtin 1988:72). Edged by low dried clay walls, these shrines were in essence a pit cut into the soil platform. Shrine objects were placed within the confines of the pit (Dmochowski 1990:175, 205). The physical parallels between these shrines and Virginia subfloor pits, both appearing as recessed areas of clay, are telling. Interestingly, none of the subfloor pits containing shrines showed any evidence of having been lined with wood or having a surfaced floor. This absence of lining may be related to the sacredness of the earth and its connection with *Ala*. Analysis also showed that the shape of most of the cellars was rectangular. Since Igbo architecture is based on a rectangular model, it is interesting to speculate that the shapes of the subfloor pits may have been culturally dictated, perhaps at a subconscious level.

The sacred and powerful nature of shrine objects explains why archaeologists find them intact in subfloor pits. In 1699, a European visitor to Andony noted attitudes toward sacred objects: "They are so superstitiously bigotted, that any person whatever, who offers to touch any of those things with his hand, is sure to be severely punished, and in danger of his life" (Barbot 1732:462). This attitude of respect toward the sacred objects of other individuals or families continues today among the Yoruba and Igbo (B. Campbell 1998, personal communication). Thurstan Shaw hypothesized that the shrine goods from Igbo-Ukwu were left intact, despite their great monetary value, because they were sacred (Shaw 1970).

Fear and respect extended to grave goods, which were placed on top of the grave rather than inside with the body of the deceased. Reverend Robert Nassau noted of the interior tribes of West Africa: "A noticeable fact about these gifts to the spirits is that, however great a thief a man may be, he will not steal from a grave. The coveted mirror will lie there and waste in the rain, and the valuable garment will flap itself to rags in the wind, but human hands will not touch them. Sometimes the temptation to steal is removed, by the donor fracturing the article before it is laid on the grave" (Nassau 1904:232). These same types of behaviors can also be seen in the decoration of African American graves in parts of the American South. Although the practice has decreased drastically during the course of the century, it was once quite common to see objects last used by the deceased—bottles, clocks, pottery, and other items—covering the grave surface (Vlach 1978). Similar to Nassau's description, the glass or pottery vessels sometimes have the bottoms broken to render them useless but otherwise appear complete.

Margaret Drewal, in her study of Yoruba ritual, gives examples of World War II gas masks being used as Yoruba spirit masks and plastic dolls being used as spiritual objects (1992:20). Similarly, in the seventeenth and eighteenth centuries, European trade goods were incorporated into the traditional repertoire of spiritual goods in West Africa, and this behavior continued in Virginia. Many objects in pit shrines are similar materially and functionally to goods the British traders used as payment for slaves in West Africa.

African American Christianity

While correlating with African ethnohistoric and ethnographic evidence, does the interpretation of some of these features as shrines also fit with historical data on slaves and Christianity? Prior to the turn of the nineteenth century, few slaves in Virginia converted to Christianity (Frey 1991, 1993; Sobel 1987). Official correspondence between Church of England and Virginia clergy is filled with references to the difficulties of inducing enslaved peoples to accept Christ as their savior (Raboteau 1978; Sobel 1979). While the clergy worried they were not fulfilling their appointed duties, planters took little notice of their slaves' spiritual lives. It was not until the late eighteenth century, with the rise of the Methodist and Baptist faiths in Virginia, that enslaved peoples began to convert to Christianity (Sobel 1979, 1987).

Interestingly, there is some evidence dating earlier in the century for conversion at the sites studied here. In 1749, four children from the Bray plantation (which contained the Utopia Quarter) were baptized at Bruton Parish Church, as were additional children from Kingsmill and Carter's Grove (Walsh 1997:158). Using these baptisms as proof that African-based spiritual traditions had no place at these plantations would be a faulty assumption, however. As Walsh points out, attending Anglican services was one of the few times the enslaved could meet openly with slaves from other plantations. Thus, it would be in the best interest of the enslaved to appear at least outwardly devout on these occasions. Accepting Christianity also did not prevent the enslaved from interpreting these teachings in their own way, refashioning Christian tenets to suit the needs of their own situations.

It is hardly surprising that the enslaved people appeared to be "working" the system—allowing members of the community to be baptized into the Christian faith while actively practicing African-based spiritual traditions. One of the defining characteristics of Igbo spirituality is creativity—including the ability to freely incorporate practices and beliefs from other spiritual traditions. Many Igbo in Nigeria incorporated Christianity into their traditional spiritual beliefs. Rather than seeing Christianity as an antithesis to their beliefs, these practitioners of Igbo traditional religion are open to multiple sources of power. This same flexibility appeared to characterize the enslaved, particularly after the Great Awakenings.

Given the overarching importance of religion in the lives of members of the African cultures from which Virginia's enslaved population was drawn, it is a mistake to believe that spiritual practices ceased until the Second Great Awakening. Indeed, evidence suggests that the enslaved drew upon beliefs brought with them across the Atlantic to comfort and sustain them. Like Bishop Thomas Secker, who wrote in 1740 that the enslaved were reluctant to abandon their "heathenish rites" (quoted in Raboteau 1995:3), the clergy lamented to their superiors that the enslaved preferred instead to practice their own traditional religions. Other whites commented on practices whose origins were clearly African. Hugh Jones remarked of the enslaved in eighteenth-century Virginia, "Africans . . . obstinately persist in their own barbarous ways" (Jones 1956 [1724]:71). Challenges to Christianity were evident in other parts of the South as well. In early eighteenth-century North Carolina, Anglican clergy noted that slaves who had converted to the Christian faith were ridiculed by their fellow bondsmen (Olwell 1998:131). Dr. Edward Warren, remembering his visits to North Carolina's Somerset Plantation in the second quarter of the nineteenth century, remarked upon older "Guinea negroes" brought from Africa who "habitually indulged in an infinitude of cabalistic rites and ceremonies, in which the gizzards of chickens, the livers of dogs, the heads of snakes, and the tails of lizards played a mysterious but very conspicuous part" (cited in Crow et al. 1992:19). Warren's interest, as that of many whites who bothered to comment on the spiritual practices of the enslaved, seemed purely academic, even if overlaid with varying degrees of derision or superiority. These practices were rarely viewed as a threat to Christianity or to planter authority.

Interestingly, the several instances found where African-based religious practices were punished were when slaves used spiritual means to intervene in plantation affairs. In one of these instances, Bristoe, an enslaved man living in Johnston County, North Carolina, was brought to trial as a conjurer in 1779. One of his alleged wrongdoings consisted of pouring brandy into a hole in the earth as part of a ritual designed to make a planter purchase another slave's wife (Johnston County Court Records [1779]). Bristoe's action of offering libations to the ancestors to petition their assistance in joining a family had clear African precedent.

Other actions prescribed by Bristoe also had West African or, more specifically, Igbo precedent. He smeared mud from the brandy-soaked hole around the ankle of his client, a practice that may be related to Igbo body painting done for spiritual or medicinal purposes (Cole and Aniakor 1984: 39). In addition, his client Tom was given a root to chew, an action reminiscent of the Igbo practices of chewing and spitting out kola nuts during morning prayers. This action forms part of the prayers of blessings for an Igbo man and his family (Metuh 1985:50). In the American South, chewing roots was part of a process aimed at protecting an individual or ensuring a desired event. George White, a Virginia ex-slave born in 1847, noted in an interview: "If you want a job wid a certain person, dere is a root dat you can chew an' den you go to de person, spit around dem, an' you will get the job, or dis root will work if you want somepin else. Dere's a root for ev'y disease" (Perdue et al. 1976:310).

A second eighteenth-century case of conjuring in Johnston County, North Carolina, revealed additional evidence of transformed Igbo practices (Johnston County Court Records [1779]). In a complicated case, evidence mounted for a whole web of conjuring actions occurring within the area's enslaved community. In this instance, two enslaved men, Harry and Cuff, traveled to visit an "ober Negro" in an adjoining county to obtain some "truck" with the intention of making the planter good to the slaves. *Obea* (also spelled *obia*) is an Igbo noun meaning diviner, doctor, or sorcerer (Chambers 1996). This word was apparently transformed in North Carolina to encompass both the individual with the spiritual powers and the objects prescribed by them. The truck used in Johnston County appeared to have been plant material and was placed on or under the doorstep of the planter, where the planter's act of walking over the material would bring about the desired effect. Marrinda Jane Singleton, who was born a slave in North Carolina in 1840 and raised in Virginia, described a similar belief: "They believed that herbs or roots of certain types where the victim would walk over 'em, he would become deathly ill soon after and perhaps die of the spell if it was not removed" (Perdue 1976 et al.:267–268). These conjuring cases were not restricted to North Carolina; a visitor to Virginia's Northern Neck in the 1820s wrote of numerous examples of slave conjurers (Chambers 1996:378).

Only when the spirituality of the slaves threatened to interfere with white authority and control was it viewed with suspicion. It is doubtful whether the white planters and court officials seriously believed that Bristoe's actions would have accomplished the desired result. Perhaps Bristoe was used instead as an example to intimidate slaves who might otherwise have been tempted to purchase his services to obtain results with far more malevolent intent.

The enslaved were continuing to practice Igbo and other West African–based beliefs on Virginia plantations. These practices were certainly no real secret to planters, although detailed knowledge about the meanings and intents behind them was probably not known. Landon Carter's search of the holes and boxes of the slaves shows quite clearly his knowledge of subfloor pits (Carter 1965:495). After all, underground pits used for the storage of foodstuffs were a tradition in British culture as well. What was probably not apparent to Carter was that some pits were serving spiritual functions. Part of the hidden power in these shrines was that the sacred objects within them were items the planter would have seen as mere utilitarian goods.

While it is possible to see the combination of Igbo shrine styles with the use of BiKongo cosmograms, the Virginia subfloor pits have so far failed to yield any positive evidence of creolized spiritual beliefs or practices that combine or transform Christian and African traditions. Evidence from Virginia shows that the enslaved were taking advantage of material goods crafted from sacred materials and in sacred colors to use in more traditional West African practices, but these practices are not evidence of creolized beliefs. The new traditions and practices sparked by creolization of Christian and West African beliefs might incorporate traditional Christian symbols like crosses with assemblages of Igbo-type shrine goods, suggesting that a combination of Christian and West African spirits was being called upon for guidance. Material absence in the archaeological record is not proof that such creolized beliefs and practices were absent in Virginia. Nonarchaeological creolized spiritual expressions, such as the ring shout found in Virginia, South Carolina, Georgia, and other parts of the American South (Sobel 1979) and the lyrics of some spirituals, are evidence of these processes at work. The conversational structures and performance patterns of improvisation in African American spirituals provide evidence of this creolization. Antebellum black preachers were often referred to as having "Royal African blood," suggesting that the Christian ministers still retained some aspects of traditional African authority (Sobel 1979:235). John Canoe (*jonkonnu*), a well-documented music and masquerade performance that occurred in nineteenth- and early twentieth-century North Carolina and parts of Virginia, is another example of a creolized tradition. This celebration was a blend of an Igbo masquerade performed during the New Yam festival (*njokku*) and Christian beliefs about Christmas (Chambers 1996).

Conversion to Christianity among African Americans followed no unilineal pattern on the quarters, and there was no distinct moment where Christianity became the religion of the quarters. It was a process best characterized by movement and flux as different individuals fashioned their own belief systems. Movement was also not toward a simple uniform blending of Christian and African components to form a homogenized creole culture. There were surely differences between "saltwater" Africans—those born in Africa—and the succeeding generations of enslaved African Americans on the same plantations. Various levels of creolized beliefs, as well as incorporation of both Christian and African components into the same belief system, were surely all part of the plantation experience. Movement could "reverse" itself, as illustrated by John McCarthy's work at a nineteenth-century African American cemetery in Philadelphia. There some burials showed a revitalization of African-based spiritual practices that he linked to growing racism, economic stress, and the in-migration of African Americans from the South (McCarthy 1997).

Christianity had difficulty taking hold among the Igbo in Virginia until it was presented in forms that were more akin to traditional Igbo beliefs about the cosmos and spirituality. In Virginia, this shift came about largely during the Second Great Awakening of the early nineteenth century. There, the expressive worship styles of the Baptists and Methodists felt more familiar to peoples of West African heritage than the formalized services of the Anglican Church (Sobel 1987).

Conclusions

The Igbo proverb "*Ike di na awaja na awaja*" ("power runs in many channels") is an appropriate adage for viewing archaeological evidence of slave spirituality in colonial Virginia. This proverb gives voice to the idea that even the smallest creature can sometimes destroy a larger, more powerful predator. Despite the unequal balance of power confronting the enslaved on Virginia's plantations, there was a cultural precedent that allowed enslaved Igbos and their descendants in Virginia the knowledge that they were not completely powerless in the face of the stronger forces confronting them. Archaeological analysis of the enslaved on the three plantations studied here suggests that Africans and African Americans were constructing and maintaining new identities based in traditions that reinforced the importance of family and household. The creation of shrines to petition ancestors for beneficence and the use of objects that appear to have functioned as personal protection and ritual items indicate that the enslaved were choosing sources of spiritual strength and power that operated at individual and family levels.

Some scholars have suggested that the social disruption of enslavement and the severing of kinship ties would have prevented ancestor-related beliefs and practices from surviving in the American colonies (Raboteau 1978: 83). If we see ancestor beliefs as intricately tied to personal identity, however, a different view holds that "the process of ethnic identity creation only comes to have its power in a situation in which pre-existing forms of identity creation and maintenance—kinship, for example—are being destroyed" (Shennan 1989:16). Ethnographic work with modern Igbo peoples also suggests that the social upheavals of war, migration, and slavery can actually prompt the creation of new founding fathers, who later attain ancestor status (McCall 1995). McCall argues that it is too simplistic to envision ancestors as a phenomenon based on unilineal descent; instead, the community plays an important role in the development and understanding of ancestors. It is just these types of communities, initially of unrelated individuals sharing a common fate and later of families, that formed on Virginia plantations. If, at first, ancestors were functioning as manifestations of ethnic identity for enslaved Africans, they could have easily been later incorporated into the spiritual beliefs of slave quarter community and family life.

Clearly, however, there are no simple answers or criteria that can be applied to archaeological data for assessing spiritual beliefs of persons long dead. Expressions of spiritual beliefs are highly personal, and only painstaking contextualizing analysis conducted at a micro-scale allowed the isolation of shrine groupings. Further complicating matters is the necessity, in the face of the scarcity of earlier data, of relying heavily on information from colonial and postcolonial Igbo culture. Igbo culture has certainly not been static over the last few centuries and has undergone a colonial period of its own during the nineteenth century. One cannot expect to find direct parallels between eighteenth-century Virginia and the Igbo culture of the nineteenth and twentieth centuries. Regional differences within Igbo culture need to be taken into account, and complications arise at the Virginia end as well. Although it appears that concentrations of Igbo were present on Virginia's York River peninsula, they were certainly not the only Africans enslaved there. Individuals from a number of different West and Central African cultures came together on Virginia's plantations and formed physical and spiritual communities with beliefs and practices that drew upon each. Contact with Native Americans and people of English or European descent must also be considered.

Despite these caveats, the picture looks promising for continued gains in our knowledge about the enslaved on the plantations of Virginia. Regional and even intraregional patterns in Virginia slavery will continue to be refined. Further advances in knowledge about where specific cultural groups were clustered on plantations of the American South are possible. With the knowledge, archaeologists can tailor their research questions and strategies to target research more adequately into specific African cultures and assess how new, creolized communities were found at slave quarters. Fitting the research questions to the data has implications far beyond the analysis of spiritual practices, with applicability for the study of, among other topics, personal and community space, foodways, and gender relations.

The discovery in coastal North Carolina of an eighteenth-century shrine group very similar to some of the Virginia examples also raises the question of how traditions spread throughout the South as the enslaved were moved within the American colonies. Because North Carolina lacked good harbors that facilitated marine transport, many of the individuals enslaved there in the eighteenth century were brought overland from Virginia and South Carolina. In the late eighteenth and early nineteenth centuries, migrations to the west and south also dispersed large numbers of Virginia slaves across the American South. Excavations in Tennessee, Kentucky, and other states have found subfloor pits in slave dwellings, as well as evidence of charms and medicine bundles. Perhaps analysis of the contents of subfloor pits in these states will also yield shrine groupings.

At this intersection of archaeology, history, anthropology, religious studies, and art history, the vitality of African cultures becomes evident. Working at individual and household scales, the enslaved coped with concerns of daily life under enslavement, using a combination of spiritual beliefs and hard work to effect change. Most likely these concerns centered primarily around personal and family matters—having enough food to feed their children, the recovery of a loved one from an illness or injury, or even having the hens continue to lay eggs that could be exchanged for cash or some other needed item at the local market. While in no way diminishing the horrors of a colonial system that affected the lives of millions of individuals, research shows that the enslaved drew upon the traditions of their forebears to effect positive change in their lives.

Note

1. *Webster's Unabridged Dictionary* defines "truck" as "miscellaneous articles of little worth; odds and ends" and "trash or rubbish."

Appendix A.
Slave Sites and Probable Slave Sites in Virginia and North Carolina

Site Name	Site Number	Structure	Beg. Date Structure (approx)	End Date Structure (approx)	No. of Pits	Occupant
Slave Sites—Known and Probable						
Kingsmill Tenement	44JC39	Structure 5	1680	1700	3	probable slave
Governor's Land	44JC298	Structure 104	1680	1700	16	probable slave
Bray Kitchen	44JC34	Structure 1	1700	1720	2	probable slave
Bray Kitchen	44JC34	Structure 2	1700	1720	0	probable slave
Governor's Land	44JC298	Structure 103a	1700	1720	1	probable slave
Governor's Land	44JC298	Structure 103b	1700	1720	2	probable slave
Atkinson Quarter	44JC648	Quarter	1700	1720	2	probable slave
Utopia Period II	44JC32	Structure 1	1700	1730	6	known slave
Utopia Period II	44JC32	Structure 10	1700	1730	12	known slave
Utopia Period II	44JC32	Structure 20	1700	1730	1	known slave

Site Name	Site Number	Structure	Beg Date Structure (approx)	End Date Structure (approx)	No. of Pits	Occupant
Jordan's Journey	44PG302	Structure 15	1700	1740	4	probable slave
Eden House	31BR52	Structure 2	1700	1750	5	probable slave
Flowerdew Christine	44PG98	Structure 35	1720	1750	4	probable slave
Harbor View	44SK192	Structure 27	1720	1760	1	probable slave
Geo. Washington Birthplace	44ST174	Structure 11	1720	1760	1	probable slave
Newport News Farm Park	44NN69	Structure 1	1720	1760	8	probable slave
Tutter's Neck	44JC45	Kitchen	1720	1760	4	probable slave
Littletown Quarter	44JC35	Structure 1	1720	1760	2	probable slave
Littletown Quarter	44JC35	Structure 2	1720	1760	4	probable slave
Woodward-Jones	44SK147	Structure 1	1720	1760	3	probable slave

Site	Site No.	Structure				
Woodward-Jones	44SK147	Structure 2	1720	1760	2	probable slave
Utopia Period III	44JC32	Structure 40	1730	1750	3	known slave
Utopia Period III	44JC32	Structure 50	1730	1750	12	known slave
Rich Neck	44WB52	Quarter	1740	1780	15	known slave
Bray Quarter	44JC34	Quarter	1740	1780	4	probable slave
Curles Neck	44HE677	Field Quarter	1740	1775	4	known slave
Palace Lands Quarter		Quarter	1740	1780	1	probable slave
Kingsmill Quarter	44JC39	Building 1	1750	1780	22	known slave
Kingsmill Quarter	44JC39	Building 2	1760	1780	6	known slave
Utopia Period IV	44JC787	Structure 140	1750	1775	22	probable slave
Utopia Period IV	44JC787	Structure 150	1750	1775	1	probable slave
Utopia Period IV	44JC787	Structure 160	1750	1775	1	probable slave
Hampton Key	44JC44	Structure	1760	1780	5	probable slave
Wilton Quarter	44HE493	Duplex One	1760	1780	2	probable slave

Site Name	Site Number	Structure	Beg Date Structure (approx)	End Date Structure (approx)	No. of Pits	Occupant
Wilton Quarter	44HE493	Duplex Two	1760	1780	4	probable slave
Stonehouse Quarter	44JC821	Structure 1	1760	1780	6	probable slave
Stonehouse Quarter	44JC821	Structure 3	1760	1780	10	probable slave
Poplar Forest	44BE94	North Hill Quarter	1760	1780	1	known slave
Mount Vernon	44FX762/ 40	House/Families	1760	1792	1	known slave
Monticello	44AB89	Negro Quarter	1770	1800	4	known slave
Rich Neck	44WB52	Structure B	1775	1815	3	probable slave
Carters Grove	44JC110	House One	1780	1800	13	known slave
Carters Grove	44JC110	House Two	1780	1800	1	known slave
Carters Grove	44JC110	House Three	1780	1800	2	known slave
Pope Site	44SN180	Structure 2	1780	1800	1	known slave
Poplar Forest Quarter Site	44BE94	Duplex 1	1780	1800	1	known slave

Site	Code	Structure			Count	Classification
Poplar Forest Quarter Site	44BE94	Duplex 2	1780	1800	1	known slave
Poplar Forest Quarter Site	44BE94	Structure 2	1780	1800	0	known slave
Poplar Forest Quarter Site	44BE94	Structure 3	1780	1800	0	known slave
North Quarter	44JC52	Structure	1780	1800	3	probable slave
Southall's Quarter	44JC969	Structure 1	1780	1800	2	probable slave
Southall's Quarter	44JC969	Structure 2	1780	1800	9	probable slave
Monticello Mulberry Row	44AB89	Building O	1780	1800	2	known slave
Monticello Mulberry Row	44AB89	Building R	1780	1800	1	known slave
Monticello Mulberry Row	44AB89	Building S	1780	1800	1	known slave
Monticello Mulberry Row	44AB89	Building T	1780	1800	1	known slave
Magnolia Grange	44CF344	Structure 1A	1780	1800	0	probable slave

Site Name	Site Number	Structure	Beg Date Structure (approx)	End Date Structure (approx)	No. of Pits	Occupant
Piney Grove	44JC643	Structure 1	c. 1800	1820	1	probable slave
Piney Grove	44JC643	Structure 5	1800	1820	1	possible slave
Magnolia Grange	44CF344	Structure 1B	1800	1830	3	probable slave
Monroe Farm	44PW80	Structure 7	1800	1830	1	probable slave
Gilliam Farm Kitchen	44G317	Kitchen	1800	1830	0	probable slave
Portici Pohoke Quarter	44PW335	Structure 1	1830	1860	1	probable slave
Monroe Farm	44PW80	Structure 8	1830	1860	0	probable slave
Monroe Farm	44PW80	Structure 9	1830	1860	0	probable slave
Valentine House	CWF 29F	House	1830	1860	0	known slave
Wilcox House	44PG114	House	1830	1860	0	known slave
Shirley Plantation	44CC135	House A	1840	1860	0	known slave

Sources: Governor's Land, Jordan's Journey, Flowerdew Christine, George Washington's Birthplace, Harbor View, Newport News Farm Park, Woodward-Jones, Curles Neck, Pope, Palace Lands Quarter, Stonehouse Quarter, Poplar Forest, Piney Grove, Monroe Farm: Fesler (2004); Atkinson: Archer et al. (2006); Kingsmill (North Quarter, Kingsmill Quarter, Hampton Key, Bray, and Littletown Quarter and Tenement): Kelso (1984); Tutter's Neck: Noel Hume (1966); Utopia: Fesler (2004); Eden House: Lautzenheiser et al.(1998); Southall's Quarter: Pullins et al. (2003); Wilton: Higgins et al. (2000); Carter's Grove: Kelso and Frank (1972); Monticello: Sanford (1991); Mt. Vernon: Pogue amd White (1991); Rich Neck: Franklin (1997); Portici/Pohoke: Parker and Hernigle (1990) Valentine: Samford (1993); Magnolia Grange: Mouer (1992); Gilliam Farm: Ryder (1991); Shirley: Leavitt (1984); and Wilcox: Deetz (1993).

Appendix B

Archaeological Narratives

Chapters 6, 7, and 8 opened with three brief narratives, included as a means to engage the reader with the past. Although based on real people and situated within specific historical and archaeological contexts, these narratives are fiction. Their creation arose from a desire to imagine more fully the lives and emotions of the people who once lived at these plantations and created these subfloor pits.

At the end of the twentieth century, the interpretive approach of storytelling became one means by which this concern with multivocality and the deprivileging of the archaeologist's voice and authority was expressed in historical archaeology (Praetzellis and Praetzellis 1998). The use of narratives as an interpretive tool represented a sharp break from processual archaeology and the scientific methods undergirding this theoretical approach. Critics of the storytelling approach lamented the downfall of methodological rigor and the resulting authority from which scientific conclusions are drawn (McKee and Galle 2000), arguing that the archaeological narratives were more a reflection of the narrator than they were of any past reality.

In response, proponents of this interpretive tool, never intending to replace rigorous archaeological analysis and interpretation, contended that all archaeological writing is a construction, even analysis done using a positivist theoretical stance (Deetz 1998; Beaudry 1998; Joyce 2002). Archaeologists who engage in the use of narrative combine the archaeological and documentary record to provide a believable context for narratives (Beaudry 1998; De Cunzo 1998; Givens 2004; Little 2000; Praetzellis and Praetzellis 1998). In this way, the stories are less apt to become mere reflections of the archaeological narrator "rather than of the historical context that he or she purports to interpret" (Praetzellis and Praeztellis 1998:1). Used judiciously and supported by documentary and archaeological findings, narratives can be an excellent device for offering windows into the past. Other archaeologists insist that narratives, being more accessible than the authoritative, privileged voice of the archaeologist in a technical report, create an opportunity for opening dialogue with general audiences (Deetz 1998; Givens 2004) and can provide an analytical tool that can bring forth "new questions and avenues of research for archaeologists" (Gibb 2000).

The author's position is that narratives can be used as a way to imagine new stories about the past. The intent in crafting these narratives is not to suggest that the described incidents occurred in exactly the manner described. These stories emerged from the sites, a product of the author's archaeological imagination coupled with detailed contextual analysis. They represent three vignettes from the innumerable stories that could have taken place and are meant to illustrate the actions of individuals making lives for themselves on these plantations.

Each of the narratives was written to highlight a particular aspect of the lives of the people who lived at these quarters: the challenges of meeting the physical demands of daily life, such as having adequate food and shelter, the roles of spirituality, and the challenges and rewards of interpersonal relationships. Details of the narratives were purposively crafted using primary and secondary sources to create a specific historical and archaeological context in which to illustrate the lives of the enslaved and to emphasize archaeology's ability to illuminate the emotional content of the past through the contextual analysis of material culture. The following paragraphs outline evidence used to create the three narratives.

Debb, the main character in the Chapter 6 vignette, lived at planter James Bray's Utopia in the 1720s. She was listed on a 1725 inventory as one of twenty-eight enslaved individuals working at three quarters owned by Bray (Bray 1725). Her role as leader of the quarter where she lived was unusual, a responsibility usually reserved for white overseers or African American foremen. At this time, the residents at the Utopia quarter were largely African-born slaves that had been purchased by the Brays in the late seventeenth and early eighteenth centuries (Walsh 1997:94). Daniel and Martin, the two children collecting grass, were also included in the 1725 list. Children were assigned tasks beginning at an early age, since the contributions of every member of the household were needed for survival. They were included as a narrative device to illustrate how African traditions were valued and shared with children born into slavery.

Debb, as an African-born female, would have memories of foods grown and prepared by family members during her childhood. Food preferences and decisions about how it is prepared and eaten are always conducted within a web of cultural meanings (Mintz 1996). In Debb's case, the cultural resonance would have been West African. Adapting remembered food preparation techniques to analogous crops grown in Virginia would have been a way to imbue these new foods with West African meanings. In Virginia, sweet potatoes were comparable to West African yams and were used as a suitable substitution for dishes, like *foo-foo*, traditionally been prepared with yams.

Knowledge of food storage strategies was an important consideration before refrigeration, modern food preservation techniques, and rapid transport made a wide range of food easily available year-round. Successful storage of the summer's crops would often be a household's only bulwark against starvation in the depths of winter.

Below-ground pits have been used by numerous cultures for centuries as a means to store food. Feature 36 was a wood-lined hearth-front pit in Structure 10 that had been used as a subterranean food storage unit. Paleobotanical analysis of soil recovered from the soil layers on the floor of the wooden box showed a high concentration of grass pollen and starch granules of a type consistent with sweet potatoes.

For Chapter 7, planter Carter Burwell's records of his labor force provided the thread from which the web of relationships between the characters in this narrative was crafted. Marcellus, a man of unknown age, arrived at Carter's Grove by 1745 (Walsh 1997:238). He had probably been born in the Niger Delta area of West Africa and arrived in Virginia speaking a dialect of one of the Niger-Congo family of languages. Given his status as a new arrival, he was likely set to work planting and tending tobacco in the agricultural fields surrounding the plantation, perhaps at the excavated quarter. The subfloor pit depicted as his personal storage space was Feature 643 in House One, interpreted as having been barracks-style housing for male slaves. The bottom layer of soil filling the pit contained several complete pieces of cutlery, buttons from clothing, and some small personal items. These items were used in reconstructing his personal possessions.

The possible thief, Lot, was hired as a carpenter at Carter's Grove in 1750. By this time, Marcellus had been in Virginia five years and would have gotten to know his fellow housemates. As an outsider who would soon be leaving the quarter, Lot stood to suffer fewer repercussions from the theft than a long-time resident of the quarter. This narrative highlights the workings of the slave economy, where the products of after-hours labor could be sold or traded for manufactured goods or food. It also considers personal property rights and how ownership of property was established and protected within the enslaved community. By suggesting that the theft had been committed by another slave, the narrative demonstrates that such conflict was a part of life within slave communities.

Chapter 8's vignette of Ebo and her shrine was created using a combination of documentary records, archaeology, and ethnohistorical sources from both Virginia and West Africa. The setting is the Utopia Quarter at Kingsmill Plantation, just outside Williamsburg, Virginia. An agreement between widowed Utopia owner Frances Bray and her father-in-law in 1745 lists an adult woman named Ebo at Utopia. Her name bespoke her Igbo cultural origins, although her age and the length of time she had been in Virginia will probably never be known. The shell-covered shrine was discovered in the bottom of a subfloor pit at Utopia. Examining the shrine contents in conjunction with information on Igbo spiritual practices from art (Cole and Aniakor 1984), literature (Achebe 1987), and ethnographies (Talbot 1969 [1926]) suggested that the shrine was built to honor Idemili, a female deity associated with water. The concentrations of grape pollen were indicative of the libations of wine poured onto the shrine consistent with Igbo spiritual customs.

By combining information from various sources, it becomes possible to reveal stories about the past that would otherwise go untold. Such an interdisciplinary approach has been used here to tell stories about African American life in eighteenth-century Virginia. Doubtless, there are some readers who will find these narratives distracting, irrelevant, or perhaps even offensive. The author would like to think that they are positive additions to this volume, creating a link between the material remains from these plantations in Virginia and individuals seeking explanations of the past.

References Cited

Abrahams, Roger D.

1968   Trickster, the Outrageous Hero. In *Our Living Traditions: An Introduction to American Folklore,* edited by Tristam Potter Coffin, pp. 170–178. Basic Books, London.

Achebe, Chinua

1987   *Anthills of the Savannah.* Anchor Press, New York.

1994   *Things Fall Apart.* Reprinted. Anchor Books, New York. Originally published 1959, Astor-Honor, New York.

Adepegba, Cornelius O.

1976   A Survey of Nigerian Body Markings and Their Relationship to Other Nigerian Arts. Unpublished Ph.D. dissertation, Fine Arts Department, Indiana University, Bloomington.

Afigbo, Adiele F.

1980   Prolegomena to the Study of the Culture History of the Igbo-Speaking Peoples of Nigeria. In *West African Culture Dynamics: Archaeological and Historical Perspectives,* edited by B. K. Swartz and Raymond Dumett, pp. 305–325. Mouton Publishers, New York.

Alagoa, E. J.

1972   The Niger Delta States and Their Neighbours, 1600–1800. In *History of West Africa,* Vol. I, edited by J.F.A. Ajayi and Michael Crowder, pp. 269–303. Columbia University Press, New York.

Allen, Captain William

1848   *A Narrative of the Expedition Sent by Her Majesty's Government to the River Niger in 1841,* Vol. I. Richard Bentley, London.

Amadiume, Ifi

1987   *Male Daughters, Female Husbands: Gender and Sex in an African Society.* Zed Books, London.

Anyanwu, Starling E. N.

1976   The Igbo Family Life and Cultural Change. Unpublished Ph.D. dissertation, University of Marburg, Marburg.

Archer, Steven N., Kevin M. Bartoy, and Charlotte L. Pearson
2006   The Life and Death of a Home; House History in a Subsurface Feature. In *Between Dirt and Discussion: Methods, Methodology and Interpretation in Historical Archaeology*, edited by Steven N. Archer and Kevin M. Bartoy, pp. 81–113. Springer, New York.

Arinze, Francis A.
1970   *Sacrifice in Ibo Religion*. Ibadan University Press, Ibadan.

Armstrong, Douglas
1990   *The Old Village and the Great House: An Archaeological and Historical Examination of Drax Hall Plantation, St. Ann's Bay, Jamaica*. University of Illinois Press, Urbana.

Awolalu, J. Omosade
1979   *West African Traditional Religion*. Onibonoje Press & Book Industries, Ibadan, Nigeria.

Bacon, Richard M.
1991   *The Forgotten Arts: Yesterday's Techniques Adapted to Today's Materials*. Yankee Books, Camden, Maine.

Baikie, William B.
1966   [1856] *Narrative of an Exploring Voyage up the Rivers Kwora and Binue, Commonly Known as the Niger and Tsadda, in 1854*. John Murray, London. 1966 reprint, Frank Cass, London.

Ball, Josiah
1754   Letter to Josiah Chinn from Josiah Ball, dated April 23, 1754. Ball Letter-book on file at Colonial Williamsburg Research Library, Colonial Williamsburg Foundation, Williamsburg, Virginia.
1755   Letter to Josiah Chinn from Josiah Ball, dated July 18, 1755. Ball Letter-book on file at Colonial Williamsburg Research Library, Colonial Williamsburg Foundation, Williamsburg, Virginia.

Barbot, James
1732   An Abstract of a Voyage to New Calabar River, or Rio Real, in the Year 1699. In *A Collection of Voyages and Travels,* compiled by Awnshawn and John Churchill. Reprinted, 1732, John Walthoe, London.

Barden, John Randolph
1993   "Flushed with Notions of Freedom": The Growth and Emancipation of a Virginia Slave Community, 1732–1812. Unpublished Ph.D. dissertation, Department of History, Duke University, Durham, North Carolina.

Baumann, Timothy E.
2001   "Because That's Where My Roots Are": Searching for Patterns of African-American Ethnicity in Arrow Rock, Missouri. Unpublished Ph.D. dissertation, Department of Anthropology, University of Tennessee, Knoxville.

Beaudry, Mary
1998   Farm Journal: First Person, Four Voices. *Historical Archaeology* 32(1):20–33.

Beaudry, Mary C., Lauren Cook, and Stephen Mrozowski

1991   Artifacts and Active Voices: Material Culture as Social Discourse. In
        The Archaeology of Inequality, edited by R. H. McGuire and R. Paynter,
        pp. 150–191. Basil Blackwell, Oxford.

Beaudry, Mary C., Janet Long, Henry M. Miller, Fraser D. Neiman, and Garry W.
Stone

1983   A Vessel Typology for Early Chesapeake Ceramics: The Potomac Typo-
        logical System. *Historical Archaeology* 17(1):18–43.

Bentor, Eli

1988   Life as Artistic Process: Igbo Ikenga and Ofo. *African Arts* 21(2):66–71, 94.

Berlin, Ira

1998   *Many Thousands Gone: The First Two Centuries of Slavery in North
        America.* Belknap Press, Cambridge, Massachusetts.

2003   *Generations of Captivity; A History of African-American Slaves.* Harvard
        University Press, Cambridge, Massachusetts.

Beverley, Robert

1947   [1705] *The History and Present State of Virginia.* 1947 reprint, University of
        North Carolina Press, Chapel Hill.

Blackburn, Robin

1997   *Making of New World Slavery: From the Baroque to the Modern, 1492–1800.*
        Verso, New York.

Blakey, Michael L.

1988   Racism Through the Looking Glass: An Afro-American Perspective.
        World Archaeological Bulletin 2:46–50.

Bockie, Simon

1993   *Death and the Invisible Powers: The World of Kongo Belief.* Indiana Univer-
        sity Press, Bloomington.

Bowen, Joanne

1993   Report on Carter's Grove Slave Quarters Faunal Remains. Unpublished
        manuscript on file, Department of Archaeological Research, Colonial
        Williamsburg Foundation, Williamsburg, Virginia.

Bowles, Samuel, and Herbert Gintis

1986   *Democracy and Capitalism: Property, Community and the Contradictions of
        Modern Social Thought.* Basic Books, New York.

Bray, James

1725   James Bray II, Will and Inventory. Unpublished manuscript on file, Co-
        lonial Williamsburg Foundation Library, Colonial Williamsburg Founda-
        tion, Williamsburg, Virginia.

Breeden, James O. (editor)

1980   *Advice Among Masters: The Ideal in Slave Management in the Old South.*
        Greenwood Press, Westport, Connecticut.

Breen, Timothy H., and Stephen Innes

1980   *"Myne Own Ground": Race and Freedom on Virginia's Eastern Shore, 1640–
        1676.* Oxford University Press, New York.

Brown, Kathleen M.

1996   *Good Wives, Nasty Wenches and Anxious Patriarchs: Gender, Race, and Power in Colonial Virginia.* University of North Carolina Press, Chapel Hill.

Brown, Kenneth L.

2001   Interwoven Traditions: Archaeology of the Conjurer's Cabins and African American Cemetery at the Jordan and Frogmore Plantations. In *Places of Cultural Memory: African Reflections on the American Landscape, Conference Proceedings,* pp. 99–114. National Park Service, Atlanta.

Brown, Kenneth L., and Doreen C. Cooper

1990   Structural Continuity in an African-American Slave and Tenant Community. *Historical Archaeology* 24(4):7–19.

Bubel, Mike, and Nancy Bubel

1979   *Root Cellaring: The Simple No-Processing Way to Store Fruits and Vegetables.* Rodale Press, Emmaus, Pennsylvania.

Burnaby, Andrew

1960   [1775] *Travels Through the Middle Settlements in North America in the years 1759 and 1760 with Observations Upon the State of the Colonies.* 1960 reprint, Great Seal Books, Ithaca, New York.

Campbell, Bolaji

1998   Personal communication, September 15, 1998.

Carson, Cary, Norman F. Barka, William Kelso, Garry W. Stone, and Dell Upton

1981   Impermanent Architecture in the Southern American Colonies. *Winterthur Portfolio* 16(2/3):135–196.

Carter Family Papers

1737   Simon Sallard to John Carter, March 1, 1737, Carter Family Papers, Virginia Historical Society, Richmond, Virginia.

Carter, Landon

1965   *The Diary of Col. Landon Carter of Sabine Hall, 1752–1778,* edited by Jack P. Greene. University Press of Virginia, Charlottesville.

Chambers, Douglas Brent

1996   "He Gwine Sing He Country": Africans, Afro-Virginians, and the Development of Slave Culture in Virginia, 1690–1810. Unpublished Ph.D. dissertation, Department of History, University of Virginia, Charlottesville.

2000   Tracing Igbo into the African Diaspora. In *Identity in the Shadow of Slavery,* edited by Paul E. Lovejoy, pp. 55–71. Continuum, New York.

2005   *Murder at Montpelier: Igbo Africans in Virginia.* Jackson: University Press of Mississippi.

Cole, Herbert M., and Chike C. Aniakor

1984   *Igbo Arts: Community and Cosmos.* Museum of Cultural History, University of California, Los Angeles.

Connah, Graham

1990   *African Civilizations: Precolonial Cities and States in Tropical Africa: An Archaeological Perspective.* Cambridge University Press, New York.

Cookey, S. J. S.

1980   An Ethnohistorical Reconstruction of Traditional Igbo Society. In *West African Cultural Dynamics: Archaeological and Historical Perspectives,* edited by B. K. Swartz, Jr., and Raymond Dummett, pp. 327–347. Mouton Publishers, New York.

Crader, Diana C.

1990   Slave Diet at Monticello. *American Antiquity* 55:690–717.

Crow, Hugh

1970   [1830] *Memoirs of the Late Captain Hugh Crow of Liverpool Comprising a Narrative of His Life Together with Descriptive Sketches of the Western Coast of Africa, Particularly of Bonny.* G. and J. Robinson, Liverpool. 1970 facsimile ed., Frank Cass and Co., Ltd.

Crow, Jeffrey, Paul D. Escott, and Flora J. Hatley

1992   *A History of African Americans in North Carolina.* North Carolina Department of Cultural Resources, Raleigh.

Cummings, Linda Scott, and Thomas E. Moutoux

1999   Pollen and Phytolith Analysis at the Utopia I Site, 44JC32, Virginia. Paleo Research Labs Technical Report 98–20. Manuscript on file, Research Laboratories of Archaeology, University of North Carolina, Chapel Hill.

Curtin, Philip

1969   *The Atlantic Slave Trade: A Census.* University of Wisconsin Press, Madison.

DAACS

2006   Artifact Query 1, June 21, 2006. The Digital Archaeological Archive of Chesapeake Slavery (http://www.daacs.org/).

Davidson, Basil

1977   *A History of West Africa 1000–1800.* Longman, London.

Davidson, James M.

2004   *Mediating Race and Class through the Death Experience: Power Relations and Resistance Strategies of an African-American Community, Dallas, Texas (1869–1907).* Unpublished Ph.D. dissertation, Department of Anthropology, University of Texas, Austin.

Dawdy, Shannon L.

2000   Preface. *Historical Archaeology* 34(3):1–4.

DeBoer, Warren

1988   Subterranean Storage and the Organization of Surplus: The View from Eastern North America. *Southeastern Archaeology* 7(1):1–20.

De Cunzo, Lu Ann

1998   A Future After Freedom. *Historical Archaeology* 32(1):42–54.

2004   *A Historical Archaeology of Delaware; People, Contexts, and the Cultures of Agriculture.* University of Tennessee Press, Knoxville.

Deetz, James

1993   *Flowerdew Hundred: The Archaeology of a Virginia Plantation, 1619–1864.* University Press of Virginia, Charlottesville.

1998   Discussion: Archaeologists as Storytellers. *Historical Archaeology* 32(1):94–96.

Delle, James A.

2000   Gender, Power, and Space: Negotiating Social Relations Under Slavery on Coffee Plantations in Jamaica, 1790–1834. In *Lines That Divide: Historical Archaeologies of Race, Class, and Gender,* edited by James A. Delle, Stephen A. Mrozowski and Robert Paynter, pp. 168–201. University of Tennessee Press, Knoxville.

Dimbleby, Geoffrey W.

1985   *The Palynology of Archaeological Sites.* Academic Press, New York.

Disraeli, Benjamin

1845   *Sybil, or, The Two Nations.* Carey and Hart, Philadelphia.

Dmochowski, Z. R.

1990   *An Introduction to Nigerian Traditional Architecture,* Vol. 3, *South-Eastern Nigeria: The Igbo-speaking Areas.* Ethnographica, London.

Douglass, Frederick

1855   *My Bondage and My Freedom.* Miller, Orton and Mulligan, New York.

Drewal, John Henry

1988   Mermaids, Mirrors, and Snake Charmers: Igbo Mami Wata Shrines. *African Arts* 21(2): 38–45, 96.

Drewal, Margaret

1992   *Yoruba Ritual: Performance, Play, Agency.* Indiana University Press, Bloomington.

Dumett, Raymond

1980   Research Trends in West African History. In *West African Cultural Dynamics: Archaeological and Historical Perspectives,* edited by B. K. Swartz and Raymond Dumett, pp. 279–304. Mouton Publishers, New York.

Edwards-Ingram, Ywone D., and Marley R. Brown III

1998   Worlds Made Together? Critical Reflections on the Use of the Creolization Model in Historical Archaeology. Paper presented at the 31st Annual Meeting of the Society for Historical Archaeology, Atlanta.

Eltis, David, Stephen D. Behrendt, David Richardson, and Herbert S. Klein, editors

2000   *The Trans-Atlantic Slave Trade; A Database on CD-ROM.* Cambridge University Press, Cambridge.

Epperson, Terrence W.

1999   Constructing Difference: The Social and Spatial Order of the Chesapeake Plantation. In *"I, Too, Am America": Archaeological Studies of African-American Life,* edited by Theresa A. Singleton, pp. 159–172. University Press of Virginia, Charlottesville.

2004   Critical Race Theory and the Archaeology of the African Diaspora. *Historical Archaeology* 38(1):101–108.

Equiano, Olaudah

1987   The Interesting Narrative of the Life of Olaudah Equiano or Gustavus

Vassa, the African. In *The Classic Slave Narratives,* edited by Henry Louis Gates, Jr., pp. 1–182. Penguin Books, New York.

Ewan, Joseph, and Nesta Ewan

1970   *John Banister and His Natural History of Virginia, 1678–1692.* University of Illinois Press, Urbana.

Fennell, Christopher

2000   Conjuring Boundaries: Inferring Past Identities from Religious Artifacts. *International Journal of Historical Archaeology* 4(4):281–313.

Ferguson, Leland

1992   *Uncommon Ground: Archaeology and Early African America, 1650–1800.* Smithsonian Institution Press, Washington, D.C.

Fesler, Garrett R.

1997   A Quantitative Study of Architectural Changes in Slave Housing in the Piedmont and Chesapeake Regions of Virginia. Manuscript on file, Department of Anthropology, University of Virginia, Charlottesville.

1998   Back to Utopia: An Interim Report on Renewed Archaeological Excavations at the Utopia Quarter, Field Seasons 1993–1996. Manuscript on file, James River Institute for Archaeology, Williamsburg, Virginia.

2004   From Houses to Homes: An Archaeological Case Study of Household Formation at the Utopia Slave Quarter, ca. 1765–1775. Unpublished Ph.D. dissertation, Department of Anthropology, University of Virginia, Charlottesville, Virginia.

Fithian, Philip Vickers

1968   *Journal and Letters of Philip Vickers Fithian 1773–1774: A Plantation Tutor of the Old Dominion,* edited with an introduction by Hunter D. Farish. Reprinted, Dominion Books, Charlottesville, Virginia. Originally published, 1943, Colonial Williamsburg Foundation, Williamsburg, Virginia.

Forde, Daryll, and G. I. Jones

1950   *The Ibo and Ibibio-Speaking Peoples of South-Eastern Nigeria.* International African Institute, London.

Fowler, J. P.

1983   *The Farming of Prehistoric Britain.* Cambridge University Press, New York.

Frank, Neil

1967   Brush-Everard House Kitchen and Surrounding Area, Block 29, Area E, Colonial Lots 164 and 165: Report on 1967 Archaeological Excavations. Manuscript on file, Foundation Library, Colonial Williamsburg Foundation, Williamsburg, Virginia.

Franklin, Maria

1997   Out of Site, Out of Mind: The Archaeology of an Enslaved Virginia Household, ca. 1740–1778. Unpublished Ph.D. dissertation, Department of Anthropology, University of California, Berkeley.

2001   Archaeological Dimensions of Soul Food: Interpreting Race, Culture and Afro-Virginian Identity. In *Race and the Archaeology of Identity,* edited by Charles E. Orser, Jr., pp. 88–107. University of Utah Press, Salt Lake City.

2004   *An Archaeological Study of the Rich Neck Slave Quarter and Enslaved Domestic Life.* Colonial Williamsburg Foundation, Williamsburg, Virginia.

Franklin, Maria, and Larry McKee

2004   African Diaspora Archaeologies: Present Insights and Expanding Discourses. *Historical Archaeology* 38(1):1–9.

Frey, Sylvia R.

1991   *Water from the Rock: Black Resistance in a Revolutionary Age.* Princeton University Press, Princeton.

1993   Shaking the Dry Bones: The Dialectic of Conversion. In *Black and White: Cultural Interaction in the Antebellum South,* edited by Ted Ownby, pp. 23–44. University Press of Mississippi, Jackson.

Gerard, John

1597   *The Herbal or General History of Plants.* 1633 edition, revised and enlarged by Thomas Johnson. Reprinted by Dover Publications, 1975.

Gibb, James

2000   Imaginary, But by No Means Unimaginable: Storytelling, Science and Historical Archaeology. *Historical Archaeology* 34(2):1–6.

Giddens, Anthony

1979   *Central Problems in Social Theory.* University of California Press, Berkeley.

Givens, Michael

2004   *Archaeology of the Colonized.* Routledge, New York.

Gomez, Michael Angelo

1998   *Exchanging Our Country Marks: The Transformation of African Identities in the Colonial and Antebellum South.* University of North Carolina Press, Chapel Hill.

Gutman, Herbert

1976   *The Black Family in Slavery and Freedom, 1750–1925.* Vintage Books, New York.

Hartle, Donald

1967   Archaeology in Eastern Nigeria. *Nigeria Magazine* 93:136–137.

Hatch, Peter J.

2001   African American Gardens at Monticello. *Twinleaf Journal* 12:14–20.

Haviser, Jay B.

1999   *African Sites Archaeology in the Caribbean.* Markus Wiener Publishers, Princeton.

Heath, Barbara J.

1991   Artisan Housing at Monticello: The Stewart/Watkins Site. *Quarterly Bulletin of the Archeological Society of Virginia* 46(1):10–16.

1994   An Interim Report on the 1993 Excavations: The Quarter Site at Poplar Forest, Forest, Virginia. Manuscript on file, Corporation for Jefferson's Poplar Forest, Forest, Virginia.

2004   Engendering Choice: Slavery and Consumerism in Central Virginia. In

Engendering African American Archaeology; A Southern Perspective, edited by Jillian E. Galle and Amy L. Young, pp. 19–38. University of Tennessee Press, Knoxville.

Henderson, Richard N.

1972   *The King in Every Man: Evolutionary Trends in Onitsha Ibo Society and Culture.* Yale University Press, New Haven.

Herman, Bernard L.

1984   Slave Quarters in Virginia: The Persona Behind Historic Artifacts. In *The Scope of Historical Archaeology: Essays in Honor of John L. Cotter,* edited by David G. Orr and Daniel G. Crozier, pp. 253–283. Temple University Laboratory of Anthropology, Philadelphia.

Higgins, Thomas F. III, Verona L. Deitrick, Charles M. Downing, Benjamin Ford, Stevan C. Pullins, Justine W. McKnight, Gregory J. Brown, and Heather A. Lapham

2000   *Wilton Speaks: Archaeology at an Eighteenth- and Nineteenth-Century Plantation, Data Recovery at Site 44HE493, Associated with the Proposed Route 895 Project, Henrico County, Virginia.* William and Mary Center for Archaeological Research, Williamsburg, Virginia. Submitted to Virginia Department of Transportation, Richmond.

Hodder, Ian

1986   *Reading the Past: Current Approaches to Interpretation in Archaeology.* Cambridge University Press, Cambridge.

1987   *The Archaeology of Contextual Meanings.* Cambridge University Press, Cambridge.

1986   Writing Archaeology. *Antiquity* 63:268–274.

Horton, Robin

1972   Stateless Societies in the History of West Africa. In *History of West Africa,* Vol. I, edited by J.F.A. Ajayi and Michael Crowder, pp. 78–119. Columbia University Press, New York.

Ifesieh, Emmanuel I.

1986   Ritual Symbolism in Igbo Traditional Religion. *Africana Marburgensia* 9(1):50–82.

Isichei, Elizabeth

1976   *A History of the Igbo People.* St. Martin's Press, New York.

1978   *Igbo Worlds: An Anthology of Oral Histories and Historical Descriptions.* Institute for the Study of Human Issues, Philadelphia.

Jackson-Opoku, Sandra

1997   *River Where Blood Is Born.* One World Ballantine Books, New York.

James City County

1768–   Taxables for Lewis Burwell IV. James City County Tax Lists, 1768–1769.

1769   Manuscript 1768:11. Manuscript on file, Virginia State Library, Richmond, Virginia.

Janson, Charles William

1807   *The Stranger in America, 1793–1806.* Reprinted from the London edition of 1807, with an introduction and notes by Carl Driver. Press of the Pioneers, New York, 1935.

Johnston County Court Records
[1779]   Court proceedings contained in Johnston County Court Records, Johnston County Miscellaneous Records, C. R. 056.928.3, Folder titled "Special Court for Negro Trials." Manuscript on file, Division of Archives and History, Department of Cultural Resources, Raleigh, North Carolina.

Jones, David
2001   Bellamy Mansion Slave Quarters Archaeology Executive Summary. Unpublished report on file at Bellamy Mansion Museum of History and Design Arts, Wilmington, North Carolina.

Jones, G. I.
1931   Photograph titled "Portable Household Shrine." In the *G. I. Jones Photographic Archive of Southeastern Nigerian Art and Culture.* Available at http://www.siu.edu/~anthro/mccall/jones/igbo/ika16.jpg.

Jones, Hugh
1956   [1724] *The Present State of Virginia from Whence Is Inferred a Short View of Maryland and North Carolina.* London. 1956 reprint, University of North Carolina Press, Chapel Hill.

Joyce, Rosemary A.
2002   *The Languages of Archaeology; Dialogue, Narrative, and Writing.* With Robert W. Preucel, Jeanne Lopiparo, Carolyn Guyer, and Michael Joyce. Blackwell, Oxford.

Kelso, William M.
1976   An Interim Report. Historical Archaeology at Kingsmill: The 1974 Season. Manuscript on file at Virginia Division of Historic Landmarks, Richmond, Virginia.

1977   Historical Archaeology at Kingsmill: The 1975 Season. Manuscript on file at Virginia Division of Historic Landmarks, Richmond, Virginia.

1984   *Kingsmill Plantations, 1619–1800: Archaeology of Country Life in Colonial Virginia.* Academic Press, New York.

1986   Mulberry Row: Slave Life at Thomas Jefferson's Monticello. *Archaeology* 39(5):28–35.

Kelso, William M., and R. Neil Frank
1972   A Report on Exploratory Excavations at Carter's Grove Plantation, James City County, Virginia (June 1970–September 1971). Manuscript on file, Colonial Williamsburg Foundation, Williamsburg, Virginia.

Killion, Ronald G., and Charles T. Waller (compilers)
1972   *A Treasury of Georgia Folk-lore.* Cherokee Publishing, Atlanta.

Kimber, Edward
1998   *Itinerant Observations in America,* edited by Kevin J. Hayes. University of Delaware Press, Newark.

Kimmel, Richard
1993   Notes on the Use of Sub-Floor Pits as Root Cellars and Places of Concealment. *African American Archaeology.* 7:11–12.

Kulikoff, Allan
   1986   *Tobacco and Slaves: The Development of Southern Cultures in the Chesapeake,*
             1680–1800. University of North Carolina Press, Chapel Hill.
Larsen, Eric L.
   2005   Situating Identity: An Archaeology and Representation of Race
             and Community in Annapolis, Maryland. Unpublished Ph.D. disser-
             tation, Department of Anthropology, State University of New York,
             Buffalo.
Lautzenheiser, Loretta, Patricia M. Samford, Jaquelin Drane Nash, Mary Ann
Holm, and Thomas Hargrove
   1998   *"I Was Moved of the Lord to Go to Carolina." Data Recovery at Eden House*
             Site 31BR52 Bertie County, North Carolina. Coastal Carolina Research.
             Submitted to the North Carolina Department of Transportation. Copies
             available from the Office of State Archaeology, Raleigh.
Leavitt, Genevieve
   1984   Slaves and Tenant Farmers at Shirley. In *The Archaeology of Shirley Plan-*
             tation, edited by Theodore Reinhart, pp. 156–188. University Press of Vir-
             ginia, Charlottesville.
Leis, Philip E.
   2002   Cultural Identity in the Multicultural Niger Delta. In *Ways of the Rivers:*
             Arts and Environment of the Niger Delta, edited by Martha G. Anderson
             and Philip M. Peek, pp. 15–21. UCLA Fowler Museum of Cultural His-
             tory, Los Angeles.
Leonard, Major Arthur G.
   1906   *The Lower Niger and Its Tribes.* Macmillan, London.
Leone, Mark P., and Gladys-Marie Fry
   2001   Spirit Management among Americans of African Descent. In *Race and*
             the Archaeology of Identity, edited by Charles E. Orser, Jr., pp. 143–157.
             University of Utah Press, Salt Lake City.
Lévi-Strauss, Claude
   1966   *The Savage Mind.* University of Chicago Press, Chicago.
Lewis, Matthew
   1834   *Journal of A West India Proprietor, Kept During a Residence in the Island of*
             Jamaica. John Murray, London. Reprinted 1999, Judith Terry, editor, Ox-
             ford University Press, New York.
Lieber, J. W.
   1971   *Ibo Village Communities.* In Human Ecology and Education Series, Vol. I,
             East Central State. Occasional Publication Number 12, Institute of Edu-
             cation, University of Ibadan, Nigeria.
Linebaugh, Donald W.
   1994   "All the Annoyances and Inconveniences of the Country": Environmental
             Factors in the Development of Outbuildings in the Colonial Chesapeake.
             Winterthur Portfolio 29(1):1–18.
Little, Barbara
   2000   Compelling Images Through Storytelling: Comments on "Imaginary, But

by No Means Unimaginable: Storytelling, Science, and Historical Archaeology." *Historical Archaeology* 34(2):10–13.

Logan, G. C., T. W. Boder, and L. D. Jones
1992   *1991 Archaeological Excavations at the Charles Carroll House in Annapolis, Maryland.* University of Maryland, College Park.

Lovejoy, Paul E., and David V. Trotman
2003   Introduction: Ethnicity and the African Diaspora. In *Trans-Atlantic Dimensions of Ethnicity in the African Diaspora*, edited by Paul E. Lovejoy and David V. Trotman, pp. 1–8. Continuum, New York.

McCall, John C.
1995   Rethinking Ancestors in Africa. *Africa* 65(2):256–270.

McCarthy, John
1997   Material Culture and the Performance of Sociocultural Identity: Community, Ethnicity, and Agency in the Burial Practices at the First African Baptist Church Cemeteries, Philadelphia, 1810–1841. In *American Material Culture: The Shape of the Field*, edited by Ann Smart Martin and J. Ritchie Garrison, pp. 359–379. Henry Francis du Pont Winterthur Museum, Winterthur, Delaware.

McCartney, Martha
1997   *James City County: Keystone of the Commonwealth.* Donning Company Publishers, Virginia Beach.

McClure, James P.
1977   *Littletown Plantation, 1700–1745.* Unpublished Master's Thesis, Department of History, College of William and Mary, Williamsburg.

McClure, Randall H.
1982   Ethnicity in Historical Archaeology. *Journal of Anthropological Archaeology* 1:159–178.

McGuire, Randall H.
1982   Ethnicity in Historical Archaeology. *Journal of Anthropological Archaeology* 1:159–178.

McKee, Larry W.
1988   *Plantation Food Supply in Nineteenth-Century Tidewater Virginia.* Unpublished Ph.D dissertation, Department of Anthropology, University of California, Berkeley.
1992   The Ideals and Realities Behind the Design and Use of 19th-Century Virginia Slave Cabins. In *The Art and Mystery of Historical Archaeology: Essays in Honor of Jim Deetz*, edited by Anne Yentsch and Mary C. Beaudry, pp. 195–213. CRC Press, Boca Raton, Florida.

McKee, Larry, and Jillian Galle
2000   Scientific Creativity and Creative Science: Looking at the Future of Archaeological Storytelling. *Historical Archaeology* 34(2):14–16.

McKnight, Justine Woodard
2000   Appendix G: Archaeobotanical Analysis. In *Wilton Speaks: Archaeology at an 18th- and 19th-Century Plantation; Data Recovery at Site 44HE493, Associated with the Proposed Route 895 Project, Henrico County, Virginia.*

Report submitted to the Virginia Department of Transportation (VDOT Project 0895-043-F01, PE101), Richmond, from the Center for Archaeological Research, The College of William and Mary, Williamsburg, Virginia.

2003   Appendix E: Botanical Analysis. In *Southall's Quarter: Archaeology at an Eighteenth-Century Slave Quarter in James City County*. Report submitted to the Virginia Department of Transportation (VDOT Project 0199-047-110, PE101), Richmond, from the Center for Archaeological Research, The College of William and Mary, Williamsburg, Virginia.

Madubuike, Ihechukwu

1974   *Structure and Meaning in Igbo Names*. Department of Black Studies, State University of New York, Buffalo.

Manning, Patrick

1990   *Slavery and African Life: Occidental, Oriental, and African Slave Trades*. Cambridge University Press, Cambridge.

Márquez, Gabriel García

1982   The Solitude of Latin America. Nobel Prize Lecture, 8   December 1982. Available at http://www.rpg.net/quail/libyrinth/gabo/gabo.nobel.html.

Martin, Ann Smart

1997   Complex Commodities: The Enslaved as Producers and Consumers in Eigtheenth-Century Virginia. Paper presented at the Omohundro Institute of Early American History and Culture Annual Conference, Winston-Salem, North Carolina.

May, Jamie, and Eric Deetz

1997   Architectural Determinates in Root Cellar Placement. Paper presented at the 30th Annual Meeting of the Society for Historical Archaeology, Corpus Christi, Texas.

Mbiti, John S.

1969   *African Religions and Philosophy*. Heinemann, Portsmouth, New Hampshire.

Menard, Russell

1980   The Tobacco Industry in the Chesapeake Colonies, 1617–1730: An Interpretation. *Research in Economic History* 5:109–177.

Metuh, Emefie Ikenga

1985   *African Religions in Western Conceptual Schemes: The Problem of Interpretation*. Pastoral Institute, Bodija, Ibadan, Nigeria.

Michel, Francis Louis

1916   [1702] Report of the Journey of Francis Louis Michel from Berne, Switzerland, to Virginia, October 2, 1701–December 1, 1702. Translated and edited by William J. Hinke. *Virginia Magazine of History and Biography* 24:1–43, 113–141, 275–288.

Miller, Daniel

1987   *Material Culture and Mass Consumption*. Basil Blackwell, New York.

Miller, Phillip

1733   *The Gardeners Dictionary: Containing the Methods of Cultivating and Im-*

proving the Kitchen, Fruit, and Flower Gardens, as Also the Physick Garden, Wilderness, Conservatory, and Vineyard. Vols. 1–3. Printed for the author and sold by C. Rivington, London.

Mintz, Sidney

1996   *Tasting Food, Tasting Freedom: Excursions into Eating, Culture, and the Past.* Beacon, New York.

Mintz, Sidney, and Richard Price

1992   *The Birth of African-American Culture: An Anthropological Perspective.* Beacon Press, Boston.

Moore, Stacy G.

1989   "Established and Well Cultivated": Afro-American Foodways in Early Virginia. *Virginia Cavalcade* 39(2):70–83.

Moore Papers

1781–   Stephen Moore Papers. 2205 Series 4.1, Volume 16. Manuscript on file,
1827   Southern Historical Collection, University of North Carolina, Chapel Hill.

Morgan, Edmund

1975   *American Slavery, American Freedom: The Ordeal of Colonial Virginia.* Norton, New York.

Morgan, Phillip

1998   *Slave Counterpoint: Black Culture in the Eighteenth-Century Chesapeake and Lowcountry.* University of North Carolina Press, Chapel Hill.

Mouer, L. Daniel

1991   "Root Cellars" Revisited. *African American Archaeology* 5:5–6.

1992   *Magnolia Grange: Archaeology of the Courthouse Plantation.* Virginia Commonwealth University Archaeological Research Center, Richmond. Submitted to the Chesterfield County Historical Society, Chesterfield, Virginia. Copies available from the Virginia Division of Historic Landmarks, Richmond.

1993   Chesapeake Creoles: The Creation of Folk Culture in Colonial Virginia. In *The Archaeology of 17th-Century Virginia,* edited by Theodore R. Reinhart and Dennis J. Pogue, pp. 105–166. The Dietz Press, Richmond, Virginia.

Moughtin, J. C.

1988   *The Work of Z. R. Dmochowski: Nigerian Traditional Architecture.* Ethnographica, London.

Mullin, Gerald W.

1972   *Flight and Rebellion: Slave Resistance in Eighteenth-Century Virginia.* Oxford University Press, New York.

Nassau, Rev. Robert Hamill

1904   *Fetichism in West Africa.* Charles Scribner's Sons, New York.

Ndubuike, D. I. I.

1994   Rituals of Identity: Examining the Cultural Context of the Art of the African Native with Implications for Multi-Cultural and Cross-Cultural

Discipline-Based Art Education. Unpublished Ph.D. dissertation, Department of Education, University of Houston, Houston.

Neaher, Nancy C.

1976   Bronzes of Southern Nigeria and Igbo Metalsmithing Traditions. Unpublished Ph.D. dissertation, Department of Art, Stanford University, Stanford, California.

Neiman, Fraser

1997   Sub-Floor Pits and Slavery in Eighteenth- and Early Nineteenth-Century Virginia. Paper presented at the 30th Annual Meeting of the Society for Historical Archaeology, Corpus Christi, Texas.

2004   An Evolutionary Game-Theoretic Perspective on Slave Housing in the Chesapeake Region. Paper presented at the Annual meeting of the Society for American Archaeology, Montreal, Quebec, Canada.

Nicholls, Michael C.

1989   Building the Virginia Southside: A Note on Architecture and Society in the Eighteenth Century. Manuscript on file, Colonial Williamsburg Foundation, Williamsburg, Virginia.

Nicholson, John

1820   *The Farmer's Assistant.* Benjamin Warner, Lancaster, Pennsylvania.

Niemcewicz, Julian U.

1965   *Under Their Vine and Fig Tree: Travels Through America in 1797–1799, 1805 with some Further Account of Life in New Jersey.* Translated and edited by Metchie J. E. Budka. Grassmann Publishing, Elizabeth, New Jersey.

Nishida, Mieko

2003   *Slavery and Identity; Ethnicity, Gender and Race in Salvador, Brazil, 1808–1888.* Indiana University Press, Bloomington.

Njoku, John E. Eberegbulam

1990   *The Igbo of Nigeria: Ancient Rites, Changes and Survival.* African Studies Vol. 14. Edwin Mellen Press, Lampeter Wales.

Noel Hume, Ivor

1966   *Excavations at Tutter's Neck in James City County, Virginia, 1960–61.* Contributions from the Museum of History and Technology, Smithsonian Institution, Washington, D.C.

1991   *Martin's Hundred.* University Press of Virginia, Charlottesville.

Nooter, Mary H.

1993   *Secrecy: African Art that Conceals and Reveals.* Museum for African Art, New York.

Offiong, D. A.

1991   *Witchcraft, Sorcery, Magic and Social Order Among the Ibibio of Nigeria.* Fourth Dimension Publishing, Enugu, Nigeria.

Ogbalu, F. C.

1965   *Ilu Igbo (The Book of Igbo Proverbs).* University Publishing Company, Nigeria.

Oguagha, Philip A.
1984   Historical and Traditional Evidence. In *History and Ethnoarchaeology in
        Eastern Nigeria: A Study of Igbo-Igala Relations with Special Reference to the
        Anambra Valley,* edited by Philip A. Oguagha and Alex. I. Ojpoko. Cam-
        bridge Monographs in African Archaeology 7, BAR International Series
        195. Cambridge.

Okehie-Offoha, Marcellina U.
1996   The Igbo. In *Ethnic and Cultural Diversity in Nigeria,* edited by
        Marcellina U. Okehie-Offoha and Matthew N.O. Sadiku. Africa
        World Press, Trenton, New Jersey.

Olwell, Robert
1998   *Masters, Slaves, and Subjects; The Culture of Power in the South Carolina
        Low Country, 1740–1790.* Cornell University Press, Ithaca.

Onwuejeogwu, M. Angulu
1981   *An Igbo Civilization: Nri Kingdom and Hegemony.* Ethnographica Ltd.,
        London.

Oramasionwu, E. U.
1994   The Enduring Power of Igbo Traditional Religion. Unpublished Ph.D.
        dissertation, University of Manitoba, Winnepeg.

Orser, Charles
1988   The Archaeological Analysis of Plantation Society: Replacing Status and
        Caste with Economics and Power. *American Antiquity* 53:735–751.
1994   The Archaeology of African-American Slave Religion in the Antebellum
        South. *Cambridge Archaeological Journal* 4(1):33–45.
2004   *Race and Practice in Archaeological Interpretation.* University of Pennsyl-
        vania Press, Philadelphia.

Osae, T. A., S. N. Nwabara, and A.T.O. Odunsi
1973   *A Short History of West Africa* A.D. *1000 to the Present.* Hill and Wang,
        New York.

Parker, Kathleen, and Jacqueline L. Hernigle
1990   *Portici: Portrait of a Middling Plantation in Piedmont Virginia.* Occasional
        Report No. 3, Regional Archaeological Program. National Park Service,
        Washington, D.C.

Penningroth, Dylan C.
2003   *The Claims of Kinfolk; African American Property and Community in the
        Nineteenth-Century South.* University of North Carolina Press, Chapel
        Hill.

Perdue, Charles L., Thomas E. Barden, and Robert K. Phillips (compilers)
1976   *Weevils in the Wheat: Interviews with Virginia Ex-Slaves.* University Press
        of Virginia, Charlottesville.

Pogue, Dennis J., and Esther C. White
1991   Summary Report on the "House for Families" Slave Quarter Site
        (44Fx762/40–47), Mount Vernon Plantation, Mount Vernon, Virginia.
        Quarterly Bulletin of the Archeological Society of Virginia 46(4):189–206.

Praetzellis, Adrian, and Mary Praetzellis
1998   Archaeologists as Storytellers. *Historical Archaeology* 32(1).
Pullins, Stevan, Joseph B. Jones, J. R. Underwood, K. A. Ettinger, and David W. Lewes
2003   Southall's Quarter: Archaeology at an 18th-Century Slave Quarter in James City County, Data Recovery at Site 44JC969 Associated with the Proposed Route 199 Project, James City County, Virginia. The Willliam and Mary Center for Archaeological Research, Williamsburg.
Quarcoopome, T.N.O.
1987   *West African Traditional Religion.* African Universities Press, Ibadan, Nigeria.
Raboteau, Albert J.
1978   *Slave Religion: The "Invisible Institution" in the Antebellum South.* Oxford University Press, New York.
1995   African-Americans, Exodus, and the American Israel. In *African-American Christianity: Essays in History,* edited by Paul E. Johnson, pp. 1–17. University of California Press, Berkeley.
Randolph, John, Jr.
1924   *A Treatise on Gardening by a Citizen of Virginia.* Edited by M. F. Warner. Reprinted from *The American Garden of John Gardiner and David Hepburn.* 3rd ed. Appeals Press, Richmond.
Rawick, George P. (editor)
1979   *The American Slave: A Composite Autobiography.* 41 vols. Greenwood, Westport, Connecticut.
Rawley, James A.
1981   *The Transatlantic Slave Trade: A History.* W. W. Norton, New York.
Ray, B. C.
1976   *African Religions: Symbol, Ritual, and Community.* Prentice-Hall, Englewood Cliffs, New Jersey.
Ray, Keith
1987   Material Metaphor, Social Interaction, and Historical Reconstructions: Exploring Patterns of Associations and Symbolism in the Igbo-Ukwu Corpus. In *The Archaeology of Contextual Meanings,* edited by Ian Hodder, pp. 66–77. Cambridge University Press, Cambridge.
Raymer, Leslie
1996   Macroplant Remains from the Jefferson's Poplar Forest Slave Quarter: A Study of African American Subsistence Practices. Manuscript on file, Jefferson's Poplar Forest, Forest, Virginia.
Reps, John
1972   *Tidewater Towns in Colonial Virginia.* University Press of Virginia, Charlottesville.
Reynolds, Peter
1974   Experimental Iron Age Storage Pits: An Interim Report. *Proceedings of the Prehistoric Society* 40:118–131.

Rosengarten, Dale

1986   *Row Upon Row: Sea Grass Baskets of the South Carolina Lowcountry.*
        McKissick Museum, University of South Carolina, Columbia.

Rucker, Walter C.

2006   *The River Flows On: Black Resistance, Culture and Identity Formation in
        Early America.* Louisiana State University Press, Baton Rouge.

Ruppel, Timothy, Jessica Neuwirth, Mark P. Leone, and Gladys-Marie Fry

2003   Hidden in View: African Spiritual Practices in North American Land-
        scapes. *Antiquity* 77:321–335.

Ryder, Robin

1991   Free African-American Archaeology: Interpreting an Antebellum Farm-
        stead. Unpublished Master's thesis, Department of Anthropology, Col-
        lege of William and Mary, Williamsburg.

Samford, Patricia M.

1993   *Archaeological Investigations at the Brush-Everard Property.* Unpublished
        report on file at the Colonial Williamsburg Foundation, Williamsburg,
        Virginia.

1999   *Archaeological Investigations at the Brush-Everard Site, Williamsburg, Vir-
        ginia.* Colonial Williamsburg Research Publications, Colonial Williams-
        burg Foundation, Williamsburg.

2004   Engendering Enslaved Communities on Virginia's and North Carolina's
        Eighteenth- and Nineteenth-Century Plantations. In *Engendering Afri-
        can American Archaeology; A Southern Perspective,* edited by Jillian E. Galle
        and Amy L. Young, pp. 151–175. University of Tennessee Press, Knoxville.

Sanford, Douglas

1991   Middle Range Theory and Plantation Archaeology: An Analysis of Do-
        mestic Slavery at Monticello, Albemarle County, Virginia, ca. 1770–1830.
        Quarterly Bulletin of the Archeological Society of Virginia 46:20–30.

Schiffer, Michael B.

1983   Toward the Identification of Formation Processes. *American Antiquity*
        48(4):675–706.

1987   *Formation Processes of the Archaeological Record.* University of New Mexico
        Press, Albuquerque.

Schuler, Monica

1979   Afro-American Slave Culture. *Historical Reflections* 6(1):121–155.

Sears, Robert

1847   Description of the State of Virginia. *The New Pictorial Family Magazine*
        4:445–492.

Shaw, Thurstan

1970   *Igbo-Ukwu: An Account of Archaeological Discoveries in Eastern Nigeria.*
        Faber and Faber, London.

1977   *Unearthing Igbo-Ukwu: Archaeological Discoveries in Eastern Nigeria.* Ox-
        ford University Press, Ibadan.

1984   Archaeological Evidence and Effects of Food-Producing in Nigeria. In
        From Hunters to Farmers: The Causes and Consequences of Food Production

in Africa, edited by J. Desmond Clark and Steven A. Brandt, pp. 152–157. University of California Press, Los Angeles.

Shennan, Stephen
1989   Introduction: Archaeological Approaches to Cultural Identity. In *Archaeological Approaches to Cultural Identity,* edited by Stephen Shennan, pp. 1–32. Unwin Hyman, London.

Sidbury, James
1997   *Ploughshares into Swords: Race, Rebellion, and Identity in Gabriel's Virginia, 1730–1810.* Cambridge University Press, New York.

Singleton, William Henry
1999   [1922] *Recollections of My Slavery Days.* Highland Democrat, Peekskill, New York. Reprinted with introduction and annotations by Katherine Mellen Charron and David S. Cecelski. Division of Archives and History, North Carolina Department of Cultural Resources, Raleigh.

Smyth, J.F.D.
1784   *A Tour in the United States of America.* Vol. I. London.

Sobel, Mechal
1979   *Trabelin' On: The Slave Journey to an Afro-Baptist Faith.* Greenwood Press, Westport, Connecticut.
1987   *The World They Made Together: Black and White Values in Eighteenth-Century Virginia.* Princeton University Press, Princeton.

Sprinkle, John H., Jr.
1991   Charles Cox's Mill Chest: A Documentary Example of Slave Material Culture. *African-American Archaeology* 3:3.

Stahl, Ann, Rob Mann, and Diana DiPaolo Loren
2004   Writing for Many: Interdisciplinary Communication, Constructionism, and the Practices of Writing. *Historical Archaeology* 38(2):83–102.

Starkweather Collection
1968   *Traditional Igbo Art: 1966. An Exhibition of Wood Sculpture Carved in 1965–66 from the Frank Starkweather Collection, August 15–October 27, 1968.* Museum of Art, University of Michigan, Ann Arbor.

Stephenson, Mary
1963   A Record of the Bray Family, 1658–ca. 1800. Manuscript on file, Foundation Library, Colonial Williamsburg Foundation, Williamsburg, Virginia.

Stewart, Marilyn
1977   Pits in the Northeast: A Typological Analysis. In *Current Perspectives in Northeastern Archaeology: Essays in Honor of William A. Ritchie: Researches and Transactions 17,* edited by R. E. Funk and C. F. Hayes III, 149–164.

Stine, Linda France, Melanie A. Cabak, and Mark D. Groover
1996   Blue Beads as African-American Cultural Symbols. *Historical Archaeology* 30(3):49–75.

Stiverson, G. A., and P. H. Butler
1977   Virginia in 1732: The Travel Journal of William Hugh Grove. *Virginia Magazine of History and Biography* 85:18–44.

Talbot, Percy A.

1967   *Life in Southern Nigeria: The Magic, Beliefs, and Customs of the Ibibio Tribe.* Barnes & Noble, New York.

1969   *The Peoples of Southern Nigeria,* Vol. II. Reprinted. Frank Cass, London. Originally published 1926, Oxford University Press, London.

Tatham, William

1800   *Communications Concerning the Agriculture and Commerce of America.* London.

Taylor, Rev. John C.

1968   [1859] Journal of the Rev. J. C. Taylor at Onitsha. In *The Gospel on the Banks of the Niger—Journals and Notices of the Native Missionaries accompanying the Niger Expedition of 1857–1859,* edited by Reverend Samuel Crowther and John C. Taylor, pp. 241–383. Church Missionary House, London. 1968 reprint by Dawsons of Pall Mall, London.

Thomas, Zach

1995   Simple Root Cellars. *Country Journal* 22 (July/August):43–48.

Thompson, Robert Farris

1983   *Flash of the Spirit: African and Afro-American Art and Philosophy.* Vintage Books, New York.

1993   *Face of the Gods: Art and Altars of Africa and the African Americas.* Museum for African Art, New York.

Thornton, John

1992   *Africa and Africans in the Making of the Atlantic World, 1400–1800.* Cambridge University Press, Cambridge.

Trigger, Bruce

1991   Constraint and Freedom: A New Synthesis for Archeological Explanation. *American Anthropologist* 95(3):551–569.

Uchendu, Victor C.

1965   *The Igbo of Southeast Nigeria.* Holt, Rinehart and Winston, New York.

1976   Ancestorcide! Are African Ancestors Dead? In *Ancestors,* edited by William E. Newell, pp. 283–296. Mouton Publishers, Paris.

Vlach, John Michael

1978   *The Afro-American Tradition in Decorative Arts.* Cleveland Museum of Art, Cleveland.

Walsh, Lorena

1993   Slave Life, Slave Society, and Tobacco Production in the Tidewater Chesapeake, 1620–1820. In *Cultivation and Culture: Labor and the Shaping of Slave Life in the Americas,* edited by Ira Berlin and Philip D. Morgan, pp. 170–199. University Press of Virginia, Charlottesville.

1997   *From Calabar to Carter's Grove: The History of a Tidewater Virginia African-American Slave Community.* University Press of Virginia, Charlottesville.

1998   Ethnicity Among Africans in North America. Paper presented at the

"Conference on Transatlantic Slaving and the African Diaspora: Using the W.E.B. Du Bois Institute Dataset of Slaving Voyages," Williamsburg, Virginia.

Washington, Booker T.
1965   *Up From Slavery*. Reprinted. The Americanist Library, Boston. Originally published 1901, Doubleday, New York.

Weld, Isaac Jr.
1799   *Travels Through the State of North America, and the Provinces of Upper and Lower Canada, During the Years 1795, 1796, and 1797.* John Stockdale, London.

Wells, Ann Camille
1976   Kingsmill Plantation: A Cultural Analysis. Unpublished Master's thesis, School of Architecture, University of Virginia, Charlottesville.

Westamacott, Richard
1992   *African-American Gardens and Yards in the Rural South.* University of Tennessee Press, Knoxville.

Westbury, Susan A.
1981   Colonial Virginia and the Atlantic Slave Trade. Unpublished Ph.D. dissertation, Department of History, University of Illinois, Urbana-Champaign.
1985   Slaves of Colonial Virgina: Where They Came From. *William and Mary Quarterly* 3rd ser. 42(2):228–237.

Wilkie, Laurie A.
1995   Magic and Empowerment on the Plantation: An Archaeological Consideration of African-American Worldview. *Southeastern Archaeology* 14(2):136–148.
2000   *Creating Freedom: Material Culture and African American Identity at Oakley Plantation, Louisiana, 1840–1950.* Louisiana State University Press, Baton Rouge.

Wilkie, Laurie, and Paul Farnsworth
2005   *Sampling Many Pots; An Archaeology of Memory and Tradition at a Bahamian Plantation.* University Press of Florida, Gainesville.

Worlidge, John
1675   *Systema Agriculturae.* 2nd ed. Printed for J. C. by T. Firing, London. Facsimile published in 1970 by Sherwin & Freutel, Los Angeles.

Wright, Dorothy
1983   *The Complete Book of Baskets and Basketry.* David and Charles, London.

Yentsch, Anne E.
1990   Minimum Vessel Lists as Evidence of Change in Folk and Courtly Traditions of Food Use. *Historical Archaeology* 24(3):24–53.
1991   A Note on a 19th-Century Description of Below-Ground "Storage Cellars" Among the Ibo. *African-American Archaeology* 4:3–4.
1994   *A Chesapeake Family and Their Slaves: A Study in Historical Archaeology.* Cambridge University Press, Cambridge.

Young, Amy L.

1996   Archaeological Evidence of African-Style Ritual and Healing Practices in the Upland South. *Tennessee Anthropologist* 21(2):139–155.

1997   Cellars and African-American Slave Sites: New Data from the Upland South. *Midcontinental Journal of Archaeology* 22(1):96–115.

Index

of in Virginia, 186; in spiritual practices, 151

Crow, Hugh: commenting on storage strategies by 19th-century Igbo, 141

de facto refuse: as way to determine personal storage function of subfloor pits, 142–143; attributes of, 119; in determining shrine function, 156–157; in subfloor pits, 119

Debb's Quarter, 43

demography of Virginia slave population, 11–12, 29–33

Desandrouins Map (1781), 67

diet: fishing and hunting, 127; foodways of enslaved, 126–129; of enslaved at Carter's Grove, 101; of enslaved at Kingsmill, 101; of enslaved at Utopia, 100–102; provisioned food for enslaved, 126–127

divination. *See* conjuring

diviners: role in Igbo culture, 36, 164

Douglass, Frederick: commenting on use of subterranean food storage, 125

earthfast construction: at Utopia, 43, 46–47, 51–52; in Virginia slave quarters, 86

Equiano, Olaudah, 35, 39, 158; commenting on significance of tobacco in Igbo culture, 158; on Igbo foodways, 131; views on ancestor veneration in Igbo culture, 152

ethnicity, 4; creation of, 13; role in identity formation, 15

ethnobotanical evidence, 133–134; at Mulberry Row, 128; at Rich Neck Quarter, 128; at Utopia, 134–136, 160; on Virginia slave sites, 128

faunal analysis. *See* diet

Fesler, Garrett, 42, 89

fishing: by enslaved to supplement diet, 127; evidence at Carter's Grove, 101; evidence at Utopia, 101

Fithian, Philip, 100, commenting on enslaved gardens, 127

food remains: Afro-Virginian foodways,

126–129; archaeological analysis of, 99–102; food preparation techniques by enslaved, 99, 128; foods provisioned to the enslaved, 126–127

foofoo: as Igbo food, 13, 200

formation of slave families in Virginia, 39–40

Frogmore Manor, S.C.: evidence of creolized spiritual practices, 172

fufu. See *foofoo*

gardens: archaeological evidence of, 127; in Igbo culture, 34–35; on slave quarters, 100, 127

gender roles: Igbo, 34; of enslaved in Virginia, 104; in work tasks, 104; role in identity formation, 15

gentry planters: role of in Virginia economy, 27

Gold Coast, 30

Governor's Land (James City Co., Virginia), 132

Grandy, Charles, 140

Grazilhier: commenting on significance of bulls in Igbo culture, 158

Great Awakening: impact on the enslaved, 183, 187

hearths: collapse of hearth front pit at Utopia, 175; configuration of hearth front pits discussed, 175–176; pit depth and hearth-front pits, 176. *See also* quarters

hoes: as part of shrine assemblage, 157; in subfloor pit at Carter's Grove, 146–147. *See also* tools

household goods: on Virginia slave quarters, 92–94

hunting: by enslaved to supplement diet, 127; evidence at Carter's Grove, 101; evidence at Utopia, 101

Ibibio people, 152; in Virginia, 11; shrines of, 154; use of libations by, 180

identity: as reflected in Afro-Virginian foodways, 128–129; as reflected in material culture, 17; collective identity, 4,

Monticello, 126, 127; archaeological excavations of Mulberry Row Quarters at, 128
Moore, Phillip: of Mount Tizrah Plantation, 143, 145
Mount Tizrah Plantation (North Carolina): sale of alcohol to enslaved, 143–144
Mount Vernon: description of slave housing at, 92, 155
Mulberry Row. *See* Monticello

Nassau, Reverend Robert: commenting on West African grave goods, 182
Native Americans. *See* subfloor pits, use of by Native Americans
New Bern, North Carolina, 126
New Calabar, 154
New Yam Festival: parallels with jonkonnu, 186
Nicholson, John: commenting in gardening manual on subterranean storage, 125
Niemcewicz, Julian: commenting on slave housing at Mt. Vernon, 92, 155
Niger Delta, 30
Niger River, 32, 38
Nomini Hall Plantation, 61
North Carolina: archaeological excavation of Eden House slave quarters, 163–164, 166; evidence of conjuring by enslaved, 160; subfloor pits in, 9, 163–164
nri: in Igbo culture, 36

obea: as Igbo conjurer, 185
obi: Igbo reception hut, 154
obia. See *obea*
Oduduwa: role in formation of Yoruba kingdom, 12
ofo: as Igbo spiritual object, 152, 154, 171
Ogun: as Yoruba deity, 157, 166, 172
okponsi: as Igbo shrine good, 154, 171
Onishe: as Igbo river spirit, 158
oral traditions: use of, 12
outbuildings: on quarters, 91, 135

paleobotanical data. *See* ethnobotanical data

Pettus family, 42
phytolith analysis: at Utopia, 134–136. *See also* ethnobotanical evidence
pollen analysis: at Rich Neck, 128; at Utopia, 134–136, 160; grape pollen recovered from subfloor pits, 135. *See also* ethnobotanical evidence
primary refuse: in subfloor pits, 175. *See also* defacto refuse

quarters: changing patterns in architecture, 86–91; changing size and form, 89–90; construction techniques, 86; co-residency versus single family homes, 86, 89; defined, 29; descriptions of, 39, 125; earthfast construction, 86; groundsill construction, 86; reduction in house size and family structure, 86, 89; similarities to West African architecture, 90–91; stick and mud chimneys at, 109
quarters, specific mentioned by name: Bremo Recess Quarter, 110; Debb's Quarter, 43; Governor's Land, 132; Jacko's Quarter, 43; Littletown Quarter, 43; Mulberry Row, 128; Rich Neck Quarter, 110, 128, 132; Tutter's Neck quarter, 43; Wilton Quarter, 137

race, 4; as social construct, 15; role in identity formation, 15
Randolph, John: commenting on garden trenches for vegetable storage, 125
Rappahannock River, 33
religion: discussed in general, 151. *See also* slave religion
resistance, 4, 177
Revolutionary War: effects on Virginia, 27
Rich Neck Quarter (Williamsburg, Virginia): slave diet at, 128; subfloor pits at, 110, 132; 5
root cellars: as a cross-cultural phenomenon, 124–126; as food preservation strategy, 125–125; conditions for success of root cellars, 129–131; historical references to in North Carolina, 126; historical references to in Virginia, 125; on late nineteenth- and early twentieth-

DGA Books
P.O. Box 201
Helena, Al 35080